MEN AND WOMEN
IN QING CHINA

The reprinting of this book is made possible through a cooperative arrangement between the University of Hawai'i Press and Brill (Leiden, The Netherlands), the purpose of which is to make available in affordable paperback editions some of the most important scholarship on Asia of recent years.

MEN AND WOMEN IN QING CHINA

GENDER IN *THE RED CHAMBER DREAM*

BY

LOUISE P. EDWARDS

UNIVERSITY OF HAWAI'I PRESS
HONOLULU

First published by Brill (Leiden, The Netherlands), 1994
© Koninklijke Brill NV, Leiden, The Netherlands

Paperback edition
© 2001 University of Hawai'i Press

Printed in the United States of America
06 05 04 03 02 01   6 5 4 3 2 1

LIBRARY OF CONGRESS CATALOGING-IN-PUBLICATION DATA

Edwards, Louise P.
Men and women in Qing China : gender in the Red
Chamber Dream / by Louise P. Edwards.
p. cm.—(Sinica Leidensia ; vol. 31)
Originally published: Leiden ; New York : E.J. Brill, 1944.
ISBN 0–8248–2468–7 (pbk. : alk. paper)
1. Cao, Xueqin, 1717–1763. Hong lou meng.
2. Sex role—China. I. Title. II. Series.

PL2727.S2 E49 2001
895.1'348—dc21
2001017132

CONTENTS

PREFACE

One can hardly describe researching *Honglou meng* as 'work' since the novel is such an immense source of pleasure and wonder. However, a process has been carried out and the current volume is the result. During the course of this process I have shifted several times and so I wish to acknowledge the support of a number of institutions. I began writing at Murdoch University, then transferred to Griffith University, Taipei's Center for Chinese Studies, Academia Sinica's Sun Yatsen Institute, University of Queensland and finally arrived at Australian Catholic University. Each of these institutions provided support for which I am particularly grateful. Over these past years, child-care centres at Murdoch, Queensland and the Academia Sinica have provided care for my children. Without their help I would not have been able to research at all.

Tim Wright, Mary Farquhar, Nick Knight, Bonrie McDougall, Bev Hooper, Ann McLaren, Anna Gibb, Charlotte Furth, Angela Leung and Lucien Miller have all commented on various sections of the book in one form or another and I would like to thank them for their advice. Anonymous readers and editors for the journals where earlier versions of chapters three, four, five and six appeared were also an enormous help, as were the readers for E.J. Brill.

I am republishing four of the chapters with the permission of editors from the following journals:

Chapter three first appeared as "Gender Imperatives in *Honglou meng*: Baoyu's Bisexuality," in *Chinese Literature: Essays, Articles and Reviews*, 12 (December, 1990). Chapter four as "Women in the *Honglou meng*: Prescriptions of Purity in the Femininity of Qing Dynasty China," in *Modern China*, 16, No. 4 (October, 1990). Chapter five as "Representations of Women and Social Power in Eighteenth Century China: The Case of Wang Xifeng," in *Late Imperial China*, 14, No. 1 (June, 1993). Chapter six as "Women Warriors and Amazons of the mid-Qing Texts *Jinghua yuan* and *Honglou meng*," in *Modern Asian Studies* (1994).

Finally, and most importantly, I would like to thank Kam Louie, who has been a constant source of inspiration and encouragement.

Louise Edwards
Australian Catholic University
Brisbane, 1994

LIST OF ABBREVIATIONS

PRC   People's Republic of China
CCP   Chinese Communist Party
RD   Zhongguo renmin daxue shubao ziliao she (Compilers of books and materials, People's University), *Fuyin baokan ziliao "Honglou meng" yanjiu* (Copied materials of journals and newspapers on *Honglou meng* research)
SS   *Story of the Stone*
JHY   *Jinghua yuan*

CHAPTER ONE

INTRODUCTION: EXPLICATION OF THEORY

As one of China's most famous novels, *Honglou meng* (*The Red Chamber Dream* or *The Story of the Stone*) has generated a considerable body of criticism in both the Chinese and Western academic spheres. Indeed this criticism carries its own august title, *Hongxue,* which literally means the 'Study of the Red.'[1] Amongst the wide variety of *Hongxue* styles, ranging from the Qing dynasty's allegorical readings to contemporary Western structuralist readings there is a lacuna that has emerged as a result of the twentieth century social phenomenon of feminism or the women's rights movement. This lacuna is, of course, feminist literary criticism and it is this space that I wish to fill in this current volume through the application of an analysis based upon gender as a prime organizing category of social systems.

The novel itself invites such an analysis as this since its tale of the intricate details of life in an aristocratic Qing family is filled with information about prescriptions regarding gender. *Honglou meng* contains a wealth of information about how sexual privilege was maintained across a range of discourses of gender and about how the tensions such privilege created were mediated. For example, one of the major themes is the triangular romance between the novel's protagonist Jia Baoyu and his two cousins, Lin Daiyu and Xue Baochai. The personal and familial concerns that influence the final selection of Baochai as Baoyu's bride are fertile ground for the critic excavating principles of gender ideologies. Similarly an equally important theme for the novel is its description of the decline of the grand and wealthy Jia clan. Here we read of notions of moral and social rectitude within a Confucian framework which necessarily implicate individuals, as gendered beings, in the context of their fulfilment or non-fulfilment of expected social functions. Another sustaining thread of the novel's structure is the outplay of the fates of twelve young women in the novel, the so called Twelve Beauties of Jinling.[2] These young women are depicted as suffering tragic

---

[1] Wu Shichang's seminal English language work on *Honglou meng* notes that *"Hongxue,"* as a term has comparatively early origins and emerged in Beijing around the mid 1870s amongst the scholarly community. See Wu Shichang, *On the Red Chamber Dream* (Oxford: Clarendon Press, 1961), p. 4.

[2] The twelve female characters known as the Twelve Beauties are Lin Daiyu, Xue Baochai, Shi Xiangyun, Wang Xifeng, Qin Keqing, Jia Yuanchun, Jia Yingchun, Jia Tanchun, Jia Xichun, Jia Qiaojie, Adamantina and Li Wan. The term "Twelve Beauties" is a translation of the phrase *Shier chai* and refers to the young women of the novel. It has, however, be-

fates and during the course of the novel each fate unravels. With over four hundred characters the novel provides a broad cross section of class and sex variations which make it unrivalled in social and moral scope. Later chapters will provide more detailed examples of the novel's generosity to the feminist critic bent on a gender analysis as they fit more appropriately the various themes.

This approach necessarily carries the danger of ahistoricism. Feminist literary criticism is a product of a specific period in time in Western history and its application to mid Qing Chinese texts may be considered a dubious endeavour whereby contemporary Western values are used to judge Qing China. However, as will become apparent in the more detailed explication of my theoretical premises, I do not judge *Honglou meng* or its author on the extent to which the values expressed measure up to our current understandings of the relationships between the sexes. Rather I examine how sexual divisions of power were enunciated in the novel and later appraised by critics across time. Indeed, the prime motivation for the book has been a reaction against the style of criticism that has emerged from time to time in the People's Republic of China (hereafter PRC) where *Honglou meng* is credited with representing what can only be considered contemporary notions of sexual equality or class struggle. The questions are then not 'Was Cao Xueqin an early Chinese feminist?' or 'Is *Honglou meng* a proto-feminist text?' but rather 'How did Cao Xueqin reflect the sexual ideologies of his time?' and 'How do sexual ideologies with their incumbent power differentials make themselves appear natural and normal?'

Thus, I will not be comparing Cao Xueqin's depiction of the distribution of power and privileges between the sexes with our own perceptions of the acceptable or the desirable. This would amount to little more than a ridicule of *Hongxue*. Rather, I will be concerned with examining the way *Honglou meng* represents gender in Qing China with a view to understanding how gender inequalities were rationalized and rendered acceptable and 'normal.' In this respect my work is not a challenge to existing analyses of the novel as much as it is a broadening of the parameters of *Hongxue*. As a polyphonic novel, *Honglou meng* eludes a single, authoritative reading and indeed invites a multiplicity of understandings. This diversity I regard as a strength rather than a weakness for *Hongxue*. Lu Xun rather caustically dismissed early

---

come customary for the phrase to refer to the twelve particular women noted above. The origins of the phrase can be traced back to a poem written in the Liang period of the Southern Dynasties (502-557). Titled "Song to the water in the river," the author, Wu Dixiao, has written a eulogy to love and a lament to the inability of individuals to marry the persons they love. Wu has used twelve head ornaments worn by women as a metaphor for a bevy of beautiful women and it is this tradition that Cao Xueqin has invoked in his use of the phrase. For more details see Wang Li, ed. *Zhongguo chengyu da cidian* (Dictionary of Chinese proverbs) (Shanghai: Shanghai cishu chubanshe, 1987), pp. 627-28 and Wang Li, ed. *Zhongguo gudai wenxue cidian: di san juan* (Dictionary of classical Chinese literature: volume three) (Nanning: Guangxi jiaoyu chubanshe, 1989), p. 982.

Hongxue as being infected by personal philosophies rather than the scientific objectivity he saw emerging in the so called New *Hongxue* of Hu Shi, Yu Pingbo and Gu Jiegang.[3] Lu Xun wrote, "Those who study the *Classics* see 'the changes,' those who study the *dao* see lust, educated people see a moving story, revolutionaries see a critique of the Manchu state, gossip mongers see the secrets of the court."[4] It follows then that those who study feminism will see the discourses of gender in *Honglou meng*. This multitude of visions about the 'meaning' of the novel reflect the strength of *Honglou meng*'s place in the literary canon. Cao's mastery is surely reflected by the multitude of various forms *Hongxue* has taken for the text has proved itself to be an immensely flexible producer of meaning.

While conducting a gender analysis of the novel itself, I have also felt it appropriate to undertake simultaneously a critique of *Hongxue*'s discourse of gender, in particular that of the PRC critics. The various meanings granted the novel over the past two hundred years are important signifiers of sexual meaning and so within my critique of *Honglou meng* is woven a critique of *Hongxue*'s discourses of gender. While the majority of these critics appear to write of a notion of gender that is unproblematized, critics from the PRC have, under the influence of socialism and the international moves towards eliminating discriminatory practices, written of gender issues, and sexual equality in particular, in a more self-conscious and overtly political fashion. Over the last decade of comparative freedom of intellectual expression, PRC critics have propounded the view that Cao Xueqin and his novel were early advocates of sexual equality. One possible explanation of the appearance of this vision of *Honglou meng* is that while the post-Mao relaxation in control over literary expression is evident, it is also partial. Scholars of *Honglou meng* are thereby careful to maintain the political and social relevance of their work to the 'modernization' of China. With the rejection of the primacy of 'class analysis' and 'class struggle' less radical visions of 'political usefulness' are being propounded. Prime among these is the vision that the novel represents early Chinese notions of sexual equality which are currently realized in a socialist system. Therefore, this view of the novel evolves not as a result of the application of feminist theory, motivated by concerns about explicating the intricacies of prescriptions of gender, but rather, as a consequence of the declining importance of class analysis within an intellectual system that still demanded political usefulness to be apparent.

---

[3] Gu Jiegang wrote in the preface to Yu Pingbo's path-breaking book *Honglou meng bian* that the appearance of Hu Shi's *Honglou meng kaozheng* and Yu Pingbo's *Honglou meng bian* represent the "overthrow of Old *Hongxue* and the establishment of New *Hongxue*." Gu Jiegang, "Gu Xu" (Gu's Preface), in Yu Pingbo, *Honglou meng bian* (Distinguishing *Honglou meng*), rpt. in *Yu Pingbo lun Honglou meng* (Yu Pingbo on *Honglou meng*), by Yu Pingbo (1922; rpt. Shanghai: Guji chubanshe, 1988), p. 79.

[4] Lu Xun, "'Jiang dong hua zhu' xiaoyin (Forward to the "Lord of the Flowers"), rpt. in *Lu Xun quanji: ji wai ji she yi* (Complete works of Lu Xun: Collected material omitted from the collections), by Lu Xun (1927; rpt. Shanghai: Lu Xun quanji chubanshe, 1938), p. 419.

Attempts at uncritically 'inheriting' *Honglou meng* as a proto-feminist text
may have the effect of perpetuating values which serve to continue the oppression of women.[5]

Zhao Rong argued in 1982 that *Honglou meng* is Cao's eulogy to equality of the sexes and a cry for freedom in marriage. Han Huiqiang similarly
described Cao Xueqin as an advocate of a revolution in sexual morality.
Huang Lixin's lengthy work on this issue encapsulates common assumptions about *Honglou meng*'s sexual ideology in the statement that "in the
history of Chinese women's liberation [*Honglou meng*] holds an important
position."[6] Western scholars have echoed this view, albeit with less vigour.
For example Moss Roberts described the novel as deeply feminist and R.
Keith McMahon suggested that the novel contained a "critique of patriarchy."[7] The *Hongxue* industry of the People's Republic has grasped this issue with enthusiasm and, in popularized television versions of Cao Xueqin's
life, have created mythical descriptions of Cao buying girls from the slave
market only to immediately release them. Cao Xueqin has been recreated as
saviour to women, and a feminist before feminism.

Invoking visions of female misery and suffering in traditional China has
served the requirements of *Hongxue* scholars in the PRC who face the need
to legitimate the current socialist system. This motivation underlies many
of the critiques written since the 1950s. An article by Guan Hua in *Renmin
ribao* of 1986 makes this sentiment obvious in its didactic tones. The article
is phrased in such as way as to suggest that the author is talking to Cao and
proceeds,

> Here the women are officials, students, teachers, engineers, scientists and
> artists who are carrying the responsibility for their own fates just as do the
> men. Their vehemence, warmth and wooing, do not have the sound of those
> trampled women who call for power. Here the laws prevent the opening of
> brothels for the cheap sale of women's flesh and spirit. All practices that

---

[5]   See Kam Louie's book *Inheriting Tradition: Interpretations of the Classical
Philosophers in Communist China* (Hong Kong: Oxford University Press, 1986) for examples
of the similar 'use' of philosophy in contemporary China and the use of the word 'inheriting.'

[6]   Zhao Rong, "Hunyin ziyou de nahan—nannü pingdeng de ouge" (A cry for freedom in
marriage and a eulogy to equality of the sexes), *Guiyang shiyuan xuebao*, no. 1 (1982), pp.
58-69, rpt. in Zhongguo renmin daxue shubao ziliao she (Compilers of books and materials,
People's University), *Fuyin baokan ziliao "Honglou meng" yanjiu* (Copied materials of journals and newspapers on *Honglou meng* research), [Hereafter *RD*], No. 4 (1982), pp. 55-65;
Han Huiqiang, "*Honglou meng* zhong de xing guannian ji wenhua yiyi" (Sexual concepts and
the cultural significance of *Honglou meng*), *Beijing daxue yanjiusheng xuekan*, No. 1 (1988),
pp. 77-82, rpt. in *RD*, No. 2 (1988), pp. 17-22; Huang Lixin, "Ming Qing nannü pingdeng de
shehui sichao yu *Honglou meng*" (*Honglou meng* and trends in social thought towards sexual
equality in the Ming and Qing), *Honglou meng xuekan* (*Honglou meng* journal), No. 2 (1986),
p. 325.

[7]   Moss Roberts, "Neo-Confucianism in the Dream of the Red Chamber: a critical note."
Bulletin of Concerned Asian Scholars, 10, No. 1 (January-March, 1978), p. 63; R.K.
McMahon, "A Case for Confucian Sexuality: the Eighteenth Century Novel 'Yesou puyan',"
Late Imperial China, 9, No. 2 (December, 1988), p. 47

seriously harm women are punishable. Here all women are sisters and loved ones of men.[8]

Honglou meng then ensures that the past is made to serve the present by legitimizing current CCP control of political power but it tells us little about the mechanisms of legitimization of the unequal distribution of power between the sexes either today or in Qing China. To say that women were oppressed is not sufficient because left at this precipice sexual inequality, focussed as it is on the ridiculous/gruesome spectacle of female suffering, becomes little more than a side-show of horrors. Such a side-show ensures that the viewer regards the object with an emotional distance which is devoid of responsibility. The viewer regards the object of 'female suffering' with a detached superiority and remains complacent and personally untroubled, indeed relieved, that 'times have changed.' *Hongxue* of this nature is simply one mechanism for normalizing or legitimizing CCP right to rule in current day China. It is my intention in chapters three through eight to examine the various mechanisms through which male right to rule was legitimized and normalized during the Qing in the text of *Honglou meng.*

As I mentioned above, this enthusiasm for discovering twentieth century values, incipient or otherwise, in an eighteenth century text carries not only the danger of ahistoricism but also can serve to perpetuate values of gender that reinforce current inequalities. So while the inclusion of sexual politics into Chinese literary criticism should be applauded, there is a tendency to embrace any works which discuss women's problems as anti-feudal, anti-patriarchal pieces. The central issue is not the fact that women's subjugation is evident in the story woven by *Honglou meng* but rather how it is portrayed. Moreover, this particular focus on women's subjugation and the complete silence on male mechanisms of domination tend to generate discourses of 'miserable, suffering females' wherein the problem is read as one of subordination and not at all one of domination. As victims of oppression the important ways in which women collude and negotiate with the patriarchal system are ignored just as are the ways in which men are limited and restrained in their roles as sexual power holders. It is for these reasons that I have broadened the study to include an analysis of both men and women in the novel and also across the broad range of ages for both sexes. Masculinity and femininity as discourses of power and control are more productively examined in unison so that the dangers of projecting one as all-powerful and the other as all-suffering is avoided.

---

[8] Guan Hua, "Cao Xueqin he nüxing" (Cao Xueqin and women), *Renmin ribao* (*People's daily*), 6.3.1986.

Feminist theory

The fundamental critical tenets of feminist literary practice include the notion that all texts embody a sexual, partial and inherently political position. Toril Moi comments that "One of the central principles of feminist criticism is that no account can ever be neutral."[9] This rejection of the notions of pure aestheticism and critical objectivity stems from the utilitarian attitude feminist literary critics adopt. Literary criticism, to the feminist critic, is a tool for exposing practices that subordinate women or alternatively is a tool for further enhancing the position of women in society. Thus, the rejection of notions of literary criticism as aesthetic appreciation is self-referential. The feminist critic recognizes the ideological and discursive function that is performed in the act of writing criticism. This partiality of purpose is consciously embraced by feminist literary critics with the aim of exploring the narrative's presentation of masculinity and femininity with the purpose of disclosing the ambiguities and contradictions in sexual ideologies. Beyond these basic visions of the place and purpose of literary criticism feminist literary methods are diverse and evolving.

A gender analysis such as that which follows, then, subverts the concept of an asexual, impartial literary text and seeks to explore the text's production of masculinity and femininity—its sexual ideology. The idea that the existence of an asexual text is an impossibility lies in direct contrast to expressive realist critiques which have reduced, and in many cases, attempted to ignore the role ideology plays in literary criticism maintaining that 'pure' literary theory is an aesthetic rather than political construct.[10] However, an analysis such as this, which seeks to explore the social production of masculinity and femininity directly, taps into what Pierre Macherey has called the "text's unconscious"—what is left unspoken in the silences and gaps— its ideology.[11]

This theoretical base also adopts the view that the authors, which in this case is Cao Xueqin, with Gao E being credited with the authorship/editorship of the last forty chapters, are not the sole keys to understanding the text. The search for the authors' intended meanings or the search for hints of the authors' lives, philosophies and grand visions are not relevant to this analysis. The New *Hongxue* of the 1920s adopted the technique of conducting extensive biographical searches into Cao Xueqin's family and life history before asserting that he was indeed the author of the first eighty chapters. The weight of importance of discovering the author of this great text can not be

---

[9] Toril Moi, *Sexual/Textual Politics: Feminist Literary Theory* (1985; rpt. London: Methuen, 1988), p. xiii.

[10] For a brief discussion of the relationship between literature and ideology see Terry Eagleton, "Literature and Politics Now," *Critical Quarterly*, 20, No. 3 (1978), pp. 65-69 or A.P. Foulkes, *Literature and Propaganda* (London Methuen, 1983), pp. 1-18.

[11] Pierre Macherey, *A Theory of Literary Production*, trans. by Geoffrey Wall, (London: Routledge and Kegan Paul, 1978), pp. 85-86.

underestimated because it has resulted in the transformation of *Hongxue* from speculative and generative critical method into a search for authorial intention. The author, Cao Xueqin, became the ultimate signifier of the text and the singular source of all meaning. The main philosophy of *Hongxue* then became the search for Cao's genius, Cao's vision and Cao's greatness. Allegorical, religious or political messages were relegated to the 'Old' and outdated *Hongxue*, and the view that the novel was the autobiography of a genius developed momentum. Complaints from some sections of the *Hongxue* community have centred on the extent of this transformation towards authorial authority, with the objection that *Hongxue* has become *Caoxue*—literally the study of the novel's author, Cao Xueqin. Certainly, a gender analysis such as this rejects the critical practice "that relies on the author as the source, origin and meaning of the text...[and] proclaims with Roland Barthes the death of the author."[12]

This is not to say that the text is analyzed regardless of its context. Indeed, meaning is at all times construed contextually but on the understanding that these are subject to change. Prescribing specific contexts for any work does not contraindicate any alternative inscription. Indeed, many different contexts can be prescribed for one text at the same time. However, the feminist critic would argue that each of these contexts is imbued with their own specific political and sexual discourses, including the feminist critique itself. No claims for objectivity or special insight are made, simply a recognition of differences and the political effects of those differences.

Thus, while Cao Xueqin may have intended readers to learn something specific and concrete from his tale, this is not the only understanding of the novel possible, nor is it the most important since each generation makes use of texts it inherits in vastly different ways, prioritizing different aspects as the needs arise. Even when the authority of the author as the ultimate signifier of meaning remains unchallenged, the author's life and views are reassessed, different features are emphasized, and new significances granted, to incorporate the fresh demands placed upon the text by a changed social situation. This is clearly the case with the PRC reassessment of Cao Xueqin. His genius was matched by his belief in class equality during the 1970s and by his belief in sexual equality in the 1980s. Critical practice is little more than the process of creating new and useful meanings for old texts that ensure that a work continues to be valued over time.

In the chapters that follow I will attempt to demonstrate how this theory of politically motivated criticism can cast an alternative light on our perceptions of *Honglou meng* and perhaps on issues of relations between the sexes in Qing China as well. In the next chapter I will trace the history of *Hongxue* (and its unproblematized invocations of gender) throughout the years since *Honglou meng* appeared, up till the introduction of Marxist

---

[12] Toril Moi, *Sexual/Textual Politics*, pp. 62-63.

methodology in 1949. The critics cited will reappear in various other forms throughout the remainder of the book when specific characters are mentioned. This first chapter is written with the intention of establishing the general principles of *Hongxue*'s lengthy past. This fundamental part of Chinese language *Hongxue*, "the history of *Hongxue*" (*Hongxue shi*) has yet to appear in English in any comprehensive form since Wu Shichang's discussion published in 1961. I hope thereby to achieve two goals in this chapter. Initially to provide a brief history of *Hongxue* and more specifically to examine the discourse of gender in *Hongxue*. The post 1949 developments of *Hongxue* form the conclusion to the book.

The following chapter will examine the character of Baoyu with specific reference to his distinct blend of gender characteristics within the one form and his professed belief in the essential nature of feminine purity. In this chapter I will be drawing heavily on the work of French feminist literary theory with its debt to psycho-linguistics and philosophy. The major argument is that Jia Baoyu embodies a metaphorical bisexuality which permits his transcendence to an enlightened state but his protestations that girls are superior to boys amount to little more than a projection of the other as sacred. Critical claims of the novels' incipient feminist stance are challenged on the grounds that this philosophical position merely reiterates the misogynist binary where women are either sacred or profane. Since many critics assume Baoyu to be Cao Xueqin, Baoyu's many utterances about the superiority of women are taken to represent the author's vision. It is important that this discussion begins the book because it provides the foundation of the critical claims of the novel's/author's incipient feminist sentiment.

The argument that Baoyu's proclamations regarding the essential purity of young girls relies intimately upon notions of female profanity is continued through to the fourth chapter in my analysis of the young women of the novel and the portrayal of purity in young girls. Here I will be arguing that *Honglou meng* has subtly revealed the manner in which notions of purity and profanity constrain women in their life choices. Pre-marital purity quickly transforms into post-marital pollution within the epistemological matrix of *Honglou meng*'s discourse of gender.

In chapter five the theme of power in marriage resulting in the pollution of women is elaborated in an analysis of the depiction of Wang Xifeng, a young but powerful daughter-in-law. Here I will show that her enthusiasm for wielding power is reified in the depiction of her as being masculine or manly. She challenges accepted realms of sexual behaviour and is depicted as suffering physically and emotionally for her 'desire to be a man.' Ultimately, she and another daughter-in-law, Qin Keqing, become dual symbols of the Jia clan's decline. Powerful women are not all regarded as harshly as Wang Xifeng has been, nor are they necessarily granted ignominious ends. As will become clear in chapter six, women warriors of the mid Qing are carefully tamed and restrained in subtle ways that ensure their complicity with broad social and sexual norms. In this sixth chapter I draw from the redaction of Lin Siniang's life in chapter seventy-eight of *Honglou meng* as well as from another Qing scholar-literati novel, *Jinghua yuan*.

Motherhood has often been described as one of the main avenues for women to exercize power, however indirectly. I will show in chapter seven that there are subtle ways in which discourse of mothering contains and restrains women as parents as well as revealing the forms in which women's dominance over a father's parenting rights is maintained. I will base this chapter on an analysis of the dichotomy of the phrase *yan fu ci mu* (severe father and indulgent mother). It will emerge that this idealized form of parenting represents a balance which relegates the *ci mu* to the position of an object of censure. In chapter eight, the men of the Jia clan will be discussed within broad notions of restraint and passivity in relation to desires. The men emerge as being completely unrestrained in their fulfilment of their desires and heedless of legal or social customs. Ultimately, the out-ward adherence to rites and rituals is exposed as being ineffectual in ensuring the continuity of clan wealth and power.

In the conclusion I will examine the problematic nature of post 1949 *Hongxue* and suggest reasons why *Hongxue* from the People's Republic of China felt the need to reconstruct *Honglou meng* and Cao Xueqin as a proto-feminist at this particular juncture of history. I will point to several features of the political climate which made sexual equality a useful tool for *Hongxue* scholars of the 1980s. In this respect the conclusion completes the chronology of *Hongxue* begun in chapter two. My own examination of *Honglou meng*'s depiction of gender then forms the central core of the volume which is framed by an exploration of the discourse of gender in *Hongxue*. The conclusion then reiterates my fundamental theoretical position that all literary criticism represents its material context and carries implicit sexual/political discourses.[13]

---

[13] The themes of the conclusion are explained in greater detail in my book on post-Mao *Hongxue*. See Louise Edwards, *Contemporary Chinese Critiques of "The Red Chamber Dream"* forthcoming with Brockmeyer's Chinathemen series.

CHAPTER TWO

HONGXUE BEFORE 1949

This chapter has two interconnected aims. At the broadest level I hope to
provide a brief overview of the various forms *Hongxue* has taken up to the
introduction of Marxist critical methods in the People's Republic of China
and at the more specific level I hope to explain how these changes embody
specific discourses of gender. While some thorough, general histories of
Hongxue are available in the Chinese language, mainly from the PRC, there
are no recent comprehensive surveys in English.[1]

Writing a brief survey of *Hongxue* is a task fraught with difficulty since
not only is there a tremendous amount of material to cover but there are also
the controversial aspects of the novels' authorship, ending and various
editions that add further tangential problems to the process. As I am
concerned primarily with the studies of the novel in this chapter I will refer
the reader to those studies in English which discuss in more detail the
various editions and versions of the novel. The most detailed and useful
explanation of the various materials of the manuscripts of *Honglou meng* is
that written by David Rolston. Here readers are provided with details of the
nature and location of the various works as well as historical notes and
points of controversy and current debate.[2]

Lu Xun's brief explanation of the evolution of the novel into its current
one hundred and twenty chapter form is that around 1765, towards the middle
of Qianlong's reign, "a novel called the *Tale of a Rock* appeared in Peking
and within five or six years became extremely popular; but all the copies
were handwritten and cost several dozen taels of silver apiece. There were
eighty chapters only... In 1792 a printed edition with one hundred and twenty
chapters appeared, in which the name of the novel was changed to *Dream of*

---

[1] The main Chinese language texts that have informed this chapter are those of Guo Yushi
and Yi Su. The former's *Honglou yanjiu xiaoshi gao* and its sequel provided the chapter's
general structure and subdivisions of authors within schools, while the latter's *Honglou meng
juan* provided ready access to almost all original complete critiques cited. Some of the
lengthier essays were excerpted by the editors and this is noted, where appropriate, by the inclusion of 'excerpts' (*jie lu*) in the footnote. Guo Yushi, *Honglou yanjiu xiaoshi gao* (A short
history of research into the red chamber) (Shanghai: Shanghai wenyi chubanshe, 1980) and
Honglou yanjiu xiaoshi xugao (A further short history of research into the red chamber)
(Shanghai: Shanghai wenyi chubanshe, 1981). Yi Su, ed. *Honglou meng juan* (Collection of
material on *Honglou meng*) (1963; rpt. Beijing: Zhonghua shuju, 1985).
[2] David Rolston, ed. *How to Read the Chinese Novel* (Princeton: Princeton University
Press, 1990), pp. 456-84.

the Red Chamber (Hung Lou Meng) and there were other minor alterations."[3]
The last forty chapters of this full version are those credited to Gao E's careful editing and emendations, although the 'rediscovery' of the missing pieces
of the novel is credited to Cheng Weiyuan. Gao E's extensive work on the
manuscript has given him co-author/editor status with Cao Xueqin for the
closing forty chapters of the novel while the hard work of rediscovering the
missing chapters remains Cheng's glory. In the Cheng preface we read:

> Surely, I thought to myself, if the table of contents lists one hundred and
> twenty chapters, a complete version must exist somewhere. I searched ev-
> erywhere, from antiquarian book-collectors to piles of old discarded papers,
> leaving no stone unturned, and over a number of years I managed with diffi-
> culty to assemble twenty-odd chapters. Then one day, by a stroke of luck, I
> acquired ten or so more chapters from a peddler. He only agreed to sell them
> to me for a high price. On perusing these chapters, I discovered to my great
> delight that the episodes in them could more or less be dovetailed into
> those in the other chapters that I had previously collected. But the
> manuscripts were in a hopeless muddle. With the help of a friend, I care-
> fully edited the material, removing what seemed superfluous and making
> good any gaps, and then transcribed the whole for publication.[4]

The friend referred to is none less than Gao E.

Although this one hundred and twenty chapter version is the version that
we read today, while the novel was still being written Cao Xueqin circulated
it among his friends and relatives in manuscript form. The margin comments on these drafts form the earliest *Hongxue* and the most influential of
the margin critics is Zhiyanzhai. The exact identity of Zhiyanzhai is un-
known and it is not clear whether the penname refers to one or more people.
Most scholars agree that it must be someone related to Cao or very close to
Cao because of the intimate knowledge of family events the margin comments reveal.[5] The Qing dynasty critic Yu Rui argued that Zhiyanzhai was

---

[3] Lu Xun, *A Brief History of Chinese Fiction*, trans. by Gladys Yang and Yang Hsien-yi
(1930; Beijing: Foreign Languages Press, 1959), p. 298 and p. 306.

[4] "Preface by Cheng Weiyuan," trans. by John Minford, in Appendix One of *The Story of
the Stone: Volume Four. The Debt of Tears*, p. 385. Minford has also included the Gao E
preface and the joint preface (see pp. 386-88). His preface to *The Debt of Tears* also includes
detailed biographical material on Gao E (see pp. 20-30). The Chinese for these three pref-
aces is included in Yi Su, *Honglou meng juan*, pp. 31-32. Unless otherwise stated, all excerpts
of the novel come from the David Hawkes and John Minford translation in five volumes—*The
Story of the Stone. Volume 1: The Golden Days* (Harmondsworth: Penguin, 1973). *Volume 2:
The Crab-Flower Club* (Harmondsworth: Penguin, 1979). *Volume 3: The Warning Voice*
(Harmondsworth: Penguin, 1981). Cao Xueqin and Gao E, *Volume 4: The Debt of Tears*
(Harmondsworth: Penguin, 1982). Cao Xueqin and Gao E, *Volume 5: The Dreamer Wakes*
(Harmondsworth: Penguin, 1986). I have also followed their lead in the translation of
characters' names. For example Daiyu remains Daiyu while Qingwen has been translated as
Skybright. I have however taken the liberty of removing the hyphen between syllables as it
use is not customary in Hanyu pinyin. For example Bao-yu becomes Baoyu.

[5] David Hawkes provides a clear path through the maze of Cao's family network in
"Introduction," *The Story of the Stone: Volume One. The Golden Days* (See pp. 22-40). Cao's
grandfather is understood to be Cao Yin and Johnathan Spence has given a detailed account

Cao's uncle or, more specifically, his father's younger brother (*shufu*).[6] Hu Shi wrote in the 1920s that it was probably one of Cao's clansmen and most likely Cao Yong but then he later changed his view on this and argued that Zhiyanzhai was none other than the author, Cao Xueqin himself. He based this later theory on the notion that *Honglou meng* is Cao Xueqin's autobiography and Cao himself is represented by Baoyu. Baoyu liked to eat cosmetics, as will be explained in the following chapter, and the phrase Zhiyanzhai sounds very similar to the phrase 'eat rouge' (*chi yanzhi*).[7] A more recent and extremely controversial claim was made by Zhou Ruchang. He argued that Zhiyanzhai is not male but female and none less than Shi Xiangyun, Baoyu's young cousin.[8]

Regardless of debates about the authorship of the margin notes, Zhiyanzhai's comments provide a wealth of information. The style and content of these margin commentaries established the fundamental matrix of *Hongxue* for the next two hundred years. A major part of the commentaries are exclamations of the author's accuracy or excellence in description as it related to Zhiyanzhai's own recollections of actual events. Thus the earliest *Hongxue* was concerned with verifying the fictional descriptions as historical events in the biography of the Jia family, just as was the 'scientific' New *Hongxue* of the 1920s, of which more will be said below. Factual accuracy was, however, not the commentator's sole concern, because moral issues and

---

of Cao Yin's life as a Textile Commissioner for the Kangxi emperor in his book *Ts'ao Yin and the K'ang-hsi Emperor: Bondservant and Master* (New Haven: Yale University Press, 1966). Probably the most interesting and authoritative introduction to the problems with the Zhiyanzhai commentary as *Hongxue* lies in Yu Pingbo's "Zhiyanzhai *Honglou meng* jiping yin yan" (Prefatory remarks to *The collected criticisms of Zhiyanzhai on "Honglou meng"*), in *Yu Pingbo lun Honglou meng*, pp. 919-32. *The collected criticisms of Zhiyanzhai on "Honglou meng"* was published in Shanghai by Zhonghua shuju in 1960.

[6] Yu Rui, "Zao chuang xian bi" (Casual jottings by the date tree window), rpt. in *Honglou meng juan*, p. 14. This view was reaffirmed by Wu Shichang in his article "Zhiyanzhai shi shei?" (Who is Zhiyanzhai?), *Guangming ribao* (Guangming daily), 14.4.1962, rpt. in *Hongxue sanshi nian lunwen xuanbian—xia* (Collected articles from thirty years of *Hongxue*—volume three) (Tianjin: Baihua wenyi chubanshe, 1984), pp. 231-37. Yu Rui requires a note as I will not be covering him in any detail in the body of the text devoted to the so called "miscellaneous critiques." His "Zao chuang xian bi" is for the most part an appraisal of the various endings written for the novel after Cao's unfinished manuscript began circulating. He judges each according to their accuracy and consistency in characterization and theme with the first eighty chapters. His comments on Gao E's version are quite disdainful. Yu Rui himself (*hao* "Si yuan zhai") was a Manchu born sometime in the Qianlong era and died during the Daoguang era. Liu Lanying et al, ed., *Honglou meng renwu cidian* (A dictionary of *Honglou meng* characters) (Nanning: Guangxi renmin chubanshe, 1989), p. 400.

[7] Compare Hu Shi, "Kaozheng *Honglou meng* de xin cailiao" (New material on textual research into *Honglou meng*), rpt. in *Hu Shi Honglou meng yanjiu lunshu quanbian* (Complete discussion and research of Hu Shi on *Honglou meng*), by Hu Shi (Shanghai: Guji chubanshe, 1988), pp. 161-66 with Hu Shi, "Ba Qianlong jiaxu Zhiyanzhai chongping "Shitou ji" yingyin ben" (Postscript to the Qianlong copy of the "Repeated commentary on the *Story of the Stone* by Zhiyanzhai"), rpt. in *Hu Shi Honglou meng yanjiu lunshu quanbian*, pp. 317-44.

[8] Zhou Ruchang, *Honglou meng xinzheng* (New evidence on *Honglou meng*) (Shanghai: Tangdi chubanshe, 1953), pp. 547-64.

family reputation were also considered. The note at the end of chapter thirteen reveals that Cao was ordered to remove references to Qin Keqing's suicide from the novel. It appears that Qin Keqing was involved with an incestuous relationship with her father-in-law, Jia Zhen, and this led her to commit suicide. Whether it be fear of the scandalous effects of the revelations or the upsetting nature of Qin Keqing's death, Zhiyanzhai was instrumental in the removal of these ten odd pages.[9]

Zhiyanzhai's margin notes also provided philosophical comments on the 'author's message.' Proposing that the major theme of the novel lies in the phrase "when happiness reaches its height tragedy finds its birth," Zhiyanzhai exclaims that "life is but a dream." "This grand book narrates a dream, Baoyu's affections are a dream, Jia Rui's lust is a dream, Qin Keqing's family calculations are a dream... What's more these criticisms are written in a dream..."[10] This style of criticism, which related the novel to major features of Buddhist and Daoist beliefs in the folly of life on earth became common later on with critics like "Er zhi dao ren" as we shall see below.

Finally, although no less significantly, the margin comments of Zhiyanzhai also provide the earliest character analysis, albeit rather brief by current standards. One of the most famous debates about the characters in the novel is the controversy over Baochai and Daiyu regarding which of these girls is the better and which should have married Baoyu. Both characters can claim to have 'mystical' rights to marry Baoyu—Daiyu as the match of the mystical Crimson Pearl Flower and Jade Boy in chapter one and Baochai as the "match between gold and jade" of their paired jewellery symbols. However, it is Baochai who eventually marries Baoyu and this has caused not inconsiderable controversy amongst *Honglou meng*'s fanatical readership. Guo Yushi notes that the disputes often became so heated that friends were forced to agree never to discuss *Honglou meng* lest fierce arguments break out.[11] The dispute begins with Zhiyanzhai's preference for Baochai, in the margins of chapter forty-five, where Baochai and Daiyu are discussing Daiyu's inability to shake her latest bout of sickness. Daiyu is concerned that she is a mere parasite on the Jia family and Baochai comforts her saying: "Your being here only means one more dowry for them to find. Surely so small an extra expense as that is hardly going to bother them? (*SS* 2.45.398)."[12] This teasing remark elicited the margin comment "In this jest Baochai directly cuts through Daiyu's own game with Baochai! Baochai's

---

[9]   David Hawkes, "Introduction," in *The Story of the Stone: Volume One*, pp. 42-43.

[10]   See the margins of chapter forty-eight when Baochai is amused at Caltrop writing poetry in her dream-sleep.

[11]   Guo Yushi, *Honglou yanjiu xiaoshi gao*, p. 4.

[12]   When citing from the Hawkes-Minford translation I have used the abbreviation *SS*, referring to *The Story of the Stone*, followed by volume number, chapter number and finally by page number.

actions are at once earnest and sincere, refined and calming. She intends no strained or far fetched significances."[13]

Similarly, Zhiyanzhai regards Baoyu's principal maid and later unofficial concubine, Aroma as a 'filial and loyal woman' (*xiao nü yi nü*). This interpretation is widely disputed since Aroma is perceived by many as being a 'traitor' who reports Baoyu's movements to his mother and subsequent *Hongxue* scholars have opposed Zhiyanzhai's appraisal.[14] Clearly, Zhiyanzhai saw Aroma's confidence in Lady Wang as being admirable in a servant girl whereas others see this 'loyalty' to Lady Wang as being 'traitorous' to Baoyu and another maid Skybright who is sent home to die as a result of Aroma's 'filial and loyal' information.

The underlying philosophy, the attention to historical accuracy and the character appraisals found in Zhiyanzhai's margin notes have all become significant parts of pre 1949 *Hongxue*. The various forms *Hongxue* has adopted beyond these brief annotations has clearly permitted a development of each feature. After the novel began circulating it generated a body of critiques written variously in the form of notes, jottings, poems and casual commentary as scholars inspired by the novel put their thoughts on paper. These have generally been grouped under three headings the 'miscellaneous critiques' (*za ping jia*), the 'small details school' (*pingdian pai*) and the 'hidden meaning school' (*suoyin pai*). Each of these belong to what became known after the New Culture Movement as Old *Hongxue*.

Miscellaneous critiques

Within the group of miscellaneous critics (1729-1815) I will turn first to Zhou Chun. Zhou Chun was from Haining in Zhejiang province and attained his *jinshi* degree in the nineteenth year of Qianlong's reign.[15] His *Yue Honglou meng suibi* is the earliest specialist *Hongxue* text extant today. His critique composed of several short essays and poems has won Zhou the honour of being called the founding father of the 'hidden meaning school.' It also set the ground rules for the 'textual criticism' (*kaozheng*) that New *Hongxue* relied so heavily upon.[16] The text's basic position is that the novel is about the aristocratic Zhang family from Jinling. In this reading Jia Yucun, a relative of the Jia clan, who assumes the post of magistrate with the patronage of the Jias during the novel, is read to be the figure of Zhang

---

[13] Zhiyanzhai cited in Guo Yushi, *Honglou yanjiu xiaoshi gao*, p. 39.

[14] See Yu Pingbo's comments on Zhiyanzhai's appraisal of Aroma in "*Zhiyanzhai Honglou meng jiping* yinyan," pp. 930-32.

[15] Liu Lanying et al, *Honglou meng renwu cidian*, p. 402.

[16] Zhou's text is eleven pages long and is made up of the essays; "Honglou meng ji" (Notes on *Honglou meng*), "Honglou meng pingli" (Critical notes on *Honglou meng*), "Honglou meng yueping" (A brief critique of *Honglou meng*) and eight poems in regulated verse. See Zhou Chun, "*Honglou meng suibi*" (Casual notes on reading *Honglou meng*), rpt. in *Honglou meng juan*, pp. 66-77.

Wujun. This view differs from contemporaneous common understandings that the tale was an allusion to the life of Nalan Xingde, a poet and son to the Prime Minister Ming Zhu who was dismissed from office in 1688.[17] This view was held by Yuan Mei (1716-1799), who also claimed that the garden he purchased, "Sui yuan," was in fact Prospect Garden. Zhang Weiping (1780-1852) was also a proponent of the Nalan Xingde view and it is against this body of opinion that Zhou Chun was writing.[18]

Zhou Chun also was one of the first to coherently link characters in the novel with the poems of portent in chapter five. Baoyu makes a dream visit to the Land of Illusion and is given a sneak preview of the fates of some of the women in his area. The poems are analyzed in typical '*kaozheng*' style. Most of his understandings are upheld today although some differences remain. For example, the last poem of the cycle is now recognized as representing Qin Keqing whose suicide was removed from the novel at Zhiyanzhai's instructions, as we saw above. The poem is accompanied by a picture of a beautiful girl hanging by her neck from the rafters of a tall building "having apparently taken her own life." The poem proceeds,

> Love was her sea, her sky; in such excess
> Love, meeting with its like, breeds wantonness.
> Say not our troubles all from Rong's side came;
> For their beginning Ning must take the blame (*SS* 1.5.135).

Zhou Chun did not however associate Keqing with suicide, perhaps he had not understood the significance of, or had not read, the margin notes. So his understanding of the poem is that it tells the fate of Grandmother Jia's maid, Faithful as well as Keqing in a doubling of characters in the one poem similar to that of Daiyu and Baochai, who share the first poem. Faithful is depicted in the novel as hanging herself after Grandmother Jia's death because she feared being forced into concubinage. Her fear was particularly poignant as Jia She had already sought her hand while Grandmother Jia was alive. Anticipating criticism of his claim on the grounds that the registers are divided upon class lines with mistresses and servants being separated, Zhou invokes Faithful's exceptional moral rectitude. Faithful, Zhou explains, is included in the Main Register with the young mistresses of the house, while all the other maids are in various Supplementary Registers, because of her exceptional loyalty. She was, according to Zhou, "prepared to die to preserve her chastity" (*zhen lie*) and this exemplary behaviour earned her promotion to the ranks of mistress after her death.[19] This opinion has been refuted since

---

[17] Lu Xun explains that Nalan Xingde was understood to be Baoyu and the Twelve Beauties were taken to be students under Nalan Xingde's tutelage. Lu Xun, *A Short History of Chinese Fiction*, pp. 309-310.

[18] Yuan Mei, "Suiyuan shi hua" (Notes on the Suiyuan poems), rpt. in *Honglou meng juan*, pp. 12-13. Zhang Weiping, "Guochao shiren zhenglue" (Brief textual notes on poets under the nation's dynasties), rpt. in *Honglou meng juan*, pp. 363-64.

[19] Zhou Chun, "Yue *Honglou meng* suibi," pp. 69-70.

the margin commentaries revealed that Keqing did indeed hang herself but it is nevertheless interesting that Zhou Chun took Faithful's ultimate defence of her chastity, suicide, as warranting her inclusion in the Main Registers. The discourses on social purity served to make sense of a seemingly improbable poem/picture sequence.

Zhou Chun's judgements on appropriate sexual codes are revealed again in his comparison of You Sanjie's death with Faithful's. You Sanjie cuts her own throat after the man she is betrothed to, Liu Xianglian, decides to call off the engagement when he hears that she has a dubious reputation through her association with the lecherous Jia men. Indeed, she has been Jia Zhen's lover for some time. Although Liu Xianglian is so impressed with You Sanjie's steadfast and suicidal maintenance of her devotion that he immediately wanders off to become a monk, Zhou Chun remains unconvinced of her virtue. Although You Sanjie does indeed commit suicide as a sign of her pure purpose, her previous licentious deeds ensure that, to Zhou, her death is "as light as a swan-goose feather while Faithful's death is as heavy as Mount Tai."[20]

The second of the 'miscellaneous critics' to be discussed is "Er zhi dao ren." The figure behind the penname remains a mystery but the twenty page critique credited to his or her name, *Honglou meng shuo meng*, appeared in 1812 and remains significant in the history of *Hongxue*. The basic philosophical line taken in this critique is that the novel is dealing with philosophical notions that life is a dream fraught with tensions between 'sensual pleasures' (*se*) and 'emptiness' (*kong*). "Er zhi dao ren" introduces the novel by comparing it to existing fictional works of note. "Pu's *Liaozhai* has a pessimistic vision which is developed through ghosts and fox fairies; Shi Naian's pessimistic vision develops through thieves and bandits; Cao Xueqin's pessimistic vision develops through young boys and girls; but they are all similar in their tearful lament at past misfortunes."[21] This tone continues through "Er zhi dao ren's" critique and s/he compares the various dreams of past figures. Zhuangzi's butterfly conundrum is described as the "dream of illusion" while Cao Xueqin is described as "never having a good dream, and so he wrote *Honglou meng*, taking the shattered dreams of an old man to summon the foolish dreams of children."[22]

On the divisive issue of Baoyu's marriage to Baochai and not Daiyu, "Er zhi dao ren" invokes the phrase "Truth becomes fiction when the fiction's true; Real becomes not-real when the unreal's real (*SS* 1.5.130)" from Baoyu's visit to the Land of Illusion in chapter five. "Er zhi dao ren" then

---

[20] Zhou Chun, "Yue *Honglou meng* suibi," p. 68. This is a quotation from the *Han Shu: Sima Qian zhuan*.

[21] "Er zhi dao ren", "*Honglou meng shuo meng*" (Dream talk on the *Honglou meng*) in *Honglou meng juan*, p. 83. "Er zhi dao ren" is referring to Pu Songling's *Liao zhai zhiyi* (Strange tales from a studio) and Shi Naian's *Shuihu zhuan* (Water Margin).

[22] "Er zhi dao ren", "*Honglou meng* shuo meng," in *Honglou meng juan*, p. 83.

draws the parallel, saying "Baoyu and Daiyu were certainly fated to marry (*yin yuan*), and yet this certain marriage turned out to be unreal; Baoyu and Baochai were certainly not fated to marry, but in the end this marriage turned out to be real. The unreal marriage was broken by death; can the real marriage therefore not be separated in life?"[23] "Er zhi dao ren" has then resolved the dispute between the two women in a dexterous philosophical reversal mimicking Cao Xueqin's own techniques and neatly avoiding the problem of personal preferences for the personalities of one or the other woman.

The last example from the 'miscellaneous critics' that I have chosen is Tu Ying or "Du hua ren". Few personal details are known except that his *Honglou meng lun zan* appeared in 1842. This twenty page critique comprises of a short essay titled "*Honglou meng lun*" (Discussing *Honglou meng*), twenty-three questions and answers in the section aptly titled "*Honglou meng wen da*" (Questions and answers on *Honglou meng*), and, most importantly, seventy-four character appraisals. These character appraisals occupy the bulk of the critique and generously cover important and insignificant characters alike. Not all of these are positive appraisals and he is one of the first to write disparagingly of Grandmother Jia, as we will see in chapter seven to follow.

In the question and answer section, Tu Ying makes a number of perceptive points. Note for example his discussion of the four prominent young girls in Baoyu's life; Baochai, Daiyu, and his two senior maids, Skybright and Aroma.

> The question: 'Of Baochai and Daiyu, who is good and who is bad?' The reply: 'Baochai is virtuous and soft (*shan ruo*) while Daiyu is virtuous and hard (*shan gang*). Baochai bends and submits (*yong qu*) while Daiyu is straight and direct (*yong zhi*). Baochai is influenced by her feelings (*xun qing*) while Daiyu is headstrong (*ren xing*). Baochai maintains "face" (*zuo mianzi*) while Daiyu flies faster than dust (*jue chen*).[24] Baochai worked on people's opinions (*shou ren xin*) while Daiyu believed in fate (*xin tian ming*)—that is all.'
>
> The question: 'Of Aroma and Skybright who is good and who is bad?' The reply: 'Aroma is virtuous and soft while Skybright is virtuous and hard. Aroma bends and submits while Skybright is straight and direct. Aroma is influenced by her feelings while Skybright is headstrong. Aroma maintains "face" while Skybright flies faster than dust. Aroma worked on people's opinions while Skybright believed in fate—that is all.'
>
> The question: 'Why did *Honglou meng* create Baochai and Aroma in this fashion?' The reply: 'Aroma is Baochai's reflection (*yingzi*). In creating Aroma, so Baochai was written.'

---

[23] "Er zhi dao ren", "*Honglou meng* shuo meng," in *Honglou meng juan*, p. 87.

[24] The phase '*jue chen*' refers to Confucius' favourite disciple Yan Hui who made remarkably quick progress.

> The question: 'Why did *Honglou meng* create Daiyu and Skybright in that fashion?' The reply: 'Skybright is Daiyu's reflection. In creating Skybright, so Daiyu was written.'[25]

For these and other comments Tu Ying has been classified as a supporter of Daiyu over Baochai. Moreover the parallels he has drawn between the four women remain unchallenged today although the significances granted each differs. In critiques written with Marxist inspiration, Daiyu and Skybright were regarded as being rebellious anti-feudal elements while Aroma and Baochai are upholders of feudal values.

Honglou meng lun zan's 'appraisal' section takes the form of paragraph length notes on either single characters or occasionally pairs of characters. There is no apparent system for selecting which characters are discussed together. For example Jia She and Lady Xing are discussed together as husband and wife while You Shi and Jia Zhen (another husband and wife pair) are discussed separately. The discussion of Aunt Zhao, Jia Zheng's resentful concubine and mother to Tanchun and Jia Huan, reveals that Tu Ying's appraisal can be colourful and combine a certain tolerance while being critical. "Even though she's a glutton and lustful that is not all there is to her... and yet if we melt her down with the five flavours she is more than bedbugs, sores, scabs and dog shit. Magic mushrooms can grow out of dung just as quails can give birth to Phoenix eggs."[26] Aunt Zhao's relentless attempts to destroy others around her earns her this rich appraisal. She is responsible for casting the spell over Baoyu and Xifeng in chapter twenty-five, which nearly causes their deaths. Xifeng has to be restrained after slaughtering some poor hapless dogs and chickens who happen to pass her way while she is under the influence of the spell. Baoyu slips into a coma and only the mysterious arrival of a monk cures him. Yet, as Tu Ying notes, Aunt Zhao is also the mother of the talented young Tanchun, and therefore capable of producing objects of goodness and virtue despite her own lack of these qualities.

Small details school

The 'small details school' critics, as will become evident below, are typified by their attention to intricate details of the text and with pointing out inaccuracies and inconsistencies in the story line or sequence of events. David Rolston's introduction to one of the members of this school, Zhang Xinzhi, provides an insightful survey of the history and critical milieu within which all three of the critics I have chosen worked.[27]

---

[25] Tu Ying, "*Honglou meng* lunzan" (An appraisal of *Honglou meng*), rpt. in *Honglou meng juan*, pp. 143-44.

[26] Tu Ying, "*Honglou meng* lun zan," rpt. in *Honglou meng juan*, pp. 139-40.

[27] David Rolston, "Chang Hsin-chih on How to Read the *Hung-lou meng* (Dream of the Red Chamber)," in *How To Read the Chinese Novel*, ed. by David Rolston, pp. 316-22.

The first representative of the 'small details school' is Wang Xuexiang (Wang Xilian) or "Hu hua zhu ren" (Protector of the Flowers). In 1832 Wang's critique, titled *Honglou meng zongping* was published. From the first line the typical features of the 'small details school' become apparent.

> *Honglou meng*'s one hundred and twenty chapters can be divided into twenty sections in a sequential construction. The first chapter is the first section as it reveals the origins of the novel, and as such it determines the work's point of departure. The second chapter is the second section since it explains the relationship of the Ning and Rong mansions to the Lin, Zhen, Wang and Shi clans, and as such it determines the commencement of the body of the work. Chapters three and four comprise the third section and it explains the origins of the meeting of Baochai, Daiyu and Baoyu. The fifth chapter is the fourth section and it forms the guiding principle for the novel. The fifth section is made up of chapters six to sixteen and it explains the case of Qin Keqing's licentious death and is the starting point of Xifeng's manipulation of power...[28]

The attention to structure is matched by the attention to individual words. Wang states that "the most crucial words in the entire text of *Honglou meng* are real and unreal, or true and false (*zhen, jia*). "The reader ought to know that the real is really the unreal, the unreal is really the real; there is unreal within the real and real within the unreal; the real is not real, and the unreal is not the unreal. To understand this destiny and purpose, Zhen Baoyu and Jia Baoyu are one and are two. This arises not from the author's cynicism but is evidence of his inventive mind."[29]

The broader discourses of socially acceptable behaviour emerge within Wang's discussion of the novel's characters. Wang selects four characteristics—wealth (*fu*), longevity (*shou*), talent (*cai*), and virtue (*de*)—and judges each of the characters upon the grounds of whether they have each of these qualities. He says "in life it is extremely difficult to have all of these qualities."[30] Of the Jia men he writes, "Jia Jing and Jia She have no virtue nor talent, Jia Zheng has virtue but not talent, Jia Lian has a little talent but no virtue, Jia Zhen has not a jot of virtue and no talent either. Of Jia Huan there is too little evidence to say, but Jia Baoyu has a talent and virtue of an unusual type and one that is no use to a career."[31] The women of the Jia clan and the Twelve Beauties are then covered in a similar fashion.

From here the remaining third of Wang's seven page text is devoted to inaccuracies and inconsistencies in the novel. These are written in the form of one or two line comments. He notes, for example, that when Baoyu visits his ailing maid Skybright in chapter seventy-seven and they exchange shirts, no comment is made of his altered clothing by Aroma when he returns. She

---

[28] Wang Xuexiang, "*Honglou meng* zongping" (General comments on *Honglou meng*), rpt. in *Honglou meng juan*, p. 146.

[29] Wang Xuexiang, "*Honglou meng* zongping," rpt. in *Honglou meng juan*, p. 147.

[30] Wang Xuexiang, "*Honglou meng* zongping," rpt. in *Honglou meng juan*, p. 149.

[31] Wang Xuexiang, "*Honglou meng* zongping," rpt. in *Honglou meng juan*, p. 150.

has in the past noted when he returns in clothes different from those he has left in and, as she is in sole charge of his personal effects and dressing, Wang suggests that this is an unlikely omission on Aroma's part. Similarly, Wang notes that the You sisters' mother disappears without mention from the novel after You Sanjie's suicide. The three women are supposedly living together but after You Sanjie's death Xifeng visits You Erjie in chapter sixty-eight, and there is no sign of the mother. Indeed, even after You Erjie transfers her place of residence to the Jia mansions there is no more said about her mother. Wang argues that this is unlikely.[32]

Zhang Xinzhi's (fl. 1828-1850) *Honglou meng du fa* is also concerned with structure and division of the novel, although his "How To Read" is closer in style to the 'miscellaneous critiques' in many other respects. For example Zhang writes, "I have posited three major structural sections [*tuan*] within the first twelve chapters: the first section wrapping up [*chieh*] the 'story of the stone,' the second section wrapping up the 'dream in the red chamber,' and the third section wrapping up the story of the 'precious mirror of love,' with the story of the 'Monk of Passion' and the "Twelve Beauties" serving as the summation and detailed outline of it all." Zhang then proceeds to stress the importance of dividing this monumental novel into sections,

> This monumental text in one hundred and twenty chapters is vast and boundless like an ocean and, yet, it still has its own structural divisions (*tuan-lo*) which one can seek out. Sometimes four chapters comprise a section (*tuan*); sometimes three chapters comprise a section; even one or two chapters can comprise a section. The divisions between them are always clearly demarcated [in my commentary]; it would never do to try to take it all in a single gulp. My pointing out of these [the structural divisions] will save the reader a considerable amount of mental effort.[33]

Zhang is also concerned that the reader should not miss other subtle messages hidden in the text. "The names of the various characters in the book, from the most important to the most insignificant, all have allegorical meaning [*yü-i*]. In the case of Chen Shih-yin and Chia Yü-ts'un, the book itself gives the proper exegesis. The others are left to the reader to grasp on his own. Some of the names are used straightforwardly, some are ironic. Some are offered in solemn earnest, others in jest."[34] Unfortunately Zhang does not take the reader further in explaining any of these significant appellations. The most distinctive feature of Zhang's critique is probably his use of the hexagrams to explain character development, plot movements and other

---

[32] Wang Xuexiang, "*Honglou meng* zongping," rpt. in *Honglou meng juan*, p. 152.

[33] Zhang Xinzhi, ""How to Read the *Dream of the Red Chamber*," trans. by Andrew H. Plaks, in *How To Read the Chinese Novel*, ed. by David Rolston, p. 330. All excerpts from Zhang Xinzhi's critique are drawn from Plaks' translation. A copy of the original is found in *Honglou meng juan*, pp. 153-59. I have used the *hanyu pinyin* system of romanization except in cases such as this when David Rolston has used the Wade-Giles system and I am citing his volume's translation.

[34] Zhang Xinzhi, "How to Read the *Dream of the Red Chamber*," p. 333.

seemingly incidental features. Yin and yang take their full significance in Zhang's critique and an intricate elaboration of the importance of each is given along with the transformation of the novel through the various hexagrams.[35]

An even more striking example of the extent to which the 'small details school' differentiates itself from other *Hongxue* is the work of Yao Xie (1805-1864). Yao Xie's *Du Honglou meng gangling* makes extensive use of numerical details. For example Yao compares the birthdays of numerous characters; "Yuanchun is born on New Years day... Baochai is born in the twenty-first of the first month, Aunt Xue and Jia Zheng are some time in the second and third months but we are not sure of the day; Lady Wang's is the first of the third month... Lin Daiyu is on the twelfth of the second month and she is born on the same day as Aroma; Baoyu, Xiuyan, Baoqin, Patience and Number Four [Citronella] all have the same birthday, probably sometime in the fourth month... Xifeng's birthday is on the second day of the ninth month and she shares it with Golden."[36]

After the intricacies of birthdays, Yao moves on to examine the various manners in which people died; listing how many committed suicide, how many died from poisoning and so on. The amounts paid to each of the main servants and mistresses for pin money is also carefully tallied, as are the monetary exchanges that occur as part of the Jia family's responsibilities to friends' funerals and weddings. Yao also provided a detailed account of the various illnesses each character suffers. The careful accounting of concurrences ensures that seemingly incidental events are given their full import.

Hidden meaning school

The years immediately after the establishment of the Republic of China saw the emergence of the 'hidden meaning school.' Guo Yushi explains that these scholars sought secret and hidden significances to elucidate the author's presumed intended messages.[37] Although this school faced the brunt of the attacks from Hu Shi and Yu Pingbo's so called scientific *Hongxue* of textual analysis its supporters continued publishing their findings well into the 1930s suggesting that some form of 'peaceful co-existence' was emerging. This pattern was of course dramatically altered after 1949, and more specifically after 1954, when both the Old and New *Hongxue* methods of critical practice were rejected in favour of the Marxist or Maoist inspired methodologies. Nevertheless, the 'hidden meaning school' remains prominent in the history of *Hongxue* both as a result of the prestige of one of its proponents, Cai Yuanpei, and because it shows a clear link to the earliest specialist

---

[35] Zhang Xinzhi, "How to Read the *Dream of the Red Chamber*," pp. 336-39.

[36] Yao Xie, "Du *Honglou meng* gangling (jie lu)" (Guiding principles for reading *Honglou meng* [excerpts]), rpt. in *Honglou meng juan*, p. 164.

[37] Guo Yushi, *Honglou yanjiu xiaoshi gao*, p. 137.

Hongxue of Zhou Chun mentioned above. In this respect, the 'hidden meaning school' can claim a more authentically traditional and authentically
Chinese methodology than can that of Hu Shi, who was inspired by Dewey's
scientific methods, or even Wang Guowei. The latter's work predates that of
the 'hidden meaning school' but as it has consciously drawn from Western
philosophy, and notably Schopenhauerian notions of tragedy, it fits less
comfortably within the Old *Hongxue* matrix that I aimed to discuss first. I
have thereby included Wang Guowei's critique of *Honglou meng* after this
final survey of the schools of Old *Hongxue*.

The first of the 'hidden meanings school' critiques to be discussed is
Wang Mengyuan's *Honglou meng suoyin tiyao*. It was published in 1916
as part of Wang's critical commentary accompanying the Shanghai zhonghua
shuju edition of the novel in its one hundred and twenty chapter form. This
edition became immensely popular and within a short time went into its thirteenth reprint.[38] It was published under Wang's penname "Wu zhen dao ren
xi bi" (The person awakened to the true path plays with a pen). As with the
other members of the 'hidden meaning school' Wang did not take the novel
on face value and expended a considerable amount of energy seeking and
proving alternative, 'real' meanings to the novel through proposals of the
novel's use of allegory. His basic position is that *Honglou meng* is the tale
of the Shunzhi emperor and his concubine Dong E. Baoyu is Shunzhi and
Daiyu is his concubine. Dong E is moreover understood to be a famous
prostitute, Dong Xiaowan, who entered the palace after changing her name to
that of a Manchu.[39] The emperor was bewitched by her talents and was broken hearted on her death. The reason why an allegory was necessary was because, "The author did not dare say what he really had on his mind.
However, because he could not suppress the urge to speak his mind, he had
no choice but to change the [true identity of] people and places."[40] The
historical events are then cleverly disguised by a tale of romance.

Wang's insistence on reading the novel as an historical allegory of the
lives of two people did not limit his analysis of the significance of the characters to Daiyu and Baoyu alone. Indeed, Wang argued that Dong E was such
a complicated figure with a complicated life that she is represented by an additional six characters. These six combine with Daiyu to present different
aspects of the one historical figure's personality and life. Qin Keqing, Xue
Baochai, Xue Baoqin, Skybright, Aroma and Adamantina are each credited
with representing different aspects of Dong E. However, the picture created
by Wang develops a further complication since he also argues that Baochai is

[38] Guo Yushi, *Honglou yanjiu xiaoshi gao*, p. 139.
[39] Wang Mengyuan, "*Honglou meng* suoyin tiyao (jie lu)" (Synopsis of the hidden meaning of *Honglou meng* [excerpts]), in *Honglou meng juan*, p. 298.
[40] Wang Mengyuan, "*Honglou meng* suoyin tiyao (jie lu)," p. 293.

the embodiment of a further two historical characters—Liu Sanxiu and Chen Yuanyuan.[41]

The problematic nature of his analysis is clear in the discussion of why Daiyu is Dong E. Similarities and contrasts between the two women are given significances which appear rather strained. "Xiaowan loved plum trees and Daiyu loved bamboo. Xiaowan was partial to *qu* while Daiyu was fond of the *qin*. Xiaowan relished illness and so Daiyu also relished her illness. Xiaowan had a weakness for the moon and so Daiyu also has a weakness for the moon. Xiaowan enjoyed planting and so Daiyu enjoys burying flowers. Xiaowan could cook and so Daiyu could cut. Xiaowan could hold her drink but didn't want to drink and so Daiyu was not able to take alcohol at all."[42] Wang's implied 'necessary' nature of the concordances he lists are extremely tenuous and could equally have been made about any number of characters.

Other representatives of this school were more restrained in their approach. For example Cai Yuanpei (1868-1940), one time President of Beijing University and Minister of Education, was a strong proponent of the 'hidden meaning school' although the allusions he described were more subtle than those of Wang. Cai's basic opinion, published in his 1917 *Shitou ji suoyin* was that the novel "is a political novel about the Kangxi era. The author was expressing his sincere nationalism."[43] In this political reading of the novel Cai was clearly informed by the recent events which saw the overthrowing of the Manchu monarchy and the establishment of the first Chinese Republic. Cai claims *Honglou meng* to be an anti-Manchu text.

He refined this vision of the novel's value with the argument that the women in the novel represented the Han and the men in the novel, the Manchu. Developed from his reading of Baoyu's statement that "boys are made of water and girls are made of mud (*SS* 1.2.76)," Cai justifies his analysis through the invocation of ancient theories of yin and yang. Citing Shi Xiangyun's brief explanation of the manifestations of yin and yang in daily life in chapter thirty-one (men are yang, women are yin; masters and mistresses are yang, servants are yin), Cai argues that yang is the controlling Manchu while yin is the Han who is controlled. This is then extrapolated to generate the notion that *Honglou meng*'s female characters represent the Han and its male characters the Manchu.[44]

Furthermore his understanding of the importance of the colour red in the text is that "Baoyu's fascination with red is saying that the Manchus loved the Han culture" because when the word red is used it is reflecting the word

---

[41] Wang cited in Guo Yushi, *Honglou yanjiu xiaoshi gao*, p. 147.

[42] Wang Mengyuan cited in Liu Lanying et al, *Honglou meng renwu cidian*, pp. 394-95.

[43] Cai Yuanpei, "*Shitou ji* suoyin (jie lu)" (Hidden meanings of the *Story of the Stone* [excerpts]) in *Honglou meng juan*, p. 319. Cai's critique went into its tenth reprint by 1930 according to Guo Yushi. Guo Yushi, *Honglou yanjiu xiaoshi gao*, p. 148.

[44] Cai Yuanpei, "*Shitou ji* suoyin (jie lu)," in *Honglou meng juan*, p. 322.

'vermilion' (*zhu*) which refers to Zhu Zheming who was Han.[45] Each of the characters is then assigned a historical figure. Baoyu is read as representing the Kangxi emperor's crown prince Yin Reng while Daiyu is Zhu Zhucha. The remainder of the Twelve Beauties are understood to represent prominent scholars of the time such as Gao Jiangcun, Chen Qinian among others.[46] His logic for allocating a character to a scholar is based upon three criteria. 1. Cai would match personality types. For example he links Baoyu with Gao Jiangcun and Adamantina with Jiang Ximing because Gao like Baochai was quiet and gentle while Jiang, like Adamantina, was arrogant and proud. 2. Cai would seek anecdotes from history that have parallels with the novel. 3. Cai would connect the names of the characters with the names of the scholars.[47] The household of the Jia clan was also taken to represent the various wings of Qing bureaucracy with individual characters symbolizing different sections. For example, Jia She represents the Board of Punishments because his wife's name, Xing, is a homophone for punishments (*xing*) and Jia Lian is the Board of Revenue and Population.[48]

Cai's work was influential in its own right but it was raised to considerable fame as a result of the attacks made upon his 'hidden meaning school' by Hu Shi. This debate split the *Hongxue* world into the two predominant camps of New and Old *Hongxue*. Cai's influence continued through his patronage of other scholars who wrote along similar lines to his own. Foremost among these is Shou Pengfei, whose *Honglou meng benshi bianzheng* appeared in 1927. Shou argued, like Cai Yuanpei, who wrote the preface for the volume, that the novel was about the Kangxi court. However, Shou regarded Grandmother Jia as being Kangxi and the twelve beauties as being the emperor's sons.[49] Similarly, Jing Meijiu's *Shitouji zhendi* of 1934 argued that the novel is a historical allegory where Daiyu represented the Ming dynasty because she was weak and in decline, while Baochai represented the Qing because she was strong and ascending. Jing associated the treachery that occurred over Baochai's marriage to Baoyu, whereby Daiyu and Baoyu are deceived by the family, as representing the court intrigue that occurred after the death of the Kangxi emperor.[50] Before I delve into the controversy that these 'hidden meaning school' advocates provoked from the Hu Shi inspired New *Hongxue*, I will trace the beginnings of Western influence in *Hongxue* by discussing Wang Guowei's

---

[45] Cai Yuanpei, "*Shitou ji* suoyin (jie lu)," in *Honglou meng juan*, p. 319.

[46] Cai Yuanpei cited in Liu Lanying et al, *Honglou meng renwu cidian*, p. 376.

[47] Cai Yuanpei cited in Guo Yushi, *Honglou yanjiu xiaoshi gao*, pp. 149-50. Guo has included lengthy extracts on characters names and how they connect to historical figures on p. 152.

[48] Cai Yuanpei cited in Guo Yushi, *Honglou yanjiu xiaoshi gao*, pp. 150-51.

[49] Shou Pengfei, *Honglou meng benshi bianzheng* (Evidence for determining the original story of *Honglou meng*) (1927; rpt. Shanghai: Shangwuyin shuguan, 1928), pp. 38-40.

[50] Jing Meijiu, *Shitouji zhendi* (The true significance of *The Story of the Stone*) (Xijing chubanshe, 1934), cited in Guo Yushi, *Honglou yanjiu xiaoshi xugao*, p. 165 and p. 175.

work. Hu Shi's work, like that of Wang Guowei, was influenced by western critical theories.

Western influence and Wang Guowei

Wang Guowei's (1877-1927) *Honglou meng pinglun* is unique for its intro-duction to *Hongxue* of comparative literary studies. It unites Schopenhauerian notions of tragedy and aesthetics with Buddhist notions of life as suffering and Daoist notions of desire. The critique is divided into five chapters. They are titled as follows: 1. Overview of life and art. 2. The spirit of *Honglou meng*. 3. *Honglou meng*'s aesthetic value. 4. *Honglou meng*'s value in the study of logic. 5. Conclusion. In chapter one of his critique Wang expounds at length upon notions of aesthetics pondering the nature of beauty, how beauty relates to life, and ultimately, the meaning of life.[51]

The following chapter then provides the supporting evidence for his theo-ries from *Honglou meng*. Wang notes that in the opening paragraphs of the novel we are shown how 'desire' exists as soon as we exist. He cites the fol-lowing section from the novel as evidence:

> Long ago, when the goddess Nüwa was repairing the sky, she melted down a great quantity of rock and, on the Incredible Crags of the Great Fable Mountains, moulded the amalgam into thirty-six thousand, five hundred and one large building blocks, each measuring seventy-two feet by a hundred and forty-four feet square. She used thirty-six thousand five hundred of these blocks in the course of her building operations, leaving a single odd block unused, which lay, all on its own, at the foot of Greensickness Peak in the aforementioned mountains. Now this block of stone, having under-gone the melting and moulding of a goddess, possessed magic powers. It could move about at will and could grow or shrink to any size it wanted. Observing that all the other blocks had been used for celestial repairs and that it was the only one to have been rejected as unworthy, it became filled with shame and resentment and passed its days in sorrow and lamentation (*SS* 1.1.47).

From this Wang argues that the jade, which the stone transforms into, repre-sents life's desire. The life of Baoyu, who is born with the jade in his mouth, reveals the path from the red dust towards enlightenment.[52] Wang contrasts this "enlightenment through life" with characters such as Golden (who throws herself in the well), and You Sanjie (who slits her own throat after Liu reneges on their betrothal) saying that these are not those who achieve enlightenment through release from life. Instead their suicides are symbolic of each woman's intense search to fulfil unattainable desires. The only characters from the novel that Wang regards as having achieved enlight-

---

[51] Wang Guowei, "*Honglou meng* pinglun" (Critique of *Honglou meng*), rpt. in *Honglou meng juan*, pp. 244-48.
[52] Wang Guowei, "*Honglou meng* pinglun," pp. 249-50.

enment are Baoyu, Xichun and Nightingale. Xichun is Baoyu's cousin and she becomes a nun at the end of the novel. Nightingale, Daiyu's principle maid, likewise joins Xichun after her mistress' death. Liu Xianglian's adoption of the religious path, (he wanders off with a monk after You Sanjie's suicide), like You Sanjie's death, is simply a response to the misery of confronting unfulfilled desires and not the true relinquishing of desire that is evidenced in Baoyu, Xichun and Nightingale, according to Wang. Among those that achieve enlightenment there are two types; those who see the suffering of others and then see the truth and those who see the truth through their own suffering.[53]

Wang regarded *Honglou meng* as fitting Schopenhauer's third type of tragedy whereby the tragedy emerges out of a complex amalgam of individual's actions and their web of relationships rather than any particular evil intent. The tragedy of Baoyu and Daiyu is then one generated by the conflicting needs and perceptions of Grandmother Jia, Lady Wang and Xifeng rather than any one character wishing to cause a tragedy.[54] In this respect *Honglou meng* is particularly poignant.

In several respects Wang Guowei's work provided a framework for the New *Hongxue* scholars who were to begin publishing a few years before Wang's own suicide. Not only did Wang introduce the possibility of the use of Western techniques to a Chinese text but he also pre-empted Hu Shi's major claim that the novel was an autobiography by Cao Xueqin. Wang Guowei's critique argued this line nearly twenty years before Hu Shi although he did not undertake the extensive proof as Hu Shi did. The first chapter in the novel states "Surely my 'number of females,' whom I spent half a lifetime studying with my own eyes and ears are preferable to this kind of stuff? [characters from romantic fiction] (*SS* 1.1.50)." Wang regards this as indicating that the novel is indeed about the author's life experiences and life companions.[55] It was not until Hu Shi took up this idea with greater force that it gained general acceptance and influence on critical style.

Hu Shi, Yu Pingbo and New "Hongxue"

The publication of Hu Shi's essay *Honglou meng kaozheng* in 1921 is a major turning point in the history of *Hongxue*. Hu Shi's adoption of Western techniques, inspired by Western thinkers like John Dewey, his promotion of the vernacular language (*baihua*), in which *Honglou meng* was written, over the classical form (*wenyan*), his vocal opposition to Cai Yuanpei's 'hidden meaning school' and his strong belief in the notion that *Honglou meng* was an autobiography by Cao Xueqin, all served to establish 1921 as a major juncture. Crucial to his work was the 'scientific' verifica-

---

[53] Wang Guowei, "*Honglou meng* pinglun," p. 251.
[54] Wang Guowei, "*Honglou meng* pinglun," pp. 254-55.
[55] Wang Guowei, "*Honglou meng* pinglun," pp. 263-65.

tion of 'facts.' The importance of method is drawn out in his essay "A briefing on my own personal thinking" where he states that his intention in *Honglou meng kaozheng* is not to tell readers how to understand *Honglou meng* but rather to learn something of the scientific method whereby one learns to "boldly hypothesize and carefully verify."[56]

His essay begins by framing his own research against previous work in the following statement:

> Completing textual research into *Honglou meng* is not an easy task; firstly because there are too few materials and secondly because the people who have studied this book up to now have all taken the wrong path. How have they taken the wrong path? They have not sought facts from those verifiable materials such as *Honglou meng*'s authorship, its social milieu, its various editions etc., but instead have gathered lots of irrelevant fragmentary historical events and drawn lots of strained analogies to the plot of *Honglou meng*. They certainly did not know how to carry out textual research on *Honglou meng*, in fact all they did was write lots of far-fetched and strained analogies for *Honglou meng*!"[57]

He then provides a brief summary of the previous *Hongxue*, which barely does justice to its diversity since it is primarily concerned with the members of the 'hidden meaning school,' Wang Mengyuan and Cai Yuanpei. This lengthy critique of Wang's and Cai's *Hongxue* completes the first chapter and outlines his major objections to Old *Hongxue*.

His second chapter then addresses the issue of the novel's authorship, stressing that in seeking out this information only reliable editions and reliable materials should be used. While Cao Xueqin is roundly presumed to be the author, Hu Shi sets out to prove this hypothesis by verifying it against the 'facts.' The first piece of evidence Hu Shi uses is drawn from comments in the novel itself. In the first chapter we read of the history of the tale, "Cao Xueqin in his Nostalgia Studio worked on it for ten years, in the course of which he rewrote it no less than five times, dividing it into chapters, composing chapter headings, renaming it *The Twelve Beauties of Jinling*, and adding an introductory quatrain (*SS* 1.1.51)." This evidence is then coupled with material from Cao's contemporaries, like Yuan Mei. As mentioned briefly above, Yuan Mei's *Suiyuan shihua* mentioned in its twenty-first *juan* that his Sui garden was indeed the garden that Cao Xueqin drew his Prospect Garden from when he wrote *Honglou meng*. From Yuan Mei's comments Hu Shi proceeds, in clear and defined fashion stating, "(1) We know that scholars of the Qianlong period thought that Cao Xueqin was the author. (2) This material said that Xueqin was Cao Lianting's son.... (but

---

[56] Hu Shi, "Jieshao wo ziji de sixiang (jielu)" (A briefing on my own personal thinking-excerpts), rpt. in *Hu Shi Honglou meng yanjiu*, p. 194.

[57] Hu Shi, "*Honglou meng* kaozheng" (Textual Research on *Honglou meng*), rpt. in *Hu Shi Honglou meng yanjiu*, p. 75.

we know this to be incorrect...). (3) This argues that Prospect Garden later became Sui Garden."[58]

Hu Shi duplicates this process, citing various scholarly notes on Cao Xueqin, the Cao family and their connection with the Kangxi emperor, and then notes where details concur and which are verifiable. At each stage the reader is presented with a numbered list of 'facts' that have been verified. Led through the maze of supporting data the reader is then reassured that,

> From the above discussion on Cao Xueqin himself and his family history we can say that in all probability *Honglou meng* is Cao Xueqin's autobiography. There is nothing extraordinary about this understanding, indeed it is quite a natural one. But the great *Hongxue* scholars of the last hundred or more years have talked and the more they talked the more minute their focus became. So that now we feel we have to seek verification for an extremely ordinary understanding.[59]

The same process is completed for Gao E and the controversy over authorship/editorship of the last forty chapters. This essay, with its attention to detail, clarity of presentation and verification of evidence has altered the style and content of *Hongxue* since.[60]

Yu Pingbo worked closely with Hu Shi, as did Gu Jiegang, and the mutual influence is evident, although Yu's critique *Honglou meng bian* is more generous in its interpretive comments and less restrained by pedantry. This is clearly a function of the difference in length between the two works, with Hu Shi's being an essay and Yu's a substantial book, however it is also a function of the difference in aims and objectives. Hu Shi wanted to use *Honglou meng* to teach and demonstrate a new textual method whereas Yu was concerned to elucidate his vision of *Honglou meng*.

Yu Pingbo's *Honglou meng bian* appeared in 1922 published by Yadong Library in Shanghai and developed from the lively discussions he and his friend Gu Jiegang became preoccupied with after reading Hu Shi's essay.[61] Yu's critique of *Honglou meng* was the first book-length piece of *Hongxue* written revealing the importance of technological change on publishing as well as the encouragement of the vernacular rather than the classical language, which amongst other features, prided itself on brevity and establishing a concise form. *Honglou meng bian* in contrast to the usually brief *Hongxue* of the past is seventeen chapters long and divided into three *juan*. The issues discussed range from an analysis of Gao E's final forty chapters,

---

[58] Hu Shi, "*Honglou meng* kaozheng," pp. 86-87.

[59] Hu Shi, "*Honglou meng* kaozheng," p. 98.

[60] This remains true even though the post 1949 reception of Hu Shi's ideas on autobiographical naturalism have been the focus for criticism by Marxist inspired *Hongxue* which advocated the primacy of realism. For more detail see the final chapter of this volume.

[61] In his introduction to the book Yu explains that he was initially rather sceptical of *Honglou meng*'s value. It was only after talking with Gu that he became infected by Gu's enthusiasm for the text and he states quite clearly that Gu's influence permeates all aspects of the study. Yu Pingbo, *Honglou meng bian*, pp. 83-85.

comparisons of the various editions through to discussions of the 'author's attitude' and analyses of Qin Keqing's death.

In a fashion clearly influenced by Hu Shi, Yu's critique is punctuated by numerically ordered lists of 'facts' or related known items. For example in his discussion of the problems related to studying an unfinished work he says, "There are special problems related to comparing *Honglou meng* with its sequels and this makes it even easier [for the critic] to be defeated. Firstly, *Honglou meng* is a literary text and not a research paper, so we cannot equate superficial comments with the whole picture. Secondly, because *Honglou meng* is a book written from actual events, those authors of the sequel do not have the same conditions, personalities or exceptional intelligence [as the original author]."[62] Hu Shi's lesson on methodology and the importance of logical thought in literary practice has clearly influenced Yu's *Hongxue*.

The effects of Hu Shi's work were not limited to style, but also to content. For example, with Hu Shi's amplification of the importance of ascertaining the author of *Honglou meng* and his certainty that it was Cao Xueqin, *Hongxue* under Yu Pingbo then similarly reflected this new authorial authority. Yu's sixth chapter is titled "The author's attitude" and here we read,

> Discussing the author's attitude is not an easy thing. We have at least two reliable paths of inquiry. Firstly, we can ascertain the author's attitude at the time of writing the book by examining what he says. This is the most believable because nobody else, except himself, can completely understand his meaning. If we don't believe the words Mr Xueqin wrote in his preface then what other evidence can we believe? So if we take this path I believe it won't be a false trail. Secondly, we can take evidence from what we know about the author's life history and environment and corroborate our conjectures. Unfortunately, at this time we know very little about Xueqin's life and affairs, but from the little we do know there is enough to corroborate results we gather from the text itself.[63]

Yu goes on to say that the first two chapters of the novel encapsulate Cao's attitude and what follows is elaboration. He then makes three points "(1) *Honglou meng* is a lament at his [Cao's] life and by comparing his life history with Baoyu's personality in the novel we can see that Xueqin was an arrogant and conceited sort of person. Moreover he laments the hardship of poverty and misfortune in life."[64] This claim is supported by textual evidence from the first few chapters where Baoyu is described as having divine origins. "(2) *Honglou meng* is written repenting passion (*qing*). Xueqin's

---

[62] Yu Pingbo, *Honglou meng bian*, p. 90.

[63] Yu Pingbo, *Honglou meng bian*, p. 180. Another interesting feature of this chapter is its brief survey of *Hongxue* up to Yu's book. Yu divides previous *Hongxue* into the 'school of riddles' (*cai mi pai*) and the 'school of leisure' (*xiao xian pai*). Yu Pingbo, *Honglou meng bian*, pp. 178-80.

[64] Yu Pingbo, *Honglou meng bian*, pp. 180-81.

original intention was to have Baoyu become a monk but only after suffering misfortune and straightened circumstances, and in this way it is a little different from Gao E's sequel."[65] This point is also verified by quotations from the first two chapters. "(3) *Honglou meng* is written to relate the biographies of the Twelve Beauties. Other than considering the two points mentioned above... the story's most important characters are the Twelve Beauties. In this respect *Shuihu* and *Honglou meng* have the same aim. As everyone knows, *Shuihu* was written to describe the author's vision of one hundred and eight heroes."[66] Yu then goes on to argue against previous *Hongxue* scholars who have held the view that none of these women were decent saying that, other than Xifeng and Keqing, all of the others are unpolluted and have nothing of which to be ashamed.

"Hongxue" of the 1940s

The greater credibility *Honglou meng* gained as a result of the work of Hu Shi and Yu Pingbo in the early Republican period also spawned a style of *Hongxue* in the later part of the era that was not solely preoccupied with the author and his vision. These critiques became concerned with the novel as a text with self-generating meanings and social relevance. Where Old *Hongxue* was interested in seeking broader political and allegorical meanings, and New *Hongxue* was preoccupied with the author, the 1940s style of criticism attempted what Guo Yushi has described as a 'comprehensive' approach.[67] This approach discussed characters' actions, motives, or personality traits and issues of current social concern that could be examined by *Honglou meng*, as well as authorship. The combination of the first two features, character analysis and social analysis was innovative for *Hongxue* because it permitted fictional characters an independence from historical events, either imperial or authorial. This style of critique judged characters on their behaviour and then sought lessons for contemporary life from their fates.

During the decade of the 1940s two books were published that represented this new era in *Hongxue*. These books were Li Chendong's *Honglou meng yanjiu* of 1942 and Tai Yu's (Wang Kunlun) *Honglou meng renwu lun* of 1948. Both engaged in a detailed analysis of the characters, their positions in the novel and their significance to current social issues, rather than exclusively attempting to link them to actual historical or political personages. Li Chendong's work is divided into five sections that reveal the breadth of subject matter included in the work of this type. These included "Cao Xueqin's life and times," "An analysis of the main characters in *Honglou*

[65] Yu Pingbo, *Honglou meng bian*, p. 182.
[66] Yu Pingbo, *Honglou meng bian*, p. 184.
[67] Guo Yushi, *Honglou yanjiu xiao shi xugao*, p. 182.

meng," "The world of *Honglou meng*," (incorporating topics such as education, family, and religion) and "The artistic value of *Honglou meng*."[68]

In his section on 'Marriage' Li writes that the clan marriage system, wherein the parents decide the fate of their children, can lead to great unhappiness. He lists all the examples of such miserable matches in the novel including the tragic death of Jia Yingchun at the hands of her husband, You Erjie's death at the hands of Wang Xifeng and, of course, the central romantic tragedy of Baoyu, Baochai and Daiyu.[69] In his detailed analysis of Daiyu, Li proposed that Lin Daiyu and Pan Jinlian of the *Jin Ping Mei*, were two types of the 'jealous' character with the difference being that one dwelt among the rougher merchant class and the other among the more refined scholars. Baochai, on the other hand, was the totality of Chinese woman's beauty and morality, whose virtues included capability in every aspect, filiality, consideration of others, warmth and compliance.[70]

Tai Yu's classic is more centrally focussed upon the characters as the chapter headings for his book make abundantly clear. Included are the following: "Qin Keqing and Li Wan," "Three Virtuous Women of *Honglou meng*," "On Shi Xiangyun," "Lin Daiyu's love," "Tanchun's political bearing." Within each chapter Tai Yu analyses each character or group of characters with a technique that has come to typify *Hongxue* character analyses, including those written in the PRC. In his chapter on Xifeng, for example, we read of her spoken manner, her background, her family connections, her activities and her motives. All personality appraisals are supported by quotations from the novel and developed from these are generalizations about the social relevance of her image. Xifeng is described as a talented, strong but evil woman whose likeness can be found in Chinese families "right up to the present time."[71] Tai Yu's analysis of the significance of the death of Baoyu's maid Skybright, is that her death portends the necessary defeat of the love between Baoyu and Daiyu and the victory of Aroma and Baochai. He then continues the theme saying, "The author wrote of Baochai, Tanchun, Patience, Aroma, and Wang Xifeng with the style of a political history but when he wrote of Daiyu, Skybright, You Sanjie and Parfumée he wrote poems of immense tragedy... The author used Li Wan to show the beauty of

---

68 Li Chendong, *Honglou meng yanjiu* (Research on *Honglou meng*) (1942; rpt. Taipei: Xinxing shuju, 1962), pp. 1-2.

69 Li Chendong, *Honglou meng yanjiu*, pp. 68-70.

70 Li Chendong, *Honglou meng yanjiu*, pp. 40-42.

71 Tai Yu, *Honglou meng renwu lun* (Discussion of characters in *Honglou meng*) (1948; rpt. Taipei: Chang'an chubanshe, 1988), p. 156. Another edition of this work was published in 1987 under the name Wang Kunlun and this text differs considerably from the Taipei edition. For example the quotation on Xifeng noted above has been deleted. The changes were part of a general re-editing carried out after 1949 as Wang republished his chapters in *Guangming ribao* (see note below). Wang Kunlun, *Honglou meng renwu lun* (1948; rpt. Hong Kong: Zhonghua shuju, 1987).

women's quietude and tenderness, and used Skybright, You Sanjie and Parfumée to reveal the beauty of women's forth-rightness and strength."[72]

Tai Yu clearly saw his analysis of the novel to have direct importance to society's notions of womanhood because versions of his chapters have appeared in the Chongqing magazine *Xiandai funü* (Modern Woman).[73] His work was republished in serial form after 1949 in national newspapers such as *Guangming ribao*, although not before some alterations were made to the text.[74]

The work of the 1940s was important for the manner in which it built on the greater respectability gained by *Honglou meng* in the previous two decades. From this platform *Hongxue* scholars, like Li Chendong and Tai Yu, were able to develop *Hongxue* into a more socially responsible form of criticism. In the decades that followed the revolutionary New Culture Movement, readers were increasingly familiar with the practice of analysing society, and family relations in particular, through literary critique. It was not enough to verify with factual evidence that Cao Xueqin was the author, as Hu Shi had done, nor was it sufficient to examine the extent to which Gao E's version followed Cao's intentions, as Yu Pingbo had done. Li Chendong and Tai Yu tried to grant meaning and social significance to the novel that would help readers of their own time understand the entire social system of late imperial China.

It is the combination of Tai Yu and Li Chendong's socially responsible criticism and Yu Pingbo's textual criticism which has survived into the late twentieth century *Hongxue* of the PRC. Each point of opinion or import is supported by citations from the text which are understood to be the author's oration. As will become clear in the concluding chapter to this volume, the introduction of Marxist and Maoist methodology to *Hongxue* also has unique ramifications for the production of new significances for *Honglou meng* but the legacy of the *Hongxue* styles from the first half of the twentieth century is also of considerable importance. However, before analyzing the *Hongxue* of the contemporary PRC and its implications for gender, I will proceed to explain in more detail my own understanding of *Honglou meng* and its discourse on gender.

---

[72] Tai Yu, *Honglou meng renwu lun*, p. 18.

[73] For example, Tai Yu's chapter on Aroma "Hua Xiren lun" (On Aroma), appeared in *Xiandai funü* (Modern women), 2, No. 1 (1.7.1943). The chapter on Skybright, "Qingwen zhi si" (Skybright's death), appeared in 2, No. 3 (1.8.1943) and that on Tanchun "Zhengzhi fengdu de Tanchun" (Tanchun's political bearing), in 2, No. 4 (1.10.1943). Other chapters appeared over the course of 1944 as well.

[74] The following are some examples of Wang Kunlun's chapters that appeared in national newspapers—"Qingwen zhi si," *Guangming ribao*, 8.12.1962; "Hua Xiren lun," *Guangming ribao*, 22,25.12.1962; "Zhengzhi fengdu de Tanchun," *Guangming ribao*, 5.1.1963; "*Honglou meng* zhong san lie nü—Yuanyang, Siqi, You Sanjie" (The three model women in *Honglou meng*: Faithful, Chess and You Sanjie), *Guangming ribao*, 2,5.2.1963; "Jiafu de laoye xiaoye men" (The masters and young masters of the Jia mansions), *Guangming ribao*, 16,19.2.1963; "Wang Xifeng lun" (Discussing Wang Xifeng), *Guangming ribao*, 25,27.4.1963.

CHAPTER THREE

GENDER IMPERATIVES: JIA BAOYU'S BISEXUALITY

Throughout the years of studies devoted to *Honglou meng*, many critics and readers have recognized the novel's potential for what Andrew Plaks has called an analysis based on complementary bipolarity.[1] His structuralist methodology has provided the basis for much fruitful discussion of the novel. Many scholars have reinforced Plaks' study by interpreting the text as representing Baoyu's existential dilemma between the dual worlds of innocence and experience, youth and non-youth, reality and utopia, realism and idealism, Daoist/Buddhist and Confucian. In keeping with this volume's focus upon gender this chapter will examine the crisis Baoyu has with the gender imperatives surrounding him, by presenting the binary masculine/feminine as a thematic paradigm. It will conclude by revealing the multifarious ways in which the text reinforces concepts of 'femininity' and 'masculinity' as distinct qualities which are divided *between* the sexes.[2]

By masculinity and femininity we are talking about all the signifying practices that inform an individual in his/her social/sexual development. That is, what exactly are the social constructs, conscious and unconscious, that project an individual into masculine or feminine modes. The terms 'femininity' and 'masculinity' are not interpreted as "real essences, biological or social in origin, but powerful myths which have had an effective function in history."[3] Masculinity and femininity do, however, interact in very concrete ways with the very corporeality of the individual's biology. Those of us born male are constrained within notions of acceptable masculinity and those of us born female are constrained within notions of acceptable femininity. In these respects, while biology does not determine an individual's gender preferences, that individual's preferences are affected by the very corporeal-

---

[1] Andrew H. Plaks, *Archetype and Allegory in the Dream of the Red Chamber* (Princeton: Princeton University Press, 1976), pp. 43-53.

[2] In the chapter "Complementary Bipolarity and Multiple Periodicity" Plaks warns of the tendency to oversimplify Levi-Strauss' concept of the binary opposition. He states that the dualism of Chinese thought is not "an absolute categorization of all phases of existence into two distinct classes of phenomena, or even to a relative distribution along a single continuum ranging between the two hypothetical poles of yin and yang." Plaks, *Archetype and Allegory*, p. 43. A gender analysis hopes to avoid the oversimplification Plaks warns us about by presenting the binary as a dialectical process of constant dynamism.

[3] Christiane Perrin Makward, "La Critique Féministe, Éléments d'une Problematique," *Revue des Sciences Humaines*, No. 168 (1977), p. 624. Cited in Meaghan Morris, "Aspects of Current French Literary Criticism," *Hecate*, 5, No. 2 (1979), p. 64.

ity of life.[4] The constraints placed upon Baoyu with regards to his behaviour then are the 'gender imperatives' that impinge upon his life. So in this chapter we shall deconstruct the text, in the Derridean sense, to explore firstly Baoyu's gender crisis—the tumultuous merging of the masculine and the feminine which has made Baoyu so socially eccentric—and secondly the many ways that the text has simultaneously reinforced the traditional hierarchical binary of masculine over feminine.

Theoretical background

The approach to the study of literature which founds itself on the masculine/feminine binary, has been most fully developed through the methodology of French feminist literary theorists like Hélène Cixous, Luce Irigaray and Julia Kristeva.[5] Through a complex composite of post-Sassaurean linguistics, psycho-analysis, post-structuralist literary theory and philosophy, these critics have attempted to investigate the social construction of masculinity and femininity. They work from the notion that "Western thought, the text, the Logos, has been founded on the structure of the binary—the dichotomy between such culturally determined oppositions as rationality and emotionality, activity and passivity, presence and absence, in a word, 'male' and 'female'."[6] This dichotomy was explained by Hegel in his *Lectures on the History of Philosophy* as a set of Pythagorean opposites: limit and infinity, unity and multiplicity, male and female, light and dark, good and evil.[7] Hélène Cixous elaborates, "The whole conglomeration of symbolic systems—everything, that is, that's spoken, everything that's organized as discourse, art, religion, the family, language, everything that seizes us, every-

---

[4] The notion of corporeality has transformed the feminist theoretical world in the last five years since it embraces the notions of biology which had been earlier rejected for fear that biological determinism and biological essentialism result. See *Australian Feminist Studies*, No. 5 (Summer, 1989), pp. 1-13 for brief discussions on why the straight-forward distinction between sex and gender (the former as biological and the later as socially constructed) has been rendered problematic. In the article that this chapter was drawn from I argued that sex and gender were distinct categories and pointed out that I was dealing with the social construct of gender. See *Chinese Literature: Essays, Articles and Reviews*, No. 12 (1990), p. 70. In this chapter the distinction between the two is collapsed on the understanding that the biological body is already a social construct.

[5] Ann Jones has noted that other feminists, such as Monique Wittig, reject this binary approach. Wittig declares that analyses based on the masculine/feminine binary have inherent weaknesses because they still take male fantasies as the central point of reference. Ann Rosalind Jones, "Inscribing femininity: French Theories of the Feminine," in Gayle Greene and Coppélia Kahn, eds. *Making a Difference: Feminist Literary Criticism* (London: Methuen, 1986), p. 90.

[6] Domna C. Stanton, "Language and Revolution: The Franco-American Dis-Connection," in Hester Eisenstein and Alice Jardine, eds. *The Future of Difference* (Boston: G.K. Hall, 1980), p. 73.

[7] G.W.F. Hegel, *Lectures on The History of Philosophy —Vol. 1*, trans. by E.S. Haldane, (London: Routledge and Kegan Paul, 1955), pp. 215-16.

thing that acts on us—it is all ordered around hierarchical oppositions that come back to the man/woman opposition."[8]

Not only do French feminist critics maintain that all texts are fundamentally 'sexual,' they also argue that the dichotomous relationship between attitudes and qualities subsumed by masculine and feminine is a hierarchical one. The binary opposition valorizes one set of principles over the other, specifically the masculine over the feminine. Thus, a method of analysis developed to deal with the female's abject specificity—that is the woman's 'negative' difference from the norm which males have co-opted. When related to the signifying practices which inform an individual's psycho-sexual development it is clear that the masculine has adopted the position of self and humanity and the feminine has been caste as his Other, as "the sex which is not one."[9] Christiane Makward elaborates by describing femininity as the 'transcendental signifier' as the "'that-which-one-must-put-aside' in order to define oneself in the masculine."[10]

Cixous and Kristeva have suggested that there exists within any individual the potential for a balance between the male and female principles. There exists, then, the potential for deconstructing the rigid classification of self/other, masculine/feminine within one person and not just between people—effectively exploding a rigid gendering of sex difference. This search for difference within rather than difference between has been described by Cixous as a metaphoric bisexuality—a "simultaneous non hierarchical presence of the feminine and the masculine, the self and the other."[11] Julia Kristeva has explored this concept of bisexuality by explaining how sexual difference is a process of dialecticization. "All speaking subjects have within themselves a certain bisexuality which is precisely the possibility to explore all the sources of signification, that which posits meaning as well as that which multiplies, pulverizes (destroys) and finally revives it."[12] In her essay "The Laugh of the Medusa" Cixous describes her notion of bisexuality as the "non exclusion either of the difference or of one sex" and differentiates it from the "classic conception of bisexuality."[13] Cixous's describes the classic bisexuality as a sexual homogeneity which merely exposes male fear of the other by allowing him to fantasize away sexual difference.[14]

---

[8] Hélène Cixous, "Castration or Decapitation?," trans. by Annette Kuhn, *Signs: Journal of Women in Culture and Society*, 7, No.1 (1981), p. 44.

[9] This phrase is the commonly accepted translation for the title of Irigaray's book. Luce Irigaray, *Ce sexe qui n'en est pas un* (Paris: Minuit, 1977).

[10] Christiane Makward, "La Critique Féministe," p. 624.

[11] Hélène Cixous, "Castration or Decapitation?," pp. 45-55.

[12] Julia Kristeva, "Oscillation Between Power and Denial," trans. by Marilyn A. August, in Elaine Marks and Isabelle de Courtivron, eds. *New French Feminisms: An Anthology* (New York: Schocken, 1980), p. 165.

[13] Hélène Cixous, "The Laugh of the Medusa," trans. by Keith Cohen and Paula Cohen, in Marks and de Courtivron, eds. *New French Feminisms*, p. 254.

[14] Toril Moi, *Sexual/Textual Politics*, pp. 108-9.

Although French feminist critics are working within the Occidental philosophical tradition, their methodology also has direct correlation to Oriental
signifying practices.[15] While the Occidental list of binary opposites can be
traced back to Aristotle and Pythagoras where "it sets male against female,
right against left and good against evil,"[16] the Oriental binary can be traced
to the ancient yin yang philosophy whereby male and female correspond to
positive and negative, active and passive, strong and weak, and constructive
and destructive.[17] Far from being an insignificant philosophical school
among the myriads of others, the yin yang doctrine has informed all aspects
of Chinese signifying discourse, including *Honglou meng*.[18] The portrayal
of the novel's protagonist Jia Baoyu reveals the interplay between yin and
yang most clearly. As a male, his character is written against the female,
and moreover Baoyu's gender preferences, those aspects of his personality
which have made him so controversial, are part of the text's invocation of
commonly held notions of the feminine and masculine, the yin and yang.

The important difference between the Occidental Pythagorean opposites
and the yin yang opposites is illuminated by Charlotte Furth's work on sexual variations in Ming-Qing China. Unlike the unalterable Western binary,
yin and yang were perceived as forces which have the potential for constant
change and interaction within the human body. She has explained that
"Chinese cosmology based on the interaction of the forces of yin and yang
made sexual difference, a relative and flexible bipolarity in natural philosophy."[19] The human body was perceived as another site where the constant
cosmic battle for ascendancy between the forces of yin and yang takes place.
Changes in the physical sex of an individual and hermaphroditism were
thereby all explained in terms of this constant dynamic interaction of yin and
yang. For followers of Daoism sexual boundaries were also relatively flexible. Daoists commonly used symbols of gender inversion (usually feminiz-

---

[15] One of the greatest philosophical problems that confronts the writer of such a cross-
cultural study (as a white Westerner looking at a Chinese novel) is that of ethnocentrism;
self/other becomes Western/Eastern. While radical thinkers such as Julia Kristeva and
Roland Barthes have both written on Asia, I hope to avoid the error both have made in their
attempt at 'understanding' a foreign culture; idealizing cultural traits on the grounds that
'they' are different. This amounts to no more than a production of the 'other' as sacred and
reinforces Asia's position as the East-negative to the West. By applying Western literary
theories to a Chinese novel on the basis of gender, this book hopes to avoid racist assumptions,
revealing the rigid gender imperatives as they appear. See Julia Kristeva, *About Chinese
Women*, trans. by Anita Barrows (1974, rpt. London: Boyars, 1977) and Roland Barthes, *The
Grain of the Voice*, trans. by Linda Coverdale (New York: Hill and Wang, 1985), pp. 113-27.

[16] K.K. Ruthven, *Feminist Literary Studies* (Cambridge: Cambridge University Press,
1984), p. 42.

[17] Wing-tsit Chan, *A Source Book in Chinese Philosophy* (Princeton: Princeton University
Press, 1963), p. 244.

[18] Indeed, as we noted in the previous chapter, readers are treated to a discourse on yin
yang theory by Baoyu's young cousin Shi Xiangyun in chapter thirty-one of the novel.

[19] Charlotte Furth, "Androgynous Males and Deficient Females: Biology and Gender
Boundaries in Sixteenth- and Seventeenth-Century China," *Late Imperial China*, 9, No. 2
(December, 1988), p. 1.

ing the male) to signify rejection of the world of dust and worldly passions. Techniques of 'internal alchemy' were used to cause a withering of the genitals.[20] However, the flexibility implied by ideas of yin/yang interrelatedness did not necessarily imply a flexibility in the social construction of gender. In fact, "Confucianism constructed gender around strict hierarchical kinship roles."[21]

The differences in systems of gender signification displayed by these philosophical schools support the analyses of *Honglou meng* which are constructed around Baoyu's choice between the worlds of Confucianism and Daoism/Buddhism. However the duality of yin and yang as presented in the novel also provides the opportunity to draw on the French feminist notions of metaphoric bisexuality and the text's production of masculinity and femininity. *Honglou meng*'s protagonist, Jia Baoyu becomes the site of conflict between masculine and feminine gender prescriptions through a manifestation of a metaphoric bisexuality.[22]

In the character of Baoyu, the metaphoric bisexuality is amplified resulting in his conflict with the society that seeks to divide masculinity and femininity between the sexes. The conflict between Confucian principles of rigid gender prescriptions, the yin yang philosophy's flexibility of corporeal sexuality and the Daoist adoption of femininity as a rejection of passion is played out in the character of Baoyu. The text has skilfully revealed the ambiguities and complexities of gender ideologies and revealed how gender imperatives stifle the exploration of a multiplicity of sexualities.

Baoyu's bisexuality

As I mentioned in the introduction the novel has presented us with numerous cues for adopting a gender analysis from very early on in its text. The most enlightening of these in relation to Baoyu's 'aberrant' preference for girls over boys and the feminine over the masculine is Leng Zixing's description of Baoyu's first birthday where the young child is presented with a choice between the objects of the feminine and those of the masculine. "But when they celebrated the First Twelve-month and Sir Zheng tested his disposition by putting a lot of objects in front of him and seeing which he would take hold of, he stretched out his little hand and started playing with some women's things—combs, bracelets, pots of rouge and powder and the like— completely ignoring all the other objects." Jia Zheng was said to be very displeased and "ever since then he hasn't felt much affection for the child (*SS* 1.2.76)." The basic psychological trauma that Baoyu faces is clearly presented to all on his first birthday; he is forced to identify his 'disposition'

---

[20] Kristopher Schipper, *Le corps Taoiste: corps physique—corps social* (Paris: Fayard, 1982), p. 161. Cited in Furth, "Androgynous Males and Deficient Females," p. 11.

[21] Charlotte Furth, "Androgynous Males and Deficient Females," p. 1.

[22] Han Huiqiang has gone as far as to say that Baoyu is a neuter, or a sexless character. Han Huiqiang, "*Honglou meng* zhong de xing guannian ji wenhua yiyi," p. 82.

with either the masculine or the feminine and is thus denied the possibility of a bisexual harmony within a sexual dialectic.

Zhen Baoyu, Jia Baoyu's double, had a similar predilection for girls. Insisting on having girls to accompany him in his studies Zhen Baoyu would also shout the word 'girls' to alleviate the pain of beatings. Leng Zixing tells the readers that Zhen would often instruct his pages on the correct handling of the word 'girls.' "The word 'girl' is very precious and very pure. It is much more rare and precious than all the rarest beasts and birds and plants in the world. So it is most extremely important that you should never, never violate it with your coarse mouths and stinking breath. Whenever you need to say it, you should first rinse your mouths out with clean water and scented tea (*SS* 1.2.80)."

Jia Baoyu's 'confused' gender preferences consistently emerge from within the text. From the earliest descriptions we see Baoyu as quite an exceptional young boy; gentle, beautiful, and considerate with a deep love of poetry. You Sanjie's description in chapter sixty-six remains the most enlightening for our analysis, "I suppose you could call him effeminate. Whether he is eating or talking or moving about, there is certainly something rather girlish about his manner. That comes from spending nearly all his time in the women's quarters with no other males around (*SS* 3.66.294)."

He seems to embody many of the qualities associated with the women of his society. Moreover, Baoyu reveals that he is quite capable of and willing to carry out household tasks normally reserved for women. His knowledge of the intricate composition of cosmetics and desire to wash his maid's clothing are considered to be quite eccentric and undesirable qualities for a young gentleman (*SS* 2.44.376-77). In several chapters Baoyu is admonished by his female companions for eating their cosmetics. His young cousins Lin Daiyu and Shi Xiangyun both acknowledge the problem although in different ways, Xiangyun by delivering Baoyu a sharp slap to the wrist just as he is about to taste her rouge and Daiyu by washing evidence of his latest consumption from his face.[23] Through the rejection of correct social behaviour and the practice of eating cosmetics Baoyu's masculinity is interfacing on a corporeal level with the feminine in a symbolic explosion of gender boundaries.

Indeed Baoyu is often spoken of as if he should have been born a girl. In chapter forty-three Baoyu's closest page Tea Leaf asks in prayer that the spirit ensure that "Master Bao is reborn in his next life as a girl... and don't

---

[23] The contrast is clear from the following two quotations. "He [Baoyu] picked up a pot of rouge, almost without realizing what he was doing, and sat with it poised in his hand, wanting to put it to his lips for a little taste, but afraid Xiangyun would rebuke him. While he hesitated, Xiangyun leaned forward...and administered a sharp slap to his hand, causing the rouge-pot to fall from it on to the dressing-table. '*Nathty* (*sic*) habit! she said. 'It's time you gave it up!' (*SS* 1.21.417)." Daiyu's approach differs—while removing a spot of rouge from his cheek Daiyu says to Baoyu "So you're up to *those* tricks again? You might at least refrain from advertizing the fact! (*SS* 1.19.394)."

let him be reborn as one of those horrible Whiskered Males he is always on about (*SS* 2.43.359)." Again in chapter seventy-eight when Grandmother Jia is trying to understand Baoyu's unusual gender preferences she wonders, "Perhaps he was a maid himself in some past life. Perhaps he ought to have been a girl (*SS* 3.78.556)."

In lamenting his lack of opportunity to visit Qin Zhong's grave Baoyu describes how he is powerless to leave the 'inner quarters' freely. Baoyu complains to Liu Xianglian "I wish I weren't so cooped up all the time at home. I can *never* do anything I want to by myself. The slightest move I make is sure to be seen and reported, and either I'm physically prevented from going where I want to or else lectured at until I promise not to go (*SS* 2.47.439)." This type of restriction on movement is usually associated with the young women of aristocratic households and not young men. Baoyu's powerlessness in this respect is particularly feminizing.

In two instances Baoyu's room is mistakenly identified as belonging to a young lady. The decor is feminine and the feel is feminine so both Granny Liu and the medical doctor called in to examine Skybright assume that they have entered a young lady's apartment. The doctor is aghast to realize that he is in a young man's room saying "Did you say 'master'? But surely that was a young lady I examined just now? The room was certainly a young lady's boudoir (*SS* 2.51.526)."[24] Similarly, Grannie Liu stumbles into Baoyu's room in a drunken stupor and on been woken by Aroma she asks "Which of the young ladies does the bedroom belong to? (*SS* 2.41.322)."

If Baoyu's personality and preferences reveal many of the qualities subsumed by the feminine, then Xue Pan provides an excellent foil as a masculine extremist. The contrast between the nature of the social relationships formed by Baoyu and Xue Pan makes a clear distinction between the differing gender projections of these two male characters. When Baoyu is drawn to make friends with other effeminate men in the clan school he is attracted to them for their grace and gentleness. The licentious Xue Pan however regards them as his 'bumcake' and jealously guards them against predators. Baoyu's friendship with Qin Zhong is jeered at in school and their subsequent attempt at friendship with the two homosexual boys in the class, nicknamed 'Darling' and 'Precious,' results in jealous tussles in the classroom.

> The two new boys, Qin Zhong and Baoyu, were both as beautiful as flowers; the other scholars observed how shrinking and gentle Qin Zhong was, blushing almost before you spoke to him and timid and bashful as a girl; they saw in Baoyu one whom nature and habit had made humble and accommodating in spite of his social position, always willing to defer to others

---

[24] Ironically, although the doctor is sure that his patient is a young lady his prescription is described by Baoyu as being suitable for a man, "you can't expect a young girl to stand up to drugs like thorny lime and ephedra (*SS* 2.51.527)." The confusion about the sex of the owner of the room coupled with this mistake in prescription only serves to amplify the confusion of gender in relation to Baoyu.

in the interest of harmony; they observed his affectionate disposition and familiar manner of speech; and they could see that the two friends were devoted to each other. Perhaps it is not to be wondered at that these observations should have given rise to certain suspicions in the minds of those ill-bred persons, and that both in school and out of it all kinds of ugly rumours should have circulated behind their backs (*SS* 1.9.206-207).

At the centre of all the friendships Baoyu forms with his young peers lies a mutual 'femininity.'

Ping-leung Chan has revealed this in his article "Myth and Psyche in *Hung lou meng*" when he states, "His superego (Baoyu's) is also represented by Ch'in Chung (Qin Zhong), Liu Hsiang-lien (Liu Xianglian), and Prince of North Tranquillity (Prince of Beijing). In these three men and in Chia Pao-yü (Jia Baoyu) too, there is one common feature. That is their femininity. It is certainly the basis of Pao-yü's good friendship with them." Furthermore, all three characters have what Chan calls 'implicit' homosexuality.[25] In fact, it is more accurate to describe this as 'classic bisexuality' for it is either implied or explicitly stated that each of these characters has relationships with women as well.[26]

An outgrowth of the phallic monosexuality represented by characters such as Xue Pan, is the depiction of the feminine-Other as the object of masculine-Self's sexual desires. Jacques Lacan, whose influence upon the French feminist theorists is undisputed, has developed his theories of psychoanalysis around notions of the Self's sexual desires.[27] Gelfand and Hules elucidate his ideas of Self/Other and desire by saying that Self is a "function of the desire and acknowledgment of the Other. But most importantly, the Other and desire are sexualized."[28] This sexualized desire of the feminine by the masculine is evident throughout *Honglou meng* and reveals the extent to which sexualized desire preoccupies any interaction between the masculine and the

---

[25] Ping-leung Chan, "Myth and Psyche in *Hung-lou meng*," in Winston L.Y. Yang and Curtis P. Adkins, eds. *Critical Essays on Chinese Fiction* (Hong Kong: Chinese University Press, 1980), p. 169. Recent articles from the PRC have raised the issue of Baoyu's 'homosexuality.' However, it is often discussed in homophobic tones. Homosexuality is regarded as a 'problem' for the aristocratic classes of feudal times and is symbolic of the ruling class' decadence and imminent decline. Ma Qin's article "Homosexuality: Clear Proof of Baoyu's Decadent Personality" is representative of this kind of sentiment. Ma Qin, "Tongxing lian: Jia Baoyu tuifei xingge de mingzheng," *Xinjiang shifan daxue xuebao* (she ke ban), No. 2 (1984), pp. 56-57.

[26] Tu Ying's Qing critique reinforces Qin Zhong's link with 'passion' or '*qing*' by saying that Qin Zhong is the 'seed of passion' (*qing zhong*) and his role is the concentration of that passion in other characters like Baoyu, with whom he has a homosexual relationship, and Sapientia, the young novice, with whom he also maintains an illicit relationship—both mentioned in chapter thirteen. Moreover, Tu argues Qin Zhong's passion is wanton and depraved. Tu Ying, "*Honglou meng* lun zan," rpt. in *Honglou meng juan*, p. 141.

[27] Jacques Lacan, *Écrits: A Selection*, trans. by Alan Sheridan (London: Tavistock, 1980), pp. 288-89.

[28] Elissa D. Gelfand and Virginia Thorndike Hules, *French Feminist Criticism: Women, Language, and Literature; An Annotated Bibliography* (New York: Garland Pub. Inc., 1985), p. xxii.

feminine. For the masculine characters the only conceivable contact with the feminine is through the sexual gratification of masculine desire. Indeed, Jia Zheng's and Xue Pan's reaction to the feminine part of Baoyu's personality is based on the assumption that he must be a libertine devoted entirely to pleasures of the flesh. For example, Leng Zixing narrated how after Baoyu makes the 'wrong' choice on his first birthday his father declared that he would grow up to be a rake and Leng agreed by saying that "He'll be a lady-killer when he grows up, no question of that (*SS* 1.2.76)."

The beating Baoyu receives from his father in chapter thirty-three confirms the applicability of this notion of sexualized desire of the Other by the Self. Baoyu was given a cummerbund from the female impersonator Bijou (Jiang Yuhan's stage name) as a token of friendship as both were pleased to meet another with equally gentle and artistic natures. Later on when Jiang is missing, his lover the powerful Prince of Zhongshan, sends out a search party which implicates Baoyu. Baoyu is then beaten by Jia Zheng for, among other crimes, the homosexual relationship he was assumed to have with Jiang. It was not the homosexual relationship that his father would have objected to but rather the fact that Jiang 'belonged' to someone of higher social standing. The homosexual relationship is expected because artists and actors belong to that 'Other' world of the feminine, and the only interaction between the two worlds that can be conceived, from the perspective of the monosexual masculine characters, is sexual.

The confusion of Baoyu's place on the Self-Other register is evident in chapter seventy-seven when Baoyu says his farewells to Skybright who is on her deathbed. While revealing their depth of mutual affection through the exchange of shirts, Skybright's lecherous sister-in-law returns and assumes that she has just caught them in the midst of a sexual tryst. She then proceeds to accost Baoyu who is left completely disarmed by the aggression. "This was something totally outside Baoyu's experience. His heart started pounding wildly, his face turned scarlet, and his whole body began to tremble. It would have been hard to say what feeling was at that moment uppermost in his mind: embarrassment, shame, fear, or annoyance." The aggressor's reaction to his rejection was one of total disbelief. "Get away with you! From what I've been told, you've had plenty of practice with other girls (*SS* 3.77.546)." She expected Baoyu's reaction to reflect the rigid phallic monosexuality projected on males by the social construction of gender. In actuality, Baoyu was placed in the reverse role by her aggression—that of sexualized Other rather than the desiring Self.

It is rather unclear from the novel exactly how much "practice with other girls" Baoyu has had. His early experience with Aroma is the one explicitly mentioned case although the text hints at several other opportunities. It is far from accidental that an otherwise sexually and morally explicit book should not dwell on Baoyu's sexual encounters with his maids. Instead emphasis has been placed on Baoyu's kind and respectful treatment of women.

It is they who desire him, albeit less aggressively than a male character would, as we see in the example of the young maid Fivey who eagerly seeks a much coveted place in his apartments. The text clearly challenges orthodox notions of sexual morality by playing on homophones for the *yu* in Baoyu's name—(jade, desire, lust)—by creating a character whose desire is portrayed so differently from the majority of other men in the text.[29] Unlike Xue Pan, Jia Baoyu subsumes both the masculine and feminine—he is at once an active and desiring male *and* a passive object of desire. Importantly he is not the object of masculine desire. Unlike other 'effeminate' characters Baoyu is not sought out by Xue Pan and his lecherous friends. His social position as a young gentleman ensures that the sexual power he loses through the adoption of feminine traits is balanced by a general social power.

Liu Xianglian, an impoverished young man from a 'good' family is not protected in the same way. Xue Pan hears that Liu is an actor and determines that Liu is thereby 'fair game' for sexual attentions. The beating Xue Pan receives at the hands of Liu Xianglian derives from Liu's revulsion at Xue Pan's repeated insistence "that he must share the same 'wind and moonlight' proclivities as himself (*SS* 2.47.437)." Liu eventually decides to punish Xue Pan for his persistent insults and tricks him into meeting alone in a deserted place beyond the city walls. Here Liu administers a beating that leaves Pan humiliated and bedridden for days.

In their work on *Honglou meng* L. and V. Sychov have revealed the importance of descriptions of clothing to the novel.[30] While their data, as they have accurately documented, does help reveal Cao's superior literary talent when compared to that of Gao E, it can also help deconstruct *Honglou meng*'s gender ideology and describe Baoyu's ambiguous place on the gender register. It is not insignificant that among all the lengthy descriptions of costume in the novel the only men who are 'objectified' in this way are these aforementioned effeminate male characters—Baoyu, Qin Zhong, Jiang Yuhan and Liu Xianglian. Part of being feminine is being appreciated aesthetically.[31] In the text's descriptions of these particular men's clothing it clearly allocates to them the status of feminine-Object. These men, like the women (particularly the young unmarried girls) then become the passive objects of Self's active desire through the intricate detailing of their costumes. In chapter fifty a description of costumes leads Grandmother Jia to participate in the textual intertwining of the gender registers. Here Grandmother Jia looks at a

---

[29] For a discussion of textual complexities in the use of lust and desire in the novel see Hsien-hao Liao, "Tai-yü or Pao-ch'ai: The Paradox of Existence as Manifested in Pao-yü's Existential Struggle," *Tamkang Review*, 15, No. 1,2,3,4 (Autumn 1984-Summer 1985), pp. 485-94.

[30] L. and V. Sychov, "The Role of Costume in Cao Xue-qin's novel *The Dream of the Red Chamber*," trans. by Cecelia Shickman, *Tamkang Review*, 11, No. 3 (Spring, 1981), pp. 287-305.

[31] Rosalind Coward, *Female Desire: Women's Sexuality Today* (London: Paladin, 1984), p. 229.

figure dressed in a red felt snow-cape and asks "Which of the girls is that?" Those around her laughingly reply, "There aren't any more girls; we're all here. That's Baoyu (*SS* 2.50.505)."

Cao's portrayal of Baoyu's intellectual preferences reveal again the problem Baoyu had in adjusting to the masculine roles it was assumed he should have. His paradox can be represented in the binary creative-feminine-Other/career-masculine-Self. As the eldest surviving son Baoyu is expected to maintain the family's position in the Imperial bureaucracy, taking the career path through years of study of the Confucian classics and culminating in the national exam for the selection of public servants. Instead, however, Baoyu prefers the more creative, poetic mode to the masculine career path. While every man must also have creative skills, particularly the ability to compose poetry to function at a high level in the world of man, they are secondary in importance to the literary aptitude needed to write the eight legged essay required in the Imperial exam. Baoyu, then, fails 'to-put-aside' the feminine when required.

Jia Zheng's relationship with Baoyu has been one of strained tolerance as he tries to encourage Baoyu to have an interest in the scholarly Confucian world of bureaucratic success. This conflict is exposed in both chapter nine and chapter seventeen. On Baoyu's first day at the clan school Jia Zheng warns his pages, "'If he read *thirty* books of the *Poetry Classic*,' said Jia Zheng, 'it would still be tomfoolery... Give my compliments to the Headmaster and tell him from me that I want none of this trifling with the *Poetry Classic* or any other ancient literature. It is of the utmost importance that he should thoroughly understand and learn by heart the whole *Four Books* before he attempts anything else' (*SS* 1.9.204)."

Later on, prompted by "a favourable report on Baoyu from his teacher Jia Dairu in which mention had been made of his skill in composing couplets," Jia Zheng asks Baoyu to name the various locations in the newly completed Prospect Garden. "Although the boy showed no aptitude for serious study, Dairu had said, he nevertheless possessed a certain meretricious talent for versification not undeserving of commendation (*SS* 1.17.326)." In the ensuing inquisition Baoyu is shown to be quite superior in this non-serious skill to both his father and the literary gentlemen who accompany them. However, this is of little consolation to Jia Zheng who primarily demands masculine scholarly skills from his heir.

Phallogocentricism reinforced

In this section it will become clear how despite Baoyu's bisexual tendencies and the text's questioning of gender imperatives, the overall tenor of the work reinforces the traditional phallogocentric binary where the masculine-

Self projects 'otherness' onto the feminine.[32] The most important way that gender imperatives are reconfirmed is in the fact that the acceptable dialecticization of sexual difference occurs in males—Baoyu, and his 'effeminate' acquaintances Qin Zhong, and Liu Xianglian.[33] These men are regarded favourably by the narrator as being superior to the stupid, oafish, licentious Jia Zhen, Xue Pan and Jia She.

The manner in which both the Confucian and Daoist systems of gender signification are invoked within the character of Baoyu render the feminine subordinate and passive. Within the Daoist frame Baoyu's femininity is part of his path to a singularly male religious enlightenment. The feminine is adopted to balance the masculine. Thus it is within the masculine that the experience of 'balancing' occurs. Alternatively Jia Zheng's Confucian ideology regarded men who take on feminine traits as libertines who are capable of extremes in an active sexuality. Charlotte Furth discusses the case of a young man who dressed himself as a woman and became a teacher of needlework to young girls.[34] When his disguise was discovered it was claimed that he adopted the feminine mode so as to debauch the girls with whom he had lived so intimately. Scholarly debate on the issue credited the impersonator with "a life of undreamed of amorous exploits" just as is assumed with Baoyu. In both the Daoist and Confucian world view invoked by *Honglou meng*, males who adopt the feminine are thereby achieving male ends; one seeking the rejection of passion and the other seeking extremes of passion. Both confirm the position of active Self as masculine and relegate the feminine to the desired/rejected Other. The concentration on male bisexuality implicitly denies the existence of females potential for bisexuality, or any form of active, and not simply responsive, sexuality by its silence on the issue. This effectively annuls sexual difference rather than expanding it. In the chapter on Xifeng it will become apparent that her desire to be a man, while balancing that of Baoyu's to become a girl, is granted negative treatment by both the novel and critics.

The role given to women in the novel is, then, subsidiary. Even though Angela Jung Palandri declares that *Honglou meng* is "fundamentally a novel about women," she more accurately relates the position of women to an analogy of a necklace where Baoyu is the string and the individual female

---

[32] The term 'phallogocentrism' is a Derridean neologism which describes "the double philosophical and Freudian paradigm that posits the male and his sexuality as the norm and the female and her sexuality as a variation." Gelfand and Hules, *French Feminist*, p. xxi.

[33] Apart from the hint at a non sexual lesbian relationship between the male impersonator and her opposite in the troop of actresses, the novel only portrays male bisexuality. When women are likened to men they hold positions of power as in the case of Wang Xifeng who has a boy's name. It is their power which is regarded as masculine, and destructive in a woman's hands, as will become evident in chapter five to follow.

[34] Charlotte Furth, "Androgynous Males and Deficient Females," pp. 22-23.

characters are the pearls.[35] The audience reads mostly of the life in the
"World of Girls"[36] but in actual fact the novel is 'fundamentally' about
Baoyu's struggle and the women exist only in so far as they help further pro-
ject this singularly male struggle.

Thus, Daiyu and Baochai are valorized primarily for their potential to reflect Baoyu's problems with, among other issues, the signification of gender
in Chinese society. In their tumultuous relationships with Baoyu, Daiyu invokes the more feminine values and Baochai the more masculine. So, while
the text creates a male protagonist that holds the dilemma of the choice
forced upon him, between masculine and feminine social constructs, his two
female protagonists are relegated to the margins as mirrors of his male
choice. Josette Féral has described this phenomenon as, "a woman does not
become the Other but *his* other, his Unconscious, his repressed, and she gets
caught in the endless and enduring circle of *his* representation. Enmeshed in
man's self-representation, woman exists only insofar as she endlessly reflects
back to him the image of his manly reality."[37]

As is revealed by his visit to the Land of Illusion in chapter five, Baoyu
admires and indeed desires both women. In this dream fantasy Baoyu is given
the fairy Combined Beauty for his lover, and it is revealed that "Her rose-
fresh beauty reminded him strongly of Baochai, but there was also something
about her of Daiyu's delicate charm (*SS* 1.5.145)." Combined Beauty initi-
ates Baoyu in the art of sex, gratifying his subconscious desires for both
women[38] while simultaneously reinforcing each woman's role as representing
one half of *Baoyu's* personality crisis.

As we noted in the previous chapter earlier analyses of the two women
have emphasized their oppositional roles in relation to an number of issues.
That the novel encouraged readers to make the choice between the two
women is evident in the earliest commentary on the novel, that of
Zhiyanzhai. As mentioned earlier, Zhiyanzhai's margin comments expressed
the view that Baochai was the better woman of the two while critics of the
Republican period adopted the view that the women were historical alle-

---

[35] Angela Jung Palandri, "Women in *Dream of the Red Chamber*," *Literature East and
West*, 12, No. 2,3,4 (1968), p. 227. The Qing critic "Er zhi dao ren" describes the primacy of
Baoyu over the Twelve Beauties with the notion that the novel is about Baoyu's life/dream and
argues that Baoyu is the "master" (*zhuzhe*) of the Twelve Beauties. See "Er zhi dao ren,"
"*Honglou meng* shuo meng," rpt. in *Honglou meng juan*, p. 85.
[36] Prospect Garden is often referred to as a "Kingdom of Girls" or a "World of Girls."
See for example Jiang Wenqin, "'Nüer shijie' de liang ge cengci—lun Daguanyuan yu
Taihuanjing" ("Girl's World" at two levels—a discussion of Prospect Garden and the Land of
Illusion), *Wenzhou shizhuan xuebao*, No. 1 (1985), pp. 15-24. In Jiang's article the concept of
a Girl's World is extended to the mythic level by incorporating the Land of Illusion as another
level.
[37] Josette Féral, "The Powers of Difference," in Eisentein and Jardine, eds. *The Future of
Difference*, p. 89.
[38] Xu Decheng, Tian Yuheng, "Qin Keqing yu Qin Zhong," *Honglou meng xuekan*, No. 1
(1985), p. 154.

gories. Daiyu being the Ming dynasty and Baochai the Qing. Daiyu, like the Ming dynasty was weak and dying, while Baochai has qualities that were associated with the Qing, those being strength and robustness.[39] Yu Pingbo's vision of the roles of the two women in his path-breaking study *Honglou meng bian* published in 1922 is however the view that has sustained critical interest. His theory that later became known as "Chai and Dai unified" (*Chai-Dai heyi*) explained the relationship of Daiyu and Baochai as one of complementary opposition and a composite of equals with neither one assuming the better or worse role. He likened their differences to rivers flowing down opposite sides of a mountain.[40] This view achieved considerable fame in the 1950s when it became the prime focus of attack from the young Marxist scholars Lan Ling and Li Xifan who argued that the two women were diametrically opposed and represented progressive and regressive social forces. Daiyu was credited with being an anti-feudal rebel while Baochai was regarded as a conservative upholder of feudalism.[41] However, while Yu Pingbo and Li Xifan can disagree about exactly what Daiyu and Baochai represent, their 'otherness' is the base of the novel in its portrayal of *Baoyu's* existential struggle.

Baoyu's dilemma between the masculine career aspirations and his own creative preferences are reflected in the personalities of the two women. Daiyu, it appears, was never encouraging of the career path, remaining firmly with the feminine world of creativity as shown by her "deep love for poetry, drama, music"[42] and her singular support of his rejection of the career path. "The exception was Daiyu, who, ever since they were little children together, had never once spoken to him about the need to 'get on in the world' or 'make a name for oneself.' This was one of the reasons why he so much respected her (*SS* 2.36.195)." This difference in the two girls' attitudes is well recognized by most *Hongxue* scholars. In 1986 the Chinese critic Zhou Yibin concluded that unlike Daiyu "Baochai did not regard poetry as a serious matter." Instead Baochai reflected the view of the Ming official Yang Shiqi who held the opinion that poetry writing was a minor skill and more time should be spent on the classics.[43] The most commonly cited example from the novel is Baochai's lecture to Daiyu on the importance of avoiding romantic books (like *Honglou meng*). "Come to that, it [reading romance] isn't a

---

[39] Jing Meijiu, *Shitouji zhendi*, p. 165 and p. 175.

[40] Yu Pingbo, *Honglou meng bian*, p. 186. For a contemporary exegesis of this theory see Wu Shaonan, *"Chai Dai heyi" xin lun*, (Hong Kong: Sanlian shudian, 1985).

[41] Lan Ling and Li Xifan, *"Honglou meng zhong liang ge duili de dianxing*—Lin Daiyu he Xue Baochai" (Two opposing types in *Honglou meng*—Lin Daiyu and Xue Baochai), *Xin guancha*, No. 23 (December, 1954), pp. 28-30.

[42] Anthony C. Yu, "Self and the Family in the *Hung-lou Meng*: A New Look at Lin Tai-yü as Tragic Heroine," *Chinese Literature, Essays, Articles and Reviews*, 2, No. 2 (July, 1980), p. 208.

[43] Zhou Yibin, "Lun Daiyu Baochai de shixue guandian yu Ming Qing shige liupai de guanxi" (Discussing Daiyu and Baochai's poetics in regard to Ming and Qing poetry schools), *Honglou meng xuekan*, No. 1 (1986), pp. 58-59.

boy's proper business either. A boy's proper business is to read books in order to gain an understanding of things, so that when he grows up he can play his part in governing the country (*SS* 2.42.333)."

Character descriptions will elucidate further the idea that each woman holds the essential elements of Baoyu's choice. Where Baochai is known for her commonsense and rationality, Daiyu is emotional and sentimental. Daiyu's overly sensitive nature has given her a reputation for being 'petty'[44] while Baochai's coolness often invites critics to call her 'feelingless.'[45] Baochai maintains a pragmatic attitude to the world while Daiyu shows no ability to turn her hand to practical affairs. Baochai enjoys good health while Daiyu's sickly constitution has become one of her most well known traits. Clearly we see the binaries appearing; strength or weakness, practical or frivolous, rational or emotional, career or creative, masculine or feminine.

These binaries are not uncomplicated however. One would not go as far as to say that Baochai was representative of yang and Daiyu representative of yin. Indeed both women embody aspects of both yin and yang. Baochai's wet, coldness represented in the 'snow' of her surname, Xue and her medicinal icon 'cold fragrance' represent her yin elements. However, the blackness in Daiyu's name, Dai, and close nexus between water and her life reveal the extreme yin of her form. She is brought back to life by the generative powers of Baoyu's water as the Crimson Pearl Flower and repays her debt to him in tears. So, Daiyu's relationship with Baoyu is one mediated by the excessive yin of water while Baochai's link with Baoyu emerges as the result of the mystical pairing of her gold clasp with his jade stone. Just as Baoyu as Jade Boy nurtured Daiyu with water, so Daiyu repays this by nurturing Baoyu with her excess of yin water. The problematic nature of applying clear demarcations between yin and yang and Daiyu and Baochai is made clear by Zhang Xinzhi's Qing critique. Zhang says,

> The element wood is assigned to the eastern quarter, where it holds sway over springtime and growth; the element gold is assigned to the western quarter, where it holds sway over autumn and death. The trees of the 'forest' ['Lin,' Tai-yü's surname] are engendered by the waters of the sea. The ocean is located in the Southeast, the domain of *yang*. Gold is engendered by the Hsüeh family [Pao-ch'ai is surnamed Hsüeh], that is to say, by snow [*hsüeh*]. This congealed and accumulated cold comes under the sign of *yin*. It is in this sense that the names of Lin and Hsüeh, referring to the elements wood and gold, take on their full significance.[46]

When the Other is no longer required to represent Baoyu's dilemma, it ceases to exist. Once he is tricked into marrying Baochai, the link with the feminine that was the essence of his relationship with Daiyu, is destroyed, and so

---

[44] Qu Mu, "Lin Daiyu de xuefeng" (Lin Daiyu's scholarly style), *Guangzhou ribao* (26 October 1983), in *RD*, No. 10 (1983), p. 53.

[45] Hsien-hao Liao, "Tai-yü or Pao-ch'ai," p. 490.

[46] Zhang Xinzhi, "How to Read the *Dream of the Red Chamber*," pp. 331-32.

Daiyu dies a tragic, lonely death. She is no longer a relevant choice for the
Self. Daiyu withers just as Samuel Richardson's Clarissa Harlowe fades
away after her rape. Neither woman committing suicide for that would be
"far too robust an action"[47] for a mere 'reflection.' Once again, when Baoyu
chooses to deny the world of masculine Confucian convention altogether by
becoming a monk, Baochai is left behind as a virtual widow. Thus, the central female characters are present only insofar as they are useful to reflect
Baoyu's dilemma. In the last instance the abjection of the feminine-Other by
the masculine-Self is confirmed by the novel's unspoken sexual ideology.
Baoyu's ultimate decision to become a wandering monk, undergoing a
metaphoric castration, is the embracing of a Daoist masculine role which
confirms the phallogocentric vision of the feminine, the sexualized Other, as
an obstacle to male spiritual freedom.

In the examination of Baoyu's 'metaphoric' bisexuality the complex and
often ambiguous interplay between the masculine and feminine symbolic
systems becomes evident. Baoyu is portrayed as a complicated and eccentric
individual who rejects the established patriarchal norms of psyho-sexual development. Manifested in his effeminate personality Cao Xueqin's character
has refused to conform to monosexual gender imperatives. That is, those
signifying practices which reject a bisexuality within, rather than between
sexes.

Jacques Derrida has described his own utopian image of a society where
individuals like Jia Baoyu are no longer considered eccentric or immoral.
This would be the area where the relationship between Self and Other is no
longer dictated by a discriminating code of sexual marks. "The relationship
[with the Other] would not be a-sexual, far from it, but would be sexual otherwise: beyond the binary difference that governs the decorum of all codes,
beyond the opposition feminine/masculine, beyond bisexuality as well, beyond homosexuality and heterosexuality which come to the same thing…I
would like to believe in the multiplicity of sexually marked voices."[48] The
deconstruction of the ubiquitous phallogocentric binary is a prerequisite for
such unfettered, unrestricted transposition of sexual signifiers. Cao Xueqin's
text has a plenitude of binaries and, most significantly for this study, the binary masculine/feminine has been intertwined in such a manner as to encourage the dismantling of the rigid gendering of the sexes within and between
characters. The task for the critic then remains to reinscribe these now dis-
mantled metaphysical and rhetorical structures in a manner such that avoids
privileging one side of the binary over the other/Other.

Lucien Miller asserts that in *Honglou meng* the reader is encouraged to
"realize a new orientation" that "human suffering results from the wilful divi-

---

[47] Ann Foreman, *Femininity as Alienation: Women and the Family in Marxism and Psychoanalysis* (London: Pluto Press, 1978), p. 97.
[48] Jacques Derrida, "Choreographies," p. 76 cited in Moi, *Sexual/Textual Politics*, p. 173.

sion of life into distinct categories."[49] This statement is indeed most apt when one considers that much of the conflict and internal anxiety suffered by Baoyu was caused by the attempts of his family and friends to distinctly categorize him as male-masculine. These "distinct categories" are necessarily imbued with a rigid set of sexually marked voices and not one of these was suitable for Jia Baoyu.

A problem that remains unresolved in this discussion is that of the nature of female challenges to the rigid sexual symbolic order within the novel. The flexibility of gender and sex in Daoism provided a path towards a singularly male religious enlightenment. By discussing the dialecticization of sexual difference in the major male character the symbolic order appears more flexible than it would if one compared this to the portrayal of a female character—Wang Xifeng for instance. The following two chapters address these issues by analyzing the depiction of women in the novel.

---

[49] Lucien Miller, *Masks of Fiction in the Dream of the Red Chamber: Myth, Mimesis, and Persona* (Tuscon: Arizona University Press, 1975), p. 36.

CHAPTER FOUR

YOUNG WOMEN AND PRESCRIPTIONS OF PURITY

Many scholars have noted that *Honglou meng* is primarily a novel about the lives of women. Relating in minute detail daily life within the inner court-yards of an aristocratic Chinese family the novel's central characters are indeed, with the exception of Jia Baoyu, primarily women. As was mentioned in the introduction, the large numbers of women included in the novel and the favourable light in which they are portrayed have often led people to assume that the novel is sympathetic to women's plight in Chinese society. In this current chapter I will examine the manner in which purity and profanity are invoked to reveal the various ways in which *Honglou meng* reflects the gender ideologies of its time rather than challenging them.

The novel describes the superiority of females over males many times. In the first instance, the narrator explains his reason for writing as the attempt to save the talented women with whom he grew up from fading into oblivion. Cao Xueqin is quoted in the introduction to the first chapter as saying:

> As I went over them [the female companions of my youth] one by one... it suddenly came over me that those slips of girls—which is all they were then—were in every way, both morally and intellectually, superior to the 'grave and mustachioed signior' I am now supposed to have become. The realization brought with it an overpowering sense of shame and remorse... I resolved that, however unsightly my own shortcomings might be, I must not, for the sake of keeping them hid, allow those wonderful girls to pass into oblivion without a memorial.[1]

However, as Lucien Miller wrote, "To assert that the theme of the novel is only life in the ladies' apartments is to contradict the author's own poignant complaint and painful lamentation."[2] The avowed concern for the women in the novel can thus be interpreted as a production of the reverse as the reader traces *Baoyu's* path to enlightenment, and *Baoyu's* painful lamentations *through* the women that are so subtly portrayed. As the novel so often suggests, "everything produces its opposite."[3]

Secondly, throughout the novel we read of how the young girls are far superior to their male counterparts in a host of different areas—including po-

---

[1] Cao Xueqin cited in David Hawkes, "Introduction," in *The Story of the Stone: Volume One*, pp. 20-21.
[2] Lucien Miller, *Masks of Fiction in Dream of the Red Chamber*, p. 218.
[3] Lucien Miller, *Masks of Fiction in Dream of the Red Chamber*, p. 86.

etry writing, literary knowledge, musical talent, philosophical understanding and morality. On the one hand, Baoyu is regarded by his teacher and other literary gentlemen as having a "certain meretricious talent for versification not undeserving of commendation" (*SS* 1.17. 326). On the other hand he is the object of the young girls' mirth during poetry club meetings for his clumsy and slow poetic skills. Indeed, in almost all matters of scholarly or cultural knowledge Baoyu shows less aptitude than his female peers. It is from this sort of reversal that critics conclude that Cao was protesting against the patriarchal feudal system. Zhao Rong describes this phenomenon as follows, "In the society where the notion of 'honouring men and disdaining women' was upheld Cao proposed 'honouring women disdaining men'."[4]

The novel has thereby reversed the openly misogynist ideology expressed in the often repeated maxims "A woman without talent is virtuous" and "A woman's hair is long but her vision and knowledge are short."[5] However, ideologies of femininity and masculinity do not form logical or closed structures. Rather they are fraught with internal contradictions and ambiguities which function simultaneously and seemingly abrasively to establish a patriarchal gender order. Indeed the greatness of Cao Xueqin's artistry lies in part in his ability to recreate these ambiguities and contradictions within his fictional text.

The simple inversion of the gender order does not, therefore, necessarily imply that the novel is expressing anti patriarchal sentiment. Rather, mere reversal of the phallogocentric female/male, yin/yang binary could reinforce the patriarchal foundation because "reversing the order only repeats the system."[6] To accomplish a complete break with a patriarchal gender order the signifying systems which smooth over its inequalities and ambiguities must be deconstructed and not simply inverted. The ways in which a simple textual reversal reinforces patriarchal dominance are many and this chapter will limit itself to one of the novel's major themes—the association of women with the binary sacred/profane and its concomitant invocation of notions of purity and pollution.[7]

Sacred women

In the first two dozen chapters of the novel, the reader is told on a number of occasions how much Baoyu reveres his young female companions. Baoyu is said to prefer female company to that of males in his well known declaration also cited in the previous chapter, "Girls are made of water and boys are made

---

[4] Zhao Rong, "Hunyin ziyou de nahan," p. 60. The phrases he is referring to are "*nanzun nübi*" and "*yangnan yinü.*"

[5] "*Nüzi wucai bian shi de*" and "*Nüren toufa chang, jianshi duan.*"

[6] Nelly Furman, "The Politics of Language: Beyond the Gender Principle?," in Greene and Kahn, eds, *Making a Difference: Feminist Literary Criticism*, pp. 74-75.

[7] Lucien Miller has noted that female purity is one of the major symbols of the novel. *Masks of Fiction in Dream of the Red Chamber*, p. 173.

of mud. When I am with girls I feel fresh and clean, but when I am with boys I feel stupid and nasty (*SS* 1.2.76)." Another example of how Baoyu sanctifies his young female friends appears in chapter twenty, "As a result of this upbringing [among girls], he [Baoyu] had come to the conclusion that the pure essence of humanity was all concentrated in the female of the species and that males were its mere dregs and off-scourings. To him, therefore, all members of his own sex without distinction were mere brutes who might just as well not have existed (*SS* 1.20.407-408)." One more example from the closing chapters of the novel allows us to see that the idealization of the feminine is a consistent theme even through to the last forty chapters written/edited by Gao E. The occasion is Baoyu's meeting with his look-a-like Zhen Baoyu. Zhen flatters Jia by describing the latter as a person of "egregious purity, refinement and grace." Jia Baoyu's response is one of bewilderment, "But why does he flatter me almost as if I were a girl? We are both of us men, and therefore creatures of impurity (*SS* 5.115.273-74)." In her discussion of the novel Angela Palandri said quite incorrectly that this sort of idealization "is against the traditional Chinese concept of women."[8] Rather, Jia Baoyu's worship of young girls throughout the novel develops from a well established pattern in the traditional representation of women.

This feature is made evident by Liao Zhongan's article, which traces the origins of the phrase considered representative of such veneration of the feminine—Baoyu's utterance "the pure essences of the universe are concentrated in the female of the species" (*Tian di jian lingshu zhi qi zhi zhong yu nüzi*). Liao followed the complex history of this phrase alone (in its various forms) back to the Southern Song dynasty in the *Tan sou* by Pang Yuanying. Here the phrase appears in a slightly different form in a discussion between a young scholar, Xie Ximeng and Lu Xiangshan.[9]

Lu Xiangshan (1139-1193) was a Neo-Confucian philosopher of considerable influence. His Neo-Confucianism was idealist, based primarily on a Mencian foundation, and directly opposed that of Cheng-Zhu rationalism. For several hundred years these two schools, the idealistic School of Mind and the rationalistic School of Principle, were the two major branches of Song Neo-Confucianism. Indeed the division between the two schools has resurfaced again in the twentieth century with Feng Youlan's *New Rational Philosophy* following the School of Principle and Xiong Shili's *New Doctrine of Consciousness-Only* expanding from the idealist branch.[10] Lu Xiangshan's philosophical teachings disdained lengthy, literary deliberation

---

[8] Angela Palandri, "Women in *Dream of the Red Chamber*," p. 229.

[9] Liao Zhongan, "*Honglou meng* sixiang suyuan yi li—'Tian di jian lingshu zhi qi zhong yu nüzi' yi yu de chuchu he yuanlai" (An example of the source of *Honglou meng*'s thinking—"The purest essences of the universe are concentrated in the female of the species" the origin of one sentence), *Guangming ribao* (December 3, 1977). The latter is a descendant of the founding fathers of the Li school of neo-Confucianism revived in the Qing.

[10] Wing-tsit Chan, *A Source Book in Chinese Philosophy*, p. 751.

and concentrated instead on the propagation of a doctrine that would guide individual students in their everyday life. Wing-tsit Chan describes Lu as advocating "the simple easy and direct method of recovering one's original good nature, by having a firm purpose, by establishing the nobler part of one's nature, and by coming to grips with fundamentals"[11] while Zhu Xi was an advocate of lengthy study and commentary on written texts.

Xie Ximeng, Lu's student, is a less famous personage. It is noted in the *Song shi ji shi* that Xie came from Huangyan in Taizhou. He passed the highest Imperial examinations in 1184 and proceeded to successfully hold several official postings. The following is a narration of the conversation between the idealist philosopher Lu Xiangshan and his student Xie Ximeng:[12]

> While at Lin'an Xie Ximeng was improperly familiar with some prostitutes. Xiangshan of the Lu clan berated him saying: "When a scholar and a gentleman passes time with base prostitutes how can he then not be shamed by the Confucian ethical code?" Ximeng apologized respectfully and pleaded that he would not offend again. Later on Xie went whoring at a brothel again and when Xiangshan heard of this he repeated his reservations. Xie replied: "Is this not a highly recommended institution in the records?" Xiangshan asked with pleasure which text he was referring to as he himself was unaware of it: "How are brothels recorded?" Xie then dictated the opening line: "From Sun, Kang, Ji and Yun's death[13], the noble spirit of departed bravery is not concentrated in the males of the world, but is concentrated in the females." Xiangshan had no reply.

There are several points that need elaboration. The timing of the recorded conversation is of importance to my argument and will be discussed first. The Song dynasty (960-1279) is recognized as being the period during which the position of women underwent dramatic changes. The Cheng-Zhu school of Neo-Confucianism propagated a highly puritanical form of an already moralistic Confucian order.[14] Many of the oppressive practices highlighted in later years, such as footbinding and widow chastity, were widely encouraged during this dynasty. That Cao Xueqin quotes from a Song dynasty text is significant when one considers that it was the revival of the Song Neo-Confucianism (particularly the restrictive Cheng-Zhu school) which resulted in the Qing dynasty being described as follows: "The values and institutions which reinforced the subordination of women in China were never stronger

---

[11] Wing-tsit Chan, *A Source Book in Chinese Philosophy*, p. 573.

[12] The excerpt from the *Tan Sou* was published in Liao Zhongan's article mentioned above. The translation is my own.

[13] Sun, Kang, Ji and Yun were all prominent members of the same Lu Clan that Xiangshan was related to. Lu Sun and Lu Kang were famous generals of the Eastern Wu while Lu Ji and Lu Yun were literati during the Western Jin.

[14] For a discussion of how Song philosophy developed a more puritanical view of the position of women see Chen Dongyuan, *Zhongguo funü shenghuo shi* (A history of the lives of Chinese women) (n.d.; rpt. Taipei: Shangwuyin, 1986), pp. 129-72.

than during the Qing dynasty."[15] Vociferous expressions of the purity and superiority of women occur most frequently in periods and cultures where their position is the most restricted.

By relating the tale of a student invoking 'the records' as justification of his attendance at a brothel the reader is aware that the followers of Zhu Xi, who prided themselves on their extensive literary knowledge through lengthy periods of textual study, clearly looked down upon the idealist school which rejected textual study. Lu Xiangshan then is herewith sneered at for being weak in textual knowledge through a facetious joke. In the context of the historically divisive debate between Lu and Zhu, Xie Ximeng's rejection of his teacher's practical advice for living and his invocation of textual evidence can imply that he had adopted the opposing school's doctrines. That our contemporary redactor Liao Zhongan can simultaneously praise Xie Ximeng for opposing Lu Xiangshan the "teacher of the *Lixue*"[16] and yet also condemn the Cheng-Zhu philosophy which ensured women's lowly place in the social scale is fundamentally contradictory given the existence of the rift between these two schools. While we have no way of predicting what the position of women would have been if Lu Xiangshan's School of the Mind had prevailed over the Cheng-Zhu school, it is clear that the Qing dynasty exegeses of the latter's works were fundamentally misogynist.

Another matter of importance to this current argument is that it is no matter of mere chance that Xie Ximeng and Lu Xiangshan's evocation of feminine virtue should take place within the vicinity of a brothel. The place of decadence and degradation juxtaposes neatly with the notion of female nobility in an invocation of the inextricable relationship within the symbolic order between the sacred and the profane. Here the elision of the venerated with the polluted is quite evident as the goddess becomes the whore and the whore the goddess.[17] This juxtaposition of notions of purity being held within a place of great pollution is echoed in *Honglou meng* through the construction of Prospect Garden. Yu Yingshi has noted that Prospect Garden is an island of purity in the sea of squalor and dirt that is the outside world. He has also noted that the Garden was built on land from both the Ning and Rong mansions. The Rong branch's donation was a section of Jia She's compound and the Ning contribution included the site of the Celestial Fragrance Pavilion (*Tian xiang lou*). Both these sites had sexually promiscuous and licentious histories. Jia She is described by the circumspect maid Aroma as being a 'sex maniac' and Celestial Fragrance Pavilion is the building where Qin Keqing's incestuous relations with Jia Zhen were conducted.

---

[15] Paul S. Ropp, "The Seeds of Change: Reflections on the Condition of Women in Early and Mid Ch'ing," *Signs: Journal of Women in Culture and Society* (Autumn, 1976), p. 5.

[16] *Lixue* is the usual name for the Neo-Confucianism of the Song and Ming times.

[17] The conflation of the goddess and the whore within Chinese culture is also revealed by the nature of the word *shennü* which served a dual linguistic function meaning at different periods both goddess and prostitute.

It is in this same building that she later hung herself. Yu writes, "He [Cao] wanted us to bear in mind that in fact the greatest purity was born of the greatest impurity. If the novel were completed by Ts'ao Hsueh-ch'in, or if a complete version were handed down to us intact, we would certainly be told that the ultimate fate of that great purity is to return to impurity."[18]

This perceptive statement reveals quite clearly the connection between the sacred and the profane that Cao Xueqin was invoking in his novel. Thereby the implications for the previously eulogized young women are grim. If these young girls are hailed as the embodiments of the "purest essences in the universe" then they must complete the circle and return to the most impure essences. The idealization does not necessarily challenge the "traditional Chinese concept of women" as Palandri suggests but is rather one of the most common forms of fictional representation of the feminine. Such idealized representation can alternatively be interpreted as another form of abjection of the female as veneration of the feminine is still a masculine privilege whereby the feminine becomes the venerated Other for the masculine Self. Veneration becomes abjection through the indifferentiation of the sacred and the unclean.[19] The idealization of the sacred and pure woman is merely one side of the phallogocentric disc to which the flip side is the polluted whore or virago.

The elevation of women to a divine position establishes them as the corporeal defenders of social morality. It may well be this very morality which subjugates them. Women thus become moral mirrors for their menfolk and are constrained within this divinity. Masculinity on the other hand, can symbolically represent the possibility of the supersession of these moral strictures to a position beyond the binary of the sacred and the profane. This potential masculine supersession of social norms is recreated in *Honglou meng* at both the mythic and mimetic realms. At the interface between the two realms it is the men like Zhen Shiyin and Liu Xianglian who through suffering achieve enlightenment and see through the vanity of worldly ways. Their rejection of the Confucian path of social responsibility follows their embracing the comparatively individualistic philosophies of Daoism and Buddhism. This is qualified by the important fact that on a worldly level those men, such as Jia Jing, who embrace a monastic and therefore more socially acceptable form of Daoism and Buddhism are also the objects of Cao's disdain. It is the ability to scorn social norms and become scabby headed wandering monks which is significantly and symbolically masculine.[20]

---

[18] Yu Yingshi, "The Two Worlds of *Hung-lou meng*," trans. by Diana Yu, *Renditions*, No. 2 (Spring, 1974), p. 13.

[19] Mary Douglas, *Purity and Danger* (London: Routledge and Kegan Paul, 1966), pp. 7-10.

[20] The nuns who appear in the novel are also portrayed in an equally sceptical and ironic light as they too are tied to a social system which is consciously seeking wisdom and this is the very activity which, in the view of the novel, inhibits enlightenment.

Alternatively, on the mimetic level the men of the Ning and Rong mansions show complete disregard for the moral standards of their time and become "more degenerate from one generation to the next (*SS* 1.2.74)." In their decadent behaviour these men flout the accepted rules of decorum upheld by society/young women. It is the potential for conflict and rejection of social norms that distinguishes the masculine. In the Confucian scheme of virtue, the man who controls and limits his desire is the model of virtue; for the Daoist, it is the man who sees the folly of human emotions and desires altogether. Through the experience and suffering caused by the ability to supersede everyday morality, these realizations are achieved. This thereby takes the masculine above social morality as it is embodied in women through such ideological prescriptions on the sacred/profane nature of femininity.

Interaction between mythic and mimetic realms

In his portrayal of both other-worldly and worldly religious paths Cao has also revealed a sexual difference that illuminates our understanding of prescriptions of purity for women in Qing China. This section discusses those characters who, deliberately seeking enlightenment, fail to achieve their goal and how those who are successful in mediating between the 'real and the unreal' realms achieve this much-sought-after status.

Those characters, both male and female who attempt to achieve enlightenment through a monastic order, are treated rather ironically in the text. The two main 'conscious seekers of immortality' are the eccentric Jia Jing and the 'over pure' Adamantina. While both the nun and the monk are treated ironically there are important differences between their eventual fates. Jia Jing dies after swallowing a potion designed to grant immortality, and Adamantina is carried away from the convent by bandits to a fate generally assumed to be prostitution. The morality directed at Adamantina and not Jia Jing reveals in part how important ideologies of purity and their invocation of the goddess/whore binary are to women in particular.

The degrading conclusion created for Adamantina by Gao E fits an already established moral pattern, a pattern that reveals the primacy of the sexualized codes of judgement established for women. For the nun, the path to the brothel follows a route noted by Kathryn Tsai in her article on the Chinese Buddhist monastic order for women. If a nun is sufficiently sincere and sufficiently determined in her resolve to remain pure, then when she is confronted by a band of knife wielding ruffians, the merciful Guanyin will step in and protect her. Adamantina, it appears, was insufficiently sincere in her resolve to remain chaste and humble when tested and this causes her to "fall into the muck." Tsai suggests that "the point of these passages seems to be that cultic practice is effective if one is sufficiently sincere in faith and attitude."[21] The important feature remains that it is the formulaic ending which, centred on a nun's chastity, that has been drawn into the fictional consciousness of *Honglou meng*. The purest essences complete the circle and return to the most impure essences. The distance between the extremely pure and the extremely impure is, within the traditional Chinese symbolic order, not a very great distance at all.

There is also a sexual difference in the manner of mediation between the two realms for those who successfully achieve this transition. Male characters like Zhen Shiyin and Liu Xianglian, who wander off to become monks and presumably immortals, do so after experiencing great suffering and shock. The male immortals wander freely between the two realms, appearing on earth and then in heaven with ease, quite readily assuming corporeal form and equally readily transforming it to ash. For the women, the method of mediating the boundaries between the real and the unreal is primarily death, and in almost every case this is achieved through suicide. Of all the suicides in the novel, only two are carried out by men, while drownings, hangings, head-dashing and throat-slitting abound among the females. As women, their suffering and the cause of their suicide are primarily related to their chastity, while the source of the men's suffering is not as singular. You Sanjie slits her throat on hearing that Liu Xianglian wished to cancel their betrothal. Golden throws herself down the well after being humiliated by Lady Wang, being accused of leading Baoyu astray into sexual knowledge. Qin Keqing is generally assumed to have hung herself as a consequence of her incestuous relationship with her father-in-law, Jia Zhen. Chess kills herself after her illicit love affair with her cousin is discovered and Faithful would rather hang than be forced into concubinage with the lecherous Jia She (although many in the mansions assume her action revealed her devotion to the Old Matriarch who had just passed away).

Zhao Rong has written that Cao was praising the young women who would die rather than lose their honour, dignity and chastity, saying these women "thought of death as returning home."[22] In a discussion of Faithful's suicide Zhao Jiaqi wrote that Faithful's spirit of "rather die than give in" (*ning si bu qu*) is an act of rebellion worthy of praise.[23] The veneration of girls who kill themselves rather than compromise their purity is supported in the novel through comments like the following by Baoyu: "What a rare girl Faithful was to choose such a death! The purest essence of

---

[21] Kathryn Tsai, "The Chinese Buddhist Monastic Order for Women: The First Two Centuries," *Historical Reflections*, 8, No. 3 (Fall, 1981), p. 14.

[22] Zhao Rong, "Hunyin ziyou de nahan," p. 61.

[23] Zhao Jiaqi, "Funü beiju mingyun de xiangxiang lishi—tan *Honglou meng* de zhongyao sixiang yinxiang (Historical images of the tragic fates of women—talking about the major trends of thought in *Honglou meng*). *Xinjiang shifan daxue xuebao: shekeban*, No. 1 (1985), pp. 99-104, rpt. in *RD*, No. 3 (1985), p. 68.

the universe is truly concentrated in her sex! She has found a fitting and noble death (*SS* 5.111.211)."

The sexual morality of those women who die of illness rather than suicide
is highlighted as well. For instance, Skybright is sent home desperately ill
under suspicion of being a fox fairy and polluting Baoyu with sexual knowledge. She later dies a lonely death in impoverished surroundings. Lin
Daiyu's death fits uncomfortably into either the death-through-illness category or the death-through-suicide category. Daiyu's willingness to allow her
recurring illness to dominate can for example be interpreted as the ultimately
passive suicide. She decides to die after she learns of plans for Baoyu's marriage. "The prophecy [of Baoyu's marriage] contained in her nightmare was
to be fulfilled after all. Bitterness and grief overwhelmed her. There was
only one way of escape left. She must die. She must not live to see this
dreaded thing take place (*SS* 4.89.208)." She, too, has an exceptional reason
for death. While she has neither been compromised sexually nor accused of
this singularly feminine crime, her love has been compromised by Baoyu's
marriage to Baochai. This emotion is not without its moral strictures.
Zhen Shiyin tells us, "while women may not commit transgressions of bodily lust, *yin*, it is equally important that they do not become infected with
romantic love, *ch'ing*".[24] Crimson Pearl's debt of tears to Jade Boy is complete as Lin Daiyu dies and ascends to the Land Of Illusion.

The women who exist in 'unreal' form appear to their worldly sisters
only as ghosts or in dreams, unlike their male counterparts, who readily assume corporeal shapes in their wanderings. The fairies' movements under
the Great Matriarch Disenchantment are as minimal as those of their earthly
sisters. They dwell in the Land of Illusion and never assume corporeal
forms.

Through this discussion of the sexual differences in the form and manner
of interaction between the real and the unreal, it is evident that the novel's
approach to sexual ideology is not as one dimensional as it superficially appears. Young women are imprisoned in both realms by discourses of feminine purity, whereas men can exploit or transcend moral/immoral and
mythic/mimetic boundaries. *Honglou meng* has revealed the pattern of sexual difference which reflects a preoccupation with feminine purity.

Married/Unmarried : The power of pollution

The allocation of positions on each side of the polluted/pure moral register is
determined with a specific, and not accidental, criterion in mind. In *Honglou
meng* the unmarried women (both the never-married girls and the widow Li
Wan) are eulogized for their virtue and purity. Placed opposite them are the
married women, who are variously described as vicious, power hungry, and

---

[24] Cited in Lucien Miller, *Masks of Fiction in Dream of the Red Chamber*, p. 243.

jealous. The symbolic split between married and unmarried women has several implications for a critique examining the text's sexual ideology.

At the level of the real, a 'girls' kingdom' in Prospect Garden is surrounded by the male world, within which dwell the maternal figures like Ladies Wang and Xing and Aunt Xue. The maternal figures are indistinguishable from the men in the symbolic structure set up by the text. At the head of the masculine world is the elderly and extremely influential Grandmother Jia in an imperfect and poorly managed 'maternal patriarchy.'

Lady Wang's harsh treatment of Skybright and Golden, resulting in their deaths, are memorable examples of the married women's imperfection and inability to manage. Lady Xing's character is established as mindless, selfish and stupid. She foolishly supports the attempt of her husband Jia She to take Grandmother Jia's principle maid Faithful as concubine and fails to see the treachery behind Qiaojie's betrothal arrangements. The foster mothers of the young actresses are also depicted as greedy and grasping in their relationships with their wards. The maternal figures are also responsible for spoiling the young boys Zhen Baoyu and Jia Baoyu, as will become evident in chapter seven.

At the mythical level, there is a matriarchy without maternity and, moreover a matriarchy without marriage. Instead a sisterhood exists in the Land of Illusion where the predominant position is that of the Fairy Disenchantment. Disenchantment holds the fate of each character's life in her registers and, to facilitate Baoyu's speedy enlightenment, reveals these to him in a dream. Above her in the broader heavenly spectrum is Nüwa, whose responsibility it is to repair the roof of heaven. In refusing to insert the Stone into heaven, she forces him to compensate by engaging in a proto-sexual encounter with Crimson Pearl, watering the latter faithfully each day. Acting in this way, Nüwa plays the causal role which gives birth to the entire novel.

In their causal and revealing roles, these two heavenly matriarchal figures are above human folly and are free of prescriptions of purity and pollution. At once they are the maternal originator of the novel and the avenue for Baoyu's sexual enlightenment through Disenchantment's sister, Two-in-one. The merger of the sexual with the maternal in a realm free of social morality is perhaps the world idealized by Cao. Indeed, in the intermingling of the mythic and the mimetic, the novel points to human desire as one of the founding principles of a worldly patriarchy and addresses the need for the abandonment of desire. In *Honglou meng*'s mythical utopia free of human desire, Baoyu's veneration of young unmarried girls is also viewed as human folly. In discounting human desire, the novel makes its critique of patriarchy by providing the key to its own deconstruction. The comparison between the earthly matriarchy headed by Grandmother Jia and the otherworldly matriarchy provides some insights into the novel's presentation of sexual ideology and the over-ruling of codes of purity and pollution in heaven. To extend this examination further, let us focus on the earthly reality of sexual politics as centred on codes of purity and pollution.

In chapter seventy-seven Baoyu laments the change in the female nature that occurs when women get married, by saying after the raid on the garden, "Strange, the way they get like this when they marry! It must be something in the male that infects them. If anything they end up even worse than the men!" In reply the gatekeepers say with a laugh, "In that case all girls must be good and all women must be bad. You don't really believe that, do you?" To which Baoyu answers, "That's precisely what I *do* believe (*S S* 3.77.534)." In his lament for young girls' loss of purity and virtue on marriage, Baoyu links the cause to infection and pollution by the male. By suggesting that it is the girls that become polluted by the males he once again inverts the commonly accepted notions of the ritually profane. It is women's bodies which are commonly thought of as the source of the most polluting substances, such substances as would offend the gods or drain vital energy from men.

Jiang Wenqin's 1985 critique of the novel concentrates heavily on the problem of male infection of the "kingdom of girls."[25] One of the ways the novel describes this infection on the symbolic level is the discovery in Prospect Garden of a purse embroidered with a pair of lovers embracing. The subsequent raid on the Garden in chapter seventy-four is the metaphoric and literal purge of any trace of the infecting masculinity. Any item of clothing or jewellery belonging to a man is sought, to track down the carrier of the polluting masculine virus of sexual knowledge. Baoyu's belongings are notably exempt from this purge. In keeping with the Daoist notion that enlightenment is facilitated by an internal balancing of yin and yang, Baoyu's masculinity is from the outset complemented with a femininity that other men, including his father, regard as signifying lecherous and wanton ways as was made evident in the preceding chapter.

The novel's notion of spoiling and corrupting the naturally pure and virtuous young woman, despite the reversal, invokes Confucian prescriptions of femininity. It supports the principle that ruled out sexual or even simple social contact between the sexes. Thus, the Qing dynasty social codes for the aristocracy demanded isolation of women from all contact with males outside of family members. To prevent infection from men, young girls were kept isolated from public affairs and thus dependent upon men. The effect of this isolation is made obvious by the case of Qiaojie, who is nearly sold into a harem by her male cousin and uncle. To deceive the elder women of the mansions, who in their isolation remained ignorant of the plot until almost too late, the men concoct a suitable tale to explain any unusual circumstances in the betrothal (*SS* 5.118.318-84). Baoyu's eulogies to the pu-

---

[25] Jiang Wenqin, "'Nüer shijie' de liang ge cengci," pp. 41-43.

rity of his virginal unmarried cousins can thereby serve to reinforce the elite interpretations of Confucian ideology.

The purity idealized by Baoyu is not as beneficial to young women as it initially appears. Zhao Rong unwittingly supported this claim by stating that young girls gain access to power and family influence after marriage and thereby sink into the mire of the masculine world.[26] This statement clearly reveals the founding principle of men's 'protection' of unmarried or widowed women from male pollution, that being, isolation from social power. It appears that within the Qing dynasty's signifying system, power is the most polluting substance that can infect a woman.

Married women face an alternative but symmetrical ideological prescription in relation to their pollution/power. The married women in the novel do have access to worldly influence beyond their husbands' control through their management of household affairs and their dominance in childbearing and rearing. The marriage bond establishes women as impure and evil because it simultaneously grants them a limited degree of power, which society counteracts with ideological prescriptions about women and power. Thus Grandmother Jia, although a widow like Li Wan, is not idealized in the same manner because, as the oldest member of the mansions, she holds considerable power as matriarch and is thereby no longer pure. As a venerated elder member of the family, Grandmother Jia could also be perceived as having transcended, through her seniority, the binary of purity/pollution that oppresses younger women.

The most *polluting* women are those who are married, because they exude polluting substances like blood or milk. Emily Ahern suggested that the most significant polluting substances issuing from women's bodies are menstrual or post-partum blood while Charlotte Furth noted that even breast milk has the potential to pollute babies through a process called foetal poisoning.[27] Significantly, the most *powerful* women are also those who are married because their blood and milk enables them to establish a uterine family which can potentially undermine the patriarchal family. The elite families of Qing China were able to reduce the power of the daughter-in-law as a new mother through invoking stringent medical/moral knowledge, a process described in detail by Charlotte Furth.[28] Because the ideal aristocratic mar-

---

[26] Zhao Rong, "Hunyin ziyou de nahan," pp. 60-61.

[27] Emily Ahern, "The Power and Pollution of Chinese Women," in *Women in Chinese Society*, ed. by Margery Wolf and Roxanne Witke (Stanford: Stanford University Press, 1979), p. 170-71 and Charlotte Furth, "Concepts of Pregnancy, Childbirth and Infancy in Ch'ing Dynasty China," *Journal of Asian Studies*, 46, No. 1 (February, 1987), pp. 8-9.

[28] See Furth's article for more detail on the inter-relationship between medical knowledge and moral prescriptions, for example, those which discouraged maternal breast-feeding and encouraged wet-nursing. By breaking the close and exclusive bond between the breast-feeding mother and her child the daughter-in-law's newly gained power is reduced. The paid wet-nurse is less of a threat to the family as she usually had working-class origins and therefore had little hope of overcoming both sexual and class domination. Charlotte Furth, "Concepts of Pregnancy, Childbirth and Infancy," pp. 21-22.

riage practice was virilocal, the daughter-in-law's allegiance to the husband's family was already in doubt. Susan Mann explains, "Like women in all male-centred family systems, Chinese women posed an implicit danger to the long-term stability of the family structure. They were liminal or marginal members who were constantly violating family boundaries: entering or exiting as brides..."[29]

To cope with this uncertainty of allegiance and access to family influence, a counter ideology exists, whereby it is regarded as unnatural and unbalanced for women to exert power. This is clearly reflected in the novel's portrayal and subsequent scholarly treatment of the 'too capable' daughter-in-law Wang Xifeng. The novel lends itself to a harsh interpretation of the powerful Xifeng, as will be revealed in more detail in the following chapter. It describes how her unwillingness to relinquish control over household affairs results in the miscarriage of a male foetus. She continues to overwork herself through fear of losing her power and, consequently, continues to lose menstrual blood throughout the remainder of the novel. Wang Xifeng's impurity as a married woman is clearly reflected in the references to her uncontrolled flow of menstrual blood. Her power is simultaneously represented by the very same post-partum blood, and its uncontrolled loss effectively symbolizes her uncontrolled, unhealthy hold on power. Xifeng's power is uncontrolled just as her blood, unstopped by male seed, flows unceasingly. Indeed through her miscarriage she rejects the male seed and begins to bleed.[30] It seems her lust for power upsets the 'natural balance' of her position as a reproductive woman. The power of menstrual blood, then, can be seen as "a symbolic representation of the actual social power of young married women. The power attributed to menstrual blood may also be the culture's way of recognizing that social power which otherwise goes virtually unacknowledged in Chinese society."[31]

In setting married women against unmarried women within the symbolic order of the polluted/pure woman, *Honglou meng* reveals many common assumptions about women in Qing China. It is on the body of Wang Xifeng that this ambiguity in ideological prescriptions is most clearly played out as she, as daughter-in-law, holds the most vulnerable and yet most powerful position.

The womanly virtue of chastity

The social standards by which women are graded into good and bad centre on the issues of chastity and fidelity, standards with historically changing implications, but never more rigid than during the Qing dynasty. The fear of

---

[29] Susan Mann, "Widows in the Kinship, Class and Community Structures of Qing Dynasty China," *Journal of Asian Studies*, 46, No. 1 (February, 1987), p. 44.

[30] Mary O'Brien, *The Politics of Reproduction* (London: Routledge and Kegan Paul, 1983), p. 151.

[31] Emily Ahern, "The Power and Pollution of Chinese Women," p. 178.

having doubt cast upon one's virtue acted as a considerable constraint on women, for even to attract male attention suggested a lack of feminine virtue and modesty. Where Qing society judged men on a variety of criteria for women the standard was based almost solely on sexual chastity. Female virtue meant chastity and purity.[32] *Honglou meng* exemplifies, in a complex manner, this feature of Qing society.

The favoured method of slandering women is through prescriptions of virtue and chastity. As a result, when women gain power doubt is cast on their sexual morality and lewd innuendoes abound. In the character of Wang Xifeng, *Honglou meng* provides a provocative example of the sexual slurring of women who hold power. Xifeng is the object of Jia Rui's lust, and by actively refusing his attentions, receives harsher judgement by critics than the aggressor himself. Wang Chaowen, for example, likens Xifeng to the Empress Lü, who was considered sexually loose and ruthlessly murderous.[33] It is 'natural' for men to respond to their sexual needs by actively seeking partners and 'unnatural' or rather immoral, for women to act at all. We learn from Patience in chapter twenty-one that Xifeng is, in fact, faithful to the adulterous Jia Lian, but she is all the same condemned by many critics for an assumed sexual transgression. The Wang Xifeng created by Cao is in fact guilty not of adultery but rather independence. Cao Xueqin's mastery gives these complex social relations an identifiable form.

As a man, Jia Rui is guilty of daring to desire the wife of someone of higher social status, and not of daring to seek a sexual partner. Assuming for himself the status of desiring Subject, Jia Rui has simultaneously placed Xifeng into the desired Object category, thus misreading the social codes where social status and sex interface. As Patience so accurately explains, this is "a case of 'the toad on the ground wanting to eat the goose in the sky' (*SS* 1.11.242)." Although Xifeng's female sex places her in a category suitable for objectification, her social rank above Jia Rui makes such a mediation repulsive and inconceivable. Her power may well be what makes Xifeng attractive to Jia Rui, and it is also the very reason why he should never have dared to flirt with her.

When looking at notions of female chastity associated with the Qing neo-Confucian order, it is clear that chastity was not prescribed for all women. Indeed, the concern was with pre-marital and post-marital chastity and not life-long sexual abstinence. It was considered rather unhealthy for women to abstain from sex; they were thought to need regular sexual relations for the

---

[32] The predominant position of chastity in codes of female virtue was a phenomenon associated with the Qing dynasty in particular according to Chien Chiao. See Chien Chao, "Female Chastity in Chinese Culture," *Bulletin of the Institute of Ethnology Academia Sinica*, No. 31 (Spring, 1971), p. 206.

[33] Wang Chaowen, *Lun Fengjie* (On Sister Feng) (Tianjin: Baihua wenyi chubanshe, 1980), pp. 456-57.

correct functioning of their body rhythms.[34] Kathryn Tsai pointed out that
there is a "general Chinese antipathy towards a deliberate celibate life."[35]
However, there are two groups for whom deliberate celibacy was a social
preoccupation: unmarried girls and widows. The encouragement of celibacy
among these two groups and the encouragement of regular sex among the
married women suggests that prescriptions of chastity were mechanisms that
ensured purity and continuity of the natal line having little to do with a
holistic Confucian sexuality.

The abundance of tales eulogizing chaste and virtuous girls and widows
suggests that their unmarried status and sexual instability were perceived as
threatening. Their unclaimed reproductive potential empowered the unmarried women, but ideologies of chaste widowhood and virginity simultaneously imprisoned them. Women who were unattached to a male, such as
unmarried daughters or young widows, thereby faced much stricter ideological controls than their married sisters.[36]

The model widow Li Wan is portrayed favourably in the novel as are the
maidens. The young pages describe Li Wan as a saint and nickname her
Lady Guanyin for her gentle nature (SS 3.65.291). Jiang Wenqin suggests
that Li Wan is placed in the "girls' world" because, even though she has a
young son she was widowed early and therefore had very little male pollution.[37] In fact, her place on the same divine level as her unmarried sisters-in-
law and girl cousins does not develop from her freedom from polluting male
contact. Rather, Li Wan, like the unmarried girls, is not under the direct
control of a husband. Therefore, her potential to disrupt the socio-sexual
order must be contained by social conventions that make it improper for her
to act independently of her husband's family.

While the novel venerates the maidens and the widowed women through
the ideology of feminine sexual purity and chastity, there is one unmarried
woman in the novel for whom chastity is not idealized: the fastidious 'too
pure' young novice Adamantina. Her exclusion from the ranks of pure virgins and chaste widows reinforces the conclusion that ensuring continuity
and purity of the natal line is the fundamental rationale for prescriptions of
purity in femininity. After the mansions are burgled, she is described by the
faithful retainer Bao Yong as "the traitor in our midst (SS 5.112.225)." His
assessment is quite accurate on a symbolic scale (though unfaithful to the
event as described in the novel): by joining a nunnery she has avoided mar-

---

[34] See for example the tale of Lady Han who falls desperately ill due to the sexual neglect
of her husband the Emperor, who is currently infatuated with his concubine An Fei. She
blooms again only after having sex with an imposter/god. C.T. Hsia, *The Classic Chinese
Novel: A Critical Introduction* (Bloomington: Indiana University Press, 1980), pp. 299-302.

[35] Kathryn Tsai, "The Chinese Buddhist Monastic Order For Women," p. 3.

[36] Lin Daiyu in her arrogant refusal to participate in family politics rejects the established
power structure. As a consequence she spits blood throughout the novel in a manner similar
to Wang Xifeng's loss of menstrual blood.

[37] Jiang Wenqin, "'Nüer shijie' de liang ge cengci," p. 41.

riage and, most importantly, shown through her vows of life-long chastity that she renounces participation in a patrilineal society.

Adamantina's ignominious end as a prostitute is directly juxtaposed with her life as a nun. Adamantina the prostitute, surrounded by dirt and pollution, is starkly contrasted with Adamantina the nun, who is portrayed as an unsurpassed snob preoccupied with maintaining her personal purity. In the character of Adamantina the novel provides yet another instructive display of the link between the pure and the polluted, the virgin and the whore. In chapter forty-one, after Adamantina is visited by Grandmother Jia and Grannie Liu, the courtyard in which the latter sat is sluiced to wash away Liu's earthly pollution. Moreover Adamantina asks that the cup used by Grannie Liu be left outside of her personal quarters because, as Baoyu explains, "Grannie Liu had drunk from it. In Adamantina's eyes the cup was now contaminated (*SS* 2.41.313)." Baoyu asks that the cup should be given to the old peasant rather than thrown out. With Adamantina's agreement he arranges to hand it over personally saying to the fastidious Adamantina, "No one would expect you to *speak* to her. That would be an even greater pollution (*SS* 2.41.315)."

The uncompromising young nun, it seems, is repulsed by the presence of an elderly peasant woman but not by that of the young man, Baoyu. Indeed she even serves him tea herself within her private quarters. For Adamantina, the peasant woman's lowly social status is more polluting than the masculinity of a member of her own class. This mocking contradiction so deftly created is the seed of Adamantina's tragedy and becomes the cause of her transformation from the pure nun to the polluted whore. Each time Adamantina is subsequently mentioned in the novel, it is in relation to Baoyu. The reader quickly gains the impression that the young nun is becoming infatuated with him. She sends him birthday greetings while forgetting the birthday of her long-time friend Xing Xiuyan. She even grants him a branch of her plum blossoms when he arrives to settle a debt incurred in losing yet another poetry competition. It is not long before her ability to meditate is hampered by the suppression of her feelings for Baoyu. She becomes delirious during meditation and imagines herself surrounded by young suitors and manhandled by ruffians.

The young men around town soon gossip lewdly about the event, "All that chastity and religion was bound to be too much for a girl of her age. Especially such an attractive, lively thing... Sooner or later she'll get soft on some lucky fellow and run away (*SS* 4.87.176)." Lewd fantasies about nuns were common in China, and established an often obvious connection between the symbolic place of purity and the symbolic place of pollution. Many are the tales where the nuns use their cloisters as fronts for brothels. The novel *Honglou meng* also provides several examples of the sexual innuendo directed at nuns. We read the salacious jokes made by men around town about the young and beautiful nuns living under the care of the Jia family.

When the nunnery is disbanded and word reaches town that the girls were to be sent off "every young rake in town fancied the idea of getting hold of one of them for himself (*SS* 4.94.283)." In chapter one hundred and eleven, the novel recounts the burglars reaction when they came upon Adamantina in the midst of her evening meditation. "After the main part of their mission was accomplished, the thieves...had been casually snooping around in Xichun's courtyard, and had caught a glimpse there of a very attractive young nun, which had put all sorts of mischievous ideas into their heads (*SS* 5.111.219-20)." The seeking of spiritual purity through meditation becomes an act of sexual significance in the burglars' minds, and Adamantina, in her conscious attempt to release herself from worldly desire becomes an object of desire.

Adamantina is even more desired than her unmarried female peers since, by entering a nunnery, she has made herself more unobtainable. As a well known homily of the time reveals 'stolen love' is better than 'legitimate love—"A wife isn't as good as a concubine, a concubine isn't as good as a maid, a maid isn't as good as a prostitute, and a prostitute isn't as good as stealing."[38] Based on the notion that the highest passion is reached only by the greatest violation of accepted morality, "the desirable woman is always unobtainable". In social notions of desirability, the nun approximates the widow in the degree to which she becomes an object of common lust. Indeed, the link between these two types of women is so close that in 1981 Liu Caonan wrote a controversial critique claiming that Adamantina is in fact a widow who retreated to a nunnery in order to preserve her chastity.[39]

Entering a nunnery was sometimes viewed as an immoral act. When Jia Xichun decides to 'leave home' her elders are horrified and try to dissuade her from such an unsavoury step. Lady Wang says that "it would look very bad for a girl from a family such as ours to enter a nunnery. That really is unthinkable (*SS* 5.118.318)." Women who enter nunneries open themselves to intense sexual speculation. When one considers that during the mid-Qing attracting male attention was enough to invite ruin for a girl, it is clear that Xichun's willingness to place herself in such a precarious position would horrify her elders. Indeed, Xichun's membership of the "Department of Ill-fated Fair" is based on the perception that her decision to enter a nunnery is tragic. Adamantina's end does not bode well for Xichun who equals Adamantina's arrogance when she declares that, unlike Adamantina, she would never be tempted by evil spirits and unholy thoughts (*SS* 4.87.177). Xichun's vow almost amounts to a premonition of disaster.

In drawing on the dual notions of purity and pollution this chapter has attempted to make the textual silences within *Honglou meng* reveal the complexity of their implicit sexual ideology and of course the intricacy of the

---

[38] R. K. McMahon, "Eroticism in Late Ming, Early Qing Fiction: The Beauteous Realm and the Sexual Battlefield," *T'oung Pao*, No. 73 (1987), p. 235.

[39] Liu Caonan, "Shixi Miaoyu de shenshi" (An attempt to analyse Adamantina's life experience), *Honglou meng xuekan*, No. 4 (1981), pp. 57-70.

novel itself. The sexual ideology within which such a significant text is produced at once smooths over ambiguity and yet simultaneously provides the seeds of its own deconstruction. The liminal characters with ambiguous socio-sexual positions like the nun Adamantina, the widow Li Wan and the daughter-in-law Wang Xifeng act in pivotal roles embodying the contradictory nature of the notions of purity implicit within ideologies of femininity.

In the intermingling of the real and the unreal around a mythical realm free of the patriarchal dominance so striking in the mimetic realm, Cao has questioned the necessity of sexual and moral distinctions. It is through posing this unspoken philosophical problem and not simply through the reversal of gender orders or the veneration of women that the novel is able to undermine comfortable assumptions about sexual ideologies.

CHAPTER FIVE

WANG XIFENG: YOUNG WOMEN AND POWER

Wang Xifeng, a young and powerful daughter-in-law, has been and is still one of the characters more frequently discussed by *Hongxue* scholars. She has been described by Angelina Yee as being "one of the most complex characters in the novel and certainly its most successful."[1] In this chapter it will become apparent that her success, in part, is a result of the tension generated by her relationship to a discourse which linked female superiority with social decline and female transgression of gender imperatives with social chaos. The legitimacy of her position as a powerful woman in the Jia mansions, as this chapter will reveal, is undermined by her symbolic position in the novel's over-riding conservative patriarchal world order. This symbolic position is attested to, and recreated, in the consistent problematization of her character in relation to issues of female power and social order by critics of *Honglou meng* over the past two centuries. This analysis of the symbolic role granted to Xifeng shows that *Honglou meng*'s reference system within the sexual ideologies of Qing China is more problematic than that theorized in terms of the dualism of opposition against or support for women's equality.

Xifeng is married to Jia Lian, eldest son of the senior branch of the Rong mansions, and she controls the management of this branch of the Jia household. She is lively, humorous, beautiful and charming but also unrivalled in her cunning, cruelty and murderous jealousy. Her importance to the novel is paramount for it is she, despite her youth, who controls with ruthless efficiency every aspect of the domestic purse. The multiformity of her character evolves from the contradiction between her relatively weak objective status as daughter-in-law and her undeniable power over the Jia's domestic affairs. Her skilful management is thereby an object of both praise and suspicion just as her confident hold on power elicits respect and disdain.

A brief examination of the body of criticism surrounding the novel reveals that literary critics have long regarded Wang Xifeng as a problematic female character. In 1812 "Er zhi dao ren" wrote, from a Buddhist inspired perspective, that the Jia family's Prospect Garden was a "sea of jealousy (vinegar)" where Wang Xifeng's "treacherous and deadly traps turn the vine-

---

[1] Angelina C. Yee, "Counterpoise in *Honglou meng*," *Harvard Journal of Asiatic Studies*, 15, No. 2 (1990), p. 638.

gar into a poisonous broth."[2] In 1832 Wang Xuexiang (Wang Xilian) de-scribed Xifeng's manipulation of power in both the Rong and Ning man-sions of the Jia clan as leading to the clan's decline and punishment.[3] Xifeng has "an ability to govern comparable to an able minister but also the ability to cause chaos of an evil hero," according to Tu Ying's essay of 1842.[4] A critique written by Huang Changlin published in 1917 likened Xifeng to the Han dynasty Empress Lü, thus linking Xifeng's dominance of the Jia family with Lü's 'irregular' reign.[5] The comparisons with figures regarded in the popular imagination as being arch villains or anti-heroes con-tinue through to 1946 when Tai Yu compared her to Cao Cao of the Three Kingdoms period.[6] By 1982 this trend had been succinctly encapsulated by Wang Yigang's chapter "The Portrayal of Xifeng and the Historical Uses of Evil." Wang states,

> From Empress Lü of the Western Han, Wu Zetian of the Tang, through to Ci Xi of the Qing, even though they occupy different historical positions and have had different historical effects, these women have all seized power through their special relationships with the emperors in order to satisfy their own fanatical desire to possess, necessarily furthering their lust for money and their lust for power simultaneously... Xifeng's fanaticism to possess can be described as the artistic incorporation and reflection of the essential nature of the feudal thinking of this type of woman.[7]

Clearly then, one hundred and fifty years of *Hongxue* have read Xifeng as a problematic powerful woman whose talent to rule is countered by the per-ceived illegitimacy of her power. Xifeng has 'worked' as a character partly

---

[2] "Er zhi dao ren", "*Honglou meng* shuo meng," p. 101.

[3] Wang Xuexiang, "*Honglou meng* zongping," p. 146.

[4] Tu Ying, "*Honglou meng* lunzan," p. 134.

[5] Huang Changlin, "*Honglou meng* erbai yong (jie lu)" (Two Hundred Odes on *Honglou meng* [excerpts]). 1917; rpt. in *Honglou meng juan*, p. 499.

[6] Tai Yu, *Honglou meng renwu lun* , p. 157.

[7] Wang Yigang, "Fengjie xingxiang de suzao yu e de lishi zuoyong" (The portrayal of Xifeng and the historical uses of evil), *Honglou meng xuekan*, No. 4 (1982), p. 242. This appraisal of Xifeng corresponds to the fundamentally negative notion of the relationship of women to social order and in particular social power noted by Lin Yutang. Lin explains that women who hold power, for example Empress Lü of the Western Han and Empress Wu of the Tang, are often referred to as nymphomaniacs or megalomaniacs. See Lin Yutang, "Feminist Thought in Ancient China," *T'ien Hsia Monthly*, 1, No. 2 (1935), p. 145. Other women who hold positions that are close to authority, although no being in authority themselves, Lin states, are often accused of causing the downfall of the social order. One such case is the beautiful Xi Shi. She is often blamed by later historians for the downfall of the State of Wu despite the historically acknowledged decadence and promiscuity of the Kingdom. Lin Yutang, "Feminist Thought in Ancient China," p. 128. Sentiment similar to those found in the Chinese histories finds echoes in the literary-political scene of the PRC. One need only look at the criticism of Jiang Qing to see familiar paradigms emerging. See Joan Grant, "Power and Pitfalls: The Possibilities of Real Political Power for Women in 20th Century China." In *Class, Ideology and Women in Asian Societies*, ed. by Gail Pearson and Lenore Manderson (Hong Kong: Asian Research Service, 1987), pp. 15-45. The translation journal *Chinese Studies in History* has also included criticisms of Jiang Qing in each of the issues for 1978 and 1979.

because critics connect her to a persistent discourse that links women in power to social chaos and decline. We need to examine the discursive triggers woven into the text that signify Xifeng as a problematic woman, despite her numerous virtues.

The absence of a victim

The portrayal of such a strong and vindictive female character creates difficulties for those critics who argue that the novel reveals how women in Qing China were 'victims' of oppression. C.T. Hsia rationalizes Xifeng's evil power with her womanhood by arguing that women are driven by their subordination to protect their interests by cunning manipulation. "This relentless struggle, whether in the form of the outwardly polite cunning of Wang Hsi-feng... or that of the undisguised ruthlessness of P'an Chin-lien, constitutes the tragedy of the Chinese woman. It is her tragedy that she has to become mean and cunning in order to cope with male domination, a condition of injustice to which she is nevertheless resigned."[8] This argument does not explain why such cunning and mean active women have repeatedly been described by literary critics as causing social chaos and family decline while attempting to 'cope' with oppression. Indeed, it is here that the portrayal of "the tragedy of the Chinese woman" plays an important part in ensuring continued male dominance.

An alternative explanation of the nature of Xifeng's role in the novel is provided by PRC critics such as Ge Chuying and Chen Shujing who argue that Xifeng is the exception to the general portrayal of women in the novel. To these critics Xifeng does not represent the typical oppressed woman in Qing China, as do Daiyu or Xiangyun, rather she is a ruthless oppressor. Ge argues that Xifeng's sex should not be taken into account when appraising her role in the novel because she is not a typical oppressed woman while Chen argues that she is an "out and out bad woman" and cannot be incorporated into *Honglou meng*'s depiction of the tragic fates of women under feudalism.[9] It will become apparent that the contradictory positions outlined above, on the one hand willing to praise the novel as progressive in its sympathy for women's plight but, on the other unwilling to incorporate Xifeng as a member of the oppressed sex into this general conception, are reinforced by the novel's own invocation of a common patriarchal duality.

---

[8] C.T. Hsia, *The Classic Chinese Novel*, p. 26. A similar argument was used by Bai Dun in his critique on Xifeng's tragedy. Bai argues that Xifeng's actions were shaped by her position as daughter-in-law in an oppressive feudal system. Bai Dun, "Lun Wang Xifeng xingge de beiju yiyi" (A discussion of the tragic significance of Wang Xifeng), *Honglou meng xuekan*, No. 1 (1982), pp. 121-36.

[9] Ge Chuying, "Wang Xifeng de beiju" (Wang Xifeng's tragedy), *Wu shi Xiaogan fenyuan xuebao* (Journal of Wuhan Teachers' College Xiaogan branch), No. 2 (1982), pp. 23-30. Rpt. in *RD*, No. 1 (1983), pp. 71-79; Chen Shujing, "Jinxiu ronghua qing ke jin—lun Qin Keqing de xiangzheng yiyi" (Good things come to an end—discussing the symbolic significance of Qin Keqing), *Honglou meng xuekan*, No. 2 (1987), pp. 224-25.

Women are regarded as being noble in their oppression when powerless and inactive while simultaneously considered to be dangerous and evil when powerful.

Another source of this contradiction is the PRC critics' general adherence to a rigid dualism of oppressor/oppressed that sets up static relations of power. In fact *Honglou meng* constructs a world of multiform power relations, in which Xifeng emerges as a woman whose relationship with the Confucian order of the Jia household was variously one of collusion, resistance, perpetuation, subversion and support.[10] Indeed Xifeng can be read as a character who negotiated her position in reference to the parameters set by her status as a young married woman, which meant sometimes stretching the boundaries and at others complying with them. One of the boundaries that she stretched was that of perceived appropriate gender distinctions.

Chaos manifested in confusing yin with yang.

From the outset of the novel the reader is aware that Xifeng is an unusual woman. In his analysis of Xifeng, Yu Pingbo notes the repeated comparisons made between her and men.[11] She is often referred to as masculine or described as being uncomfortable with the rigid gender imperatives of her milieu. Ann Waltner has noted that within Confucian lore "gender confusion is symbolic of larger disorder: it is the blurring of distinctions that make social order possible."[12] Xifeng's confused gender can thereby be seen to invoke social disorder.

We read that Xifeng was "brought up from earliest childhood just like a boy, and had acquired in the schoolroom, the somewhat boyish-sounding name of Wang Xifeng." As a child she was nicknamed "Brother Feng" [*Feng ge*] (*SS* 1.3.91-92, 1.6.156). The masculinity of her name is a motif brought back to the reader twice again in the novel. The story tellers of chapter fifty-four offer the tale of a young man called Wang Xifeng who journeys to the capital to sit for the Imperial exams (*SS* 3.54.29). In chapter one

---

[10] Dorothy Ko has discussed the importance of reaching beyond such rigid dichotomies in the attempt to write a version of women's history that is able to appreciate the shifting alliances, collusion and resistance that were an inevitable part of women's relationship to social power. Dorothy Ko, "Pursuing Talent and Virtue: Education and Women's Culture in Seventeenth and Eighteenth-Century China," *Late Imperial China*, 13, No. 1 (1992), p. 13.

[11] Yu Pingbo, "Honglou meng zhong guanyu 'Shi er chai' de miaoxie," Rpt. in *Yu Pingbo lun "Honglou meng*," p. 1018. An alternative view is that of Angelina Yee who has discussed Xifeng's masculinity as an artistic device that counterpoises Xifeng's masculine traits with Baoyu's feminine ones. Angelina Yee, "Counterpoise in *Honglou meng*," pp. 636-49.

[12] Ann Waltner, "On Not Becoming a Heroine: Lin Dai-yu and Cui Ying-ying," *Signs*, 15, No. 1 (1989), p. 65. Of course the equally Chinese lore of the yin yang cosmology was more flexible in its attitude to gender boundaries. Charlotte Furth has noted that "it is well known that Chinese cosmology based on the interaction of the forces of yin and yang made sexual difference, a relative and flexible bipolarity in natural philosophy. On the other hand, Confucianism constructed gender around strict hierarchical kinship roles." Charlotte Furth, "Androgynous Males and Deficient Females," p. 1.

hundred and one the nun who tells Xifeng's fortune ominously relates the details of [the scholar] Wang Xifeng's 'return home' from officialdom—thus foreshadowing the imminent end of Xifeng's [the daughter-in-law] dominance (*SS* 5.101.62).

Many of Xifeng's own activities are described as being masculine. In chapter forty she attempts to punt the boat on the lake at Prospect Garden (without success). In chapter fifty-four during the New Year's celebrations she consciously takes the male role by acting the 'dickey bird' saying that if the menfolk will not oblige and entertain their parents then she will have to perform this task for them. In the same chapter she boasts to her sister-in-law, Youshi, that she can let the firecrackers off better than the boys (*SS* 3.54.32,42). The theme is further enhanced by descriptions of her smoking and drinking heavily (*SS* 1.16.310; 5.101.57). Ling Jiefang regards Xifeng's religious scepticism as being unusual for her sex since the practise of cult superstitions was a predominantly female pastime (and one that men abhorred). As Xifeng said to the Prioress of Wheatcake Priory, Euergesia, "You know that I've never believed all that talk about hell and damnation (*SS* 1.15.298)."[13]

Wang Xifeng's name, upbringing and behaviour all suggest a masculinized woman who would prefer to be a man. Thus we read Xifeng's statement, "If I'm a good girl in this life, I might be reborn as a man (*SS* 2.46.426)." In this way the text has established a contrast with Jia Baoyu, the novel's main male protagonist, who is often described as desiring to be reborn a girl, as we saw in earlier discussion. Where Baoyu has always rejected the trappings of masculinity that are associated with careers and power, Xifeng is active in seeking them out.

Juxtaposed with the masculine Xifeng who consciously expresses the preference to be a man is the text's elaboration of the negative consequences of such gender bending. Indeed, the cost for her desire to become a man is high. Comments about Xifeng's omni-competence are paired with details of how she is crumbling and weak, implying that the desire to become a powerful man is unnatural and unbalanced and thereby leads Xifeng to illness and madness. Moreover, the novel links the unbalanced yin and yang essences within Xifeng with corporeal abnormalities and irregularities that are specifically related to the female body.

The most prominent symbol of her corporeal and spiritual imbalance is flowing blood. Charlotte Furth's work on female blood and a woman's gender is instructive for our discussion. Here we read that blood is the ruling aspect in women.[14] Blood served as a dual symbol of femininity, at once

[13] Ling Jiefang, "Fenghuang chao he fang huan chao: ling yi ge Wang Xifeng" (The Phoenix nest and the phoenix returns to the nest: another Wang Xifeng), *Honglou meng xuekan*, No. 4 (1983), p. 157.

[14] Charlotte Furth, "Blood, Body and Gender: Medical Images of the Female Condition in China," *Chinese Science*, No. 7 (1986), p. 44.

emphasizing woman's weakness and woman's power. Ailments resulting from menstrual irregularity dwelt on woman's nature as the 'sickly sex' while blood was also symbolic of the reproductive power of the young fertile woman. Menstrual blood was both highly polluting and representative of a young woman's power and, as evidence of its importance, considerable medical attention was given to regularity of the menses.

In *Honglou meng* Wang Xifeng's state of health is mentioned several times and it is made clear that she suffered a miscarriage and subsequently endured chronic haemorrhaging with an uncontrolled loss of menstrual blood. In chapter sixty-one we read that she lost a "man-child" at six or seven months through worry (*SS* 3.61.183). Later an unceasing dripping of menstrual blood causes Xifeng to become more and more ill. Patience confides to Faithful, "During this past month, ever since she had her last period, it's been drip-drip, drip-drip all the time. Surely that's serious, isn't it? (*SS* 3.72.420)." Unable to forgo her household duties, Xifeng supervises the raid on the garden in chapter seventy-four and this exertion has dire consequences, "...but during the course of the night she was several times obliged to get out of bed, and each time she did so she found that she was losing blood. By the time next morning came, she was too weak and dizzy to get up (*SS* 3.74.479)."

Unwilling to relinquish the power of managing the household, Xifeng is overworked and overstressed. Her trusted servant, Patience, comments that Xifeng will not admit to being ill nor to seeing a doctor. "Surely you know our Mrs Lian [Xifeng] better than that? It's not just calling a doctor or taking medicine that she objects to.... She says there's nothing wrong with her and that I'm trying to make her ill by talking about it. In spite of feeling so poorly, she still insists on keeping up with everything that goes on in the household (*SS* 3.72.420)." Xifeng's denial of illness and her refusal to adopt the sickly/weaker sex role in these instances is in direct contrast to the more passive acceptance of illness by characters such as Lin Daiyu. This active assertion of dominance, and the continued desire for self-control and control over others, are constructed problematically through the invocation of the symbol of unrestrained, flowing menstrual blood. Andrew Plaks has noted that the connection between Wang Xifeng and blood represents her place in the Southern quarter, a yang quarter, of the cycle of elements[15] but we can also see that Wang Xifeng's uncontrolled loss of menstrual blood symbolizes her inappropriate relationship to power and her inappropriate connection to yang. Her very body manifests the effects of her challenge to conservative Confucian gender imperatives.

Gao E did not continue the theme of dripping menstrual blood but chose to have her "vomit up quantities of bright red blood" during the debacle of Grandmother Jia's funeral. This funeral was meant to demonstrate Xifeng's

---

[15] Andrew Plaks, *Archetype and Allegory*, pp. 64-65.

management prowess, equalling her success with Qin Keqing's funeral in chapters thirteen and fourteen, but instead it proves to be a signifier of her vulnerability as a young daughter-in-law. With her patron, Grandmother Jia, dead and her wealth stripped away, Xifeng lacked the authority to ensure obedience and support from those around her. Indeed, her mother-in-law and many of the servants simply refused to co-operate. Xifeng's enemies were at last able to seek their revenge. Her vulnerability as a daughter-in-law, symbolized by the loss of blood, had become evident as early as chapter seventy-one when Faithful explains to the young widow, Li Wan, Xifeng's predicament. "She's in a bad way at the moment. During all the years she has been managing things she may not have put a foot wrong as far as Their Ladyships are concerned, but she has given a great deal of offence elsewhere. A daughter-in-law's life must be pretty impossible. If she is too meek and mild her in-laws will complain that she is stupid and the servants won't respect her, yet if she shows any initiative, there is always another set of problems rising up behind her back (*SS* 3.71.412)."

After a period of persecution and failure over Grandmother Jia's funeral Xifeng suffers a collapse. "The strength ebbed from her legs and she sank to the ground. Luckily Patience was at hand and hurried over to support her mistress as she crouched there, blood gushing from her mouth in an unstaunchable stream (*SS* 5.110.206)." The uncontrollable loss of blood is symbolic of Xifeng's internal corporeal disharmony. Within the Neo-Confucian order of this period a young woman who seeks to wield the influence and power 'naturally' bestowed upon men, can cause physical disorder to herself and chaos to the household within which she lives. Blood stands at once as symbolic of her power and her vulnerability as a young daughter-in-law.

Her corporeal dysfunction further establishes Xifeng as a problematic wife and daughter-in-law. Wang Xifeng has already given birth to a young daughter, Qiaojie, and, as we saw above, miscarries a male foetus mid-way through the novel.[16] Her lack of a son places her in an extremely vulnerable position within the family. Significantly for our discussion problematic childbirth was not simply regarded as a bodily malfunction but a reflection of a woman's poor morality. Charlotte Furth has explained the close connection between a woman's physical well-being and her moral state. "Bodily conditions are inseparable from emotions and influence can act in either direction."[17]

Xifeng's failure to carry a male foetus through to full term can thereby be perceived as indicative of her transgressive morality. Van Gulik's work on

---

[16] Angelina Yee notes that the novel is inconsistent in respect to the number of Xifeng's children, because a second daughter is mentioned, however, importantly there is no confusion over their sex. Angelina Yee, "Counterpoise in *Honglou meng*," p. 623.

[17] Charlotte Furth, "Blood, Body and Gender," p. 59.

sexuality in China notes that it was perceived that "wives who are lewd by nature and whose passion is easily stirred...shall not obtain children."[18] Furth explains the connection between moral and medical knowledge and women as follows,

> They [medical authorities] taught that successful child bearing, like successful wifehood, was a matter of moral discipline and restraint. Maternal and child health depended on the same virtues of passionless calm that served the patriarchal family well in the social regulation of its wives. On the other hand, those vices that socially were held responsible for family disruption—resentment and anger, lust and passion, indulgence and immoderate desires—all were implicated in the pathological disorders of pregnancy and neonatal disease.[19]

If miscarriages were caused by anger and lust or immoderate desires, Xifeng's failure to carry a male child to full term can be regarded as symbolic of her lack of moral restraint. Similarly early childhood illnesses were understood to be caused by deviant maternal behaviour patterns. Qiaojie is described by Xifeng as a sickly child, "pursued by countless ailments and afflictions (SS 5.113.249)," and this can also be perceived as linked to Xifeng's transgressive lifestyle.

Xifeng is certainly not depicted as a moderate and retiring woman and the text provides tantalizing hints of her sexual indiscretions. Her relationship with her nephew Jia Rong remains ambiguous—whether it be idle flirtation or unbridled adultery is left for the reader to ponder. Angelina Yee's interpretation of the scene when Rong comes to borrow a screen from Xifeng draws the ambiguity out most clearly. Here we see the subtle comparisons between Xifeng and Rong's wife, Qin Keqing, figuratively referred to as 'stuff.'

> "I don't know what's so special about [the Wang] family's things. Heaven knows, you have enough stuff of your own over there; [you don't see the goodness of what you have, but keep turning to me.]" Jia Rong's smile flashed again. "[How could mine even compare!] Please, Auntie! Be merciful!" "If it's the tiniest bit chipped [If you dare lay your hands on me]," said Xifeng, "I'll have the hide off you!"[20]

Patience, Xifeng's principle maid, is made to insist upon her mistress's fidelity but, as we also noted in the previous chapter, recent critical opinion has generally assumed this to be inaccurate and indicative only of Patience's loyalty to her mistress.[21] More reliable opinions are considered to be those of characters such as the drunken servant, Big Jiao, who accuses Rong and Xifeng of adultery and incest by saying "Auntie has it off with nevvy" (SS 1.7.183). Some other contemporary PRC critics have gone to extent of say-

---

[18] R.H. Van Gulik, *Sexual Life in Ancient China* (Leiden: E.J. Brill, 1974), p. 274.

[19] Charlotte Furth, "Concepts of Pregnancy, Childbirth and Infancy, p. 9.

[20] Angelina Yee, "Counterpoise in *Honglou meng*," p. 643.

[21] Li Junxia, *Honglou meng renwu jieshao* (An introduction to the characters in *Honglou meng*) (Taipei: Shangwuyin, 1988), p. 1.

ing that Xifeng helped to murder Qin Keqing out of her desire for Keqing's husband Jia Rong.[22]

Xifeng's sexually indiscreet conduct is also highlighted in the comic-tragedy of Jia Rui. After visiting the ailing Qin Keqing, Xifeng is approached by Jia Rui, a distant relation to the Jias, who 'ogled her' and insinuated that the two of them might meet in private later. Xifeng decides to teach him a lesson through humiliation. She thereupon arranges a series of false rendezvous with Rui where he finds himself locked outside in an alley, humiliated by Rong and Jia Qiang, doused with manure and kept out in the freezing cold of the night. He becomes so ill from these non-encounters that he is bedridden. After a year or so when his illness had reached its apex, two wandering monks present the family with a mirror which will cure him of his illness if he only looks at its front. Rui can not resist looking in the back of the mirror and here he sees the image of Xifeng beckoning him and after repeated fantasies of their sexual encounters, he dies in a pool of semen. Although Xifeng is not responsible for Rui's immoderate lust, her flirtation is not the behaviour of the moderate, pure young wife.

Thus, Xifeng's stretching of gender boundaries and the 'acceptable' behavioural codes attached to these can be read as symbolic of social chaos. Her body manifests these transgressions in its inability to bear heirs and the poor health of her daughter. The social disorder invoked by these corporeal signals is in turn supported by repeated hints of her immoderate relationships with young men. The connection between Xifeng and the masculine world, described by Yee in terms of the dualistic technical structure of the novel, can thereby be granted a discursive significance as well. Not only does Xifeng's relationship with the masculine world complement and contrast with Baoyu's but it can also reveal the complex matrix of Qing sexual ideologies and their ambiguous appraisal of women who wield power.

Chaos manifested in yin subduing yang

As well as being described as having masculine qualities Xifeng is also depicted as superior to the men around her. Lucien Miller has explained that "the motif of decline and the related disregard of the family is connected to the inferiority of men and the superiority of women."[23] This state of affairs, where women dominate and prove themselves to be superior to men, in itself indicates decay within the Chinese world view for, as PRC critic Fan Yang has noted, one of the features of a declining family is the imbalance in male and female power, that is "when yin is ascending yang is decaying."[24] The

---

[22] Wang Zhiyao and Tong Haitian, "Lun Qin Keqing zhi si" (On Qin Keqing's death), *Henan daxue xuebao: zhe she ban*, No. 5 (1984), pp. 103-107. Rpt. in *RD*, No. 5 (1984), pp. 83-87.

[23] Lucien Miller, *Masks of Fiction*, p. 280.

[24] Fan Yang, *Yanggang de huichen* (The demise of yang) (Beijing: Guoji wenhua chubangongsi, 1988), pp. 62-63. The phrase translated is *"yin sheng er yang shuai."*

tale of the Jia mansions as invoked by *Honglou meng* uses the dominance of women as a symbol of social decline.

Within *Honglou meng* the household is dominated by two women, Grandmother Jia and Wang Xifeng, and is noted for its especially weak and degenerating male leadership. The novel suggests a link between the dominance of the Grandmother Jia over the entire household and the struggles for an expansion of power by Xifeng. Baochai makes a comparison between the two women in chapter thirty-five and Grandmother Jia's response is, "when I was the age that Feng is now, I could have taught her a thing or two. Still, though she may not be as sharp as I was then, she doesn't do so badly (*SS* 2.35.180)." Again in chapter seventy-one Li Wan says "Cousin Feng may not quite come up to Lady Jia's standard [of effectiveness in household management] but she doesn't do too badly (*SS* 3.71.412)." These comments suggest that Grandmother Jia's dominance of the family grew not only from her status as the oldest member of the household but developed early on and was based on her quick-witted intelligence.

Xifeng is repeatedly shown in competition with men. Leng Zixing, who provides the reader with the first descriptions of many major members of the Jia household, tells Jia Yucun that Xifeng is "more than a match for most men (*SS* 1.2.83)." She is able to "talk down ten grown men any day of the week" according to the senior household servant (*SS* 1.6.156). Her sister-in-law Qin Keqing returns to her in a dream and describes Xifeng as "a paragon among women that even strong men find more than their match (*SS* 1.13.255)." Later in the novel Zhou Rui's wife flatters Xifeng by saying that "a grown man with six arms and three heads would crumple under the strain of what you have to bear (*SS* 4.83.81-82)."

Not only is Xifeng compared favourably to the men around her but she is also set up in direct contrast to other women. The comparison between her and other women of her age and status is emphasized in chapter thirteen when she manages the arrangements for Keqing's funeral. "When a servant announced 'The Master is here,' all these females jumped up with little shrieks of alarm and rushed off to hide themselves—all, that is, except Xifeng, who rose slowly to her feet and imperturbably stood her ground (*SS* 1.13.266)." Later during the funeral preparations Wang Xifeng's competence is again contrasted to that of her female peers. "There were, to be sure, a number of other young married women in the clan, but all were either tongue tied or giddy, or they were so petrified by bashfulness or timidity that the presence of strangers or persons of higher rank threw them into a state of panic. Xifeng's vivacious charm and social assurance stood out in striking contrast (*SS* 1.14.283)." Wang Guowei's 1904 critique wrote that Xifeng herself was nervous of competition from other women and suggested that Xifeng's betrayal of Daiyu in supporting the secret plan to marry Baoyu to

Baochai evolved in part because Xifeng feared that "Daiyu's talent would lead to her own decline in family status."[25]

The ambiguity of this praise for her talents is an integral part of the success of Xifeng as a literary figure. Wang Xuexiang noted this contradiction in his critique written in the 1830s by writing "Wang Xifeng has no virtue but she has talent, with the result that she uses her talent in incorrect ways."[26] Readers and critics alike are encouraged to admire her multifarious skills and her considerable ability to cheerfully cope with strain where "grown men would crumple." She remembers numerous minutiae of the location of household items, details of the granting and receiving of presents, and still has time to help establish the Poetry Club and perform the many duties of attendance and serving expected of a daughter-in-law. However, her aptitude is undermined in the subtext because of the readers' knowledge that the men she surpasses are dissolute, licentious, lazy, and irresponsible. Angelina Yee states "her brilliance exposes men for what they are, ridiculous and ineffectual" but also notes that Xifeng is "more than masculine. She is a female who conquers men. The role reversal carries itself into the realm of supernatural admonitions."[27] Thus, while the critic Yu Pingbo's Republican era analysis is that the text censures the men of the Jia clan for being eclipsed by Xifeng, it is also the case that Xifeng is admonished by the text for her transgression of gender boundaries as well. Significantly Yu describes Xifeng as "a hero among women" or "a scarfed hero" (*jin guo yingxiong*) in a bid to establish her difference from the womanly norm.[28]

Xifeng's relationship with her husband, Jia Lian, is indicative of the disruption to Confucian concepts of family life her superiority to men represents. Wang Chaowen declares that the portrayal of Xifeng and Jia Lian satirizes the Confucian relationship between husband and wife, and describes Lian in terms designed specifically for the description of a weak husband and a strong wife—*mei guqi*.[29] Their marriage abounds with conflicts and competition in which Lian generally emerges as the loser. The vulnerability of her position, as wife, is reinforced if one supports the reading of the text that Lian finally divorces Xifeng.[30]

---

[25] Wang Guowei, "*Honglou meng* pinglun," in *Honglou meng juan*, p. 255.

[26] Wang Xuexiang, "*Honglou meng* zongping," in *Honglou meng juan*, p. 150. This section of his critique is interesting for it appraises each of the novel's foremost female characters, the Twelve Beauties, based on the criteria of relative talent and virtue. Both Yuanchun, the Imperial Concubine, and Xue Baochai are regarded as having both talent and virtue.

[27] Angelina Yee, "Counterpoise in *Honglou meng*," p. 639 and p. 641.

[28] Yu Pingbo, "*Honglou meng* zhong guanyu 'Shi er chai' de miaoxie," p. 1020. Yu draws his phrase from the Qing dynasty scholar Xiang Lingzi whose poem "Xuanting yuan: shang hua" (Aggrieved pavilion: appreciating the flowers) mentions the 'scarfed hero.'

[29] Wang Chaowen, *Lun Fengjie*, p. 206.

[30] This reading draws support from the poems portending Xifeng's fate in chapter five. Here the phrase *yi cong er ling san ren mu* is taken as referring to the three stages of her relationship with Lian with the final 'third' one being divorce because when the characters *ren*

Our introduction to Xifeng by Leng Zixing in chapter two describes the contrast between the two as follows: "However, ever since he [Jia Lian] married this young lady I mentioned [Xifeng], everyone high and low has joined in praising *her*, and he has been put into the shade rather (*SS* 1.2.83)." Lian and Xifeng's competition for praise continues throughout the novel. For example, Xifeng is actually described snatching the limelight from Lian in chapter ninety-five after Baoyu's precious jade was lost. When someone arrives with a similar jade Jia Lian brings the parcel in to Grandmother Jia only to have Xifeng snatch the parcel from his hands. To this he replies with a sneer, "Can't you even let me take the credit for a small thing like this? (*SS* 4.95.320)." Their marriage is filled with endless arguments about allocation of power and responsibility with both attempting to take credit for success and neither willing to shoulder blame for failure.

Wang Chaowen describes their relationship as indicating the competitive greed typical of the marriages among the oppressor class of feudal China.[31] An alternative reading could stress the mulitvalency of the text's depiction of Xifeng's and Lian's marriage and in this manner draw out more of the complexity of Xifeng's image in relation to the problematic of women in power. For example, Xifeng's consistent opposition to Lian's wish to take a concubine reveals the contradictory features of her portrayal. She is at once powerful and yet vulnerable in relation to her husband and this contradiction signifies familial instability.

The rumpus caused by Xifeng on her birthday when she discovers Jia Lian in bed with Bao Er's wife is one of the most memorable moments in the novel, and reveals in a similar fashion the precarious position in which Wang Xifeng is placed. Xifeng's loss of temper over her discovery evokes a reprimand from Grandmother Jia—Xifeng should not be jealous about such a common and expected occurrence. "Young men of his age are like hungry pussy-cats, my dear. There's simply no way of holding them. This sort of thing has always happened in big families like ours (*SS* 2.44.373)." Thus, it is Xifeng who was acting improperly by causing such a scene when her husband was conducting an affair that he had every right to have. Xifeng herself understood this fact and so exaggerated the description of her argument with Lian by suggesting to Grandmother Jia that Lian had used gross physical violence on her. The violence evoked a reprimand from the Matriarch but not the adultery.

---

and *mu* combine they form the word for divorce, *xiu*. See Yu Pingbo, *Honglou meng bian*, pp. 235-36. Recent discussions of this reading are found in Wu Shaoping, "'Yi cong er ling san ren mu' xi" (Analysis of "Two makes my riddle with a man and a tree"), *Honglou meng xuekan*, No. 1 (1990), pp. 279-89; Wan Zhaofeng, "'Yi cong er ling san ren mu' xin jie" (A new explanation of "Two makes my riddle with a man and a tree"), *Honglou meng xuekan*, No. 2 (1980), pp. 191-92, 234.

[31] Wang Chaowen, *Lun Fengjie*, p. 215.

The contradictory nature of Xifeng's position, at once more talented than men and yet subordinate to men, is also reflected in the issue of her education. Her skill and flare at organizing are broadly recognized and yet we are told several times in the novel that Xifeng is illiterate. This is a weighty indictment of her right to wield power in the eighteenth-century Confucian conception of the world. Jennifer Holmgren has noted that "education and morality were inseparable concepts in traditional or orthodox Confucian thinking...moral virtue and education are rarely mentioned separately."[32] Indeed, homophones for Xifeng's name imply a censure of her illiteracy. Wang Xifeng is homophonous for 'Go to School' with the pun on *xi* and yet her "somewhat boyish sounding name" was "acquired in the schoolroom (*SS* 1.3.91-92)."

Xifeng's illiteracy, despite her schoolroom experience, is juxtaposed with the literary and philosophical talent of the young widow, Li Wan, who is described as having been given a restricted, inferior education founded on the "good old maxim 'a stupid woman is a virtuous one' (*SS* 1.4.108)."[33] Indeed Li Wan was named "Fine Silk" to exemplify her father's hope for her to be skilled in the womanly arts of spinning and weaving. The description of Li Wan's inferior education contrasts with her actions throughout the novel in the same way that Xifeng's schoolroom experience belies her illiteracy. It is Li Wan who judges the poetry competitions held in the garden and Li Wan who is primarily responsible for the education of her son Jia Lan, who later goes on to pass the Imperial examinations. Li Wan's position is directly parallel to Xifeng's and the former's outstanding modesty and virtue are written in direct, if ironic, contrast to the sonless, immoderate, uneducated Xifeng.

Wang Xifeng's inability to read and write makes her unusual amongst the cultivated mistresses of the Jia mansions and even more broadly amongst other women of her social class, drawing her closer to the stupidity and barbarism of many of the Jia men. Dorothy Ko argues that the separation of talent and morality implied by the "good old maxim" is merely "one vision or ideal of women's education, not the reality that many daughters of the gentry class experienced in the seventeenth and eighteenth centuries." Instead "talent and virtue were compatible and in fact mutually reinforcing" and "women themselves played crucial roles in this education."[34] That Xifeng's talent develops without the benefits of the education that would propagate virtue and moderation, symbolically places her in a precarious position in

---

[32] Jennifer Holmgren, "Myth, Fantasy or Scholarship: Images of Women in Traditional China," *The Australian Journal of Chinese Affairs*, No. 6 (1981), p. 154.

[33] Susan Mann notes that this "good old maxim" "seems genuinely to have been out of fashion by the eighteenth century" and uses *Honglou meng*'s ironic invocation of it to support her claim. Susan Mann, "*Fuxue* (Women's Learning) by Zhang Xuechang (1738-1801): China's First History of Women's Culture," *Late Imperial China*, 13, No. 1 (1992), p. 54.

[34] Dorothy Ko, "Pursuing Talent and Virtue," p. 9.

terms of the legitimacy and propriety of her managing techniques and also in terms of her 'immoderate' relationship with her husband and other men.

Indeed, Wang Xifeng's competence as a manager of the huge Rong household is hindered by her illiteracy and this point springs up several times in the novel. She relies heavily on an astute memory and also on literate servants to perform her multifarious daily tasks. She is made to comment that Tanchun's ability to read and write would make her better equipped to run the household than Xifeng herself (*SS* 2.30.99, 3.55.64). Baochai mentions early on in the novel that other people are lucky that Xifeng cannot read for her sharp wit is hindered only by her lack of literary puns. "'If one wants to hear the demotic at its most forceful,' said Baochai, 'one has to listen to Cousin Feng. Fortunately for us she can't read, so her jokes are somewhat lacking in finesse and the language she uses can never rise above the level at which it is commonly spoken' (*SS* 2.42.334-35)." This comment is at once satirical of Baochai's obsession with female virtue and an indictment of Xifeng's unrestrained and untutored talent.

The notion that Wang Xifeng's superiority to men, despite her illiteracy, reads as signifying social decline can be supported by a discussion of her irregular position in the allocation of responsibility in the family hierarchy. She is granted power over men because of their incompetence, but she is also granted power over an older woman, Lady Xing, because of the latter's ineptitude. Thus, Xifeng's superiority and her subsequent hold on power represents disharmony among the women of the family as well as disorder in the male-female hierarchy. In terms of yin/yang cosmology, where Lady Xing is yang and Xifeng is yin, the latter's dominance can also be read as indicative of disruption and instability.

Xifeng's position as household manager emerges as the result of a complex negotiation of family responsibility with the central problematic being the moral failure of Xifeng's father-in-law, the eldest son, Jia She. Jia She was known to be morally decrepit and incompetent and his wife, Lady Xing, was also regarded by all as being rather stupid and lacking in 'breeding.' Consequently, responsibility for the household was switched to the head of the junior branch of the Rong mansions, Jia Zheng, and his wife Lady Wang, an aunt of Xifeng's. Xifeng's competence and her Wang family connections ensure that she is 'transferred' to the more junior (but more powerful) side of the household. Instead of acting with suitable filiality towards her parents-in-law, Xifeng spends most of her time and energies ensuring that Lady Wang and Grandmother Jia are pleased by her behaviour. See Xifeng's comment to Jia Lian when he asks her to help him persuade Faithful to secretly lend him some of Grandmother Jia's money. "Then suppose Grandmother finds out? Her confidence in me, that has taken me all these years to build up, will be completely shattered (*SS* 3.72.424)." This reveals the conscious efforts she has made to ensure her place in Grandmother Jia's affections. Lady Xing is acutely aware of this breech in decorum and reveals her hatred and jealousy of Xifeng several times in the novel.

The public humiliation of Xifeng by Lady Xing over the treatment of the domestic servants in chapter seventy-one was an outcome of Lady Xing's increasing hatred of Xifeng and had little to do with her supposed concern for the aging servants. Lady Xing's success in degrading Xifeng in front of all the senior women of the mansions is clear as Xifeng rushed back to her apartment to weep alone (SS 3.71.408-409). Again, in chapter seventy-three when Lady Xing is called to see her daughter Yingchun regarding misbehaviour by her servants, she is told of Wang Xifeng's arrival. Her response is as follows: "'Huh!' said Lady Xing scornfully; and then again 'Huh!' 'Tell her to go back home and take care of her illness,' she said to the waiting servant. 'Tell her I have no need of her services' (SS 3.73.445)." Xifeng's attitude to Lady Xing is also portrayed as being far from filial as we see when she gives Lady Xing a lecture on how Jia She should be conducting his life. Jia She had instructed his wife to arrange for Faithful, Grandmother Jia's principle maid, to become his concubine and Lady Xing seeks Xifeng's advice on how best to approach the matter. Xifeng rather abruptly declares "Father is inclined to be a bit ga-ga at times nowadays. It's up to you to talk him out of it, Mother. This sort of thing is all very well in a younger man, but in someone of Father's years, with children and grandchildren of his own, it really is too shaming! (SS 2.46.407)." The competition between the two women, despite the objective superiority of the mother-in-law, becomes a major feature of the politics of the inner chambers as indicated by the narrator's comment that, "Ever since the Faithful fiasco Grandmother Jia's attitude towards Lady Xing seemed to have hardened, whilst Xifeng's stature seemed to have grown at her mother-in-law's expense (SS 3.71.406)." As will become apparent below, her ambiguous position as a daughter-in-law, at once powerful and vulnerable, is pivotal in constructing her as symbolic of social chaos.

Daughters-in-law as motifs of decay

The 'problematic of daughters-in-law' is an integral part of *Honglou meng*'s sexual ideology. On comparing Xifeng's symbolic role with that of Qin Keqing, the senior daughter-in-law of the Ning branch of the Jia clan, this problematic defines daughters-in-law as motifs of decay and decline. Xifeng, it will emerge, is a motif of the Jias' immoderate financial practices while Keqing is a motif of the Jias' immoderate sexual practice.

Their twin role as motifs of decline, and active participants in this decline, is emphasized by descriptions of events on the night of Keqing's death. Xifeng is just about to fall asleep when the ghost of Keqing walks into her room to warn her of the clan's impending catastrophe and decline in fortunes. Keqing makes two concrete suggestions on how Xifeng can protect the Jia clan's long-term reputation despite the inevitable disaster they will experience. She suggests that money be invested to ensure the continued existence of the clan school and the continued regularity of the seasonal offerings to the ancestors (*SS* 1.13.256-57). It is uncertain whether or not Xifeng acts on this advice as she had promised, but that readers are alerted to the imminence of the Jias' decline through the discussions of these two daughters-in-law is important.

The poems of portent read by Baoyu in chapter five are similarly revealing of the duality of the figurative role of these daughters-in-law. It is possible to read Keqing as representing the decline of the clan's sexual morals and Xifeng as the decline of their wealth by comparing their songs. Keqing's song includes the following lines.

> Her sportive heart
> And amorous looks
> The ruin of a mighty house portended (*SS* 1.5.144).

Xifeng's song likewise links her personal decline to the broad fate of the Jia family.

> Fall'n the great house once so secure in wealth,
> Each scattered member shifting for himself;
> And half a life-time's anxious schemes
> Proved no more than the stuff of dreams (*SS* 1.5.143).

The motifs linking the two women can be supported with other textual evidence as well, as will become apparent below.

Xifeng's questionable financial management is of major importance to the novel and subsequent critiques. Credited with both theft and illegal usury, Xifeng's "lust for money" is often regarded as rivalling her "lust for power."[35] Throughout the novel we are told of the doubts other characters have about Xifeng's honesty. The jealous concubine Aunt Zhao suggests that Xifeng is actually stealing from the Jia family in chapter twenty-five. In a discussion with the mystic Mother Ma she says, "if that woman doesn't end up by carrying off every stick of property belonging to this family to line her own nest with, my name's not Zhao! (*SS* 1.25.496)." In her conversation with Zhou Rui's wife, Xifeng is discussing the financial problems of the household and says, "Some people are under the illusion that it's all caused by bad management on my part. Some even have the nerve to suggest that I am lining the Wang nest at the Jia family's expense (*SS* 4.83.81)." Her precarious position as a 'newcomer' to the Jia family is made clear when she argues with Lian about money.

> Well, what of it? The "four or five thousand taels" is my own money, isn't it? I haven't cheated you Jias out of it...Why do you always assume that any money I have must be Jia money? I haven't noticed that your family is

---

[35] Wang Yigang, "Fengjie xingxiang de suzao," p. 242.

so staggeringly rich. You're not exactly millionaires, are you? We Wangs could probably keep you going for the rest of your lives just with the sweepings from our floor! (*SS* 3.72.425).

In fact, it appears that her financial indiscretions further her own personal wealth through usury at illegally high interest rates. Patience, Xifeng's trusted senior maid, describes the situation in a private conversation with Aroma when the latter queries the non-payment of the month's allowances. "Mrs Lian has already put the money for this month's allowances out at interest. She's waiting for the interest on some of her other loans to pay your allowances with." Later in the conversation Patience reveals the extent of Xifeng's financial interest saying, "just in the few years since she started doing this, the amount she has got out on loan must have grown to several hundred times the original premium... Why, just her profits alone after she's deducted the allowances from the interest must be in the region of a thousand taels a year (*SS* 2.39.263)."

It is the discovery of her chest of promissory notes and usury receipts during the Imperial raid that draws the family into further major political strife and financial ruin in the closing chapters of the novel. On the discovery the Commissioner of the Embroidered Jackets the Imperial Secret Police, Zhao, reveals the gravity of this find. "'Usurers!' hissed Zhao. 'They deserve to lose everything... allow me to order the immediate confiscation of the entire contents of the mansion' (*SS* 5.105.115)." In contrast to such a major indiscretion, shifting Jia money into Wang coffers would be a minor problem and one of little interest to Imperial investigators.

The raid was prompted by the wanton behaviour of Zhen and She, and not Xifeng's usury, but the gravity of her illegal ventures into the masculine world of finance beyond the household places severe doubt upon her reliability and trustworthiness and has brought disgrace to the family. Jia Zheng reprimanded Jia Lian in the strongest terms for the discovery of usury notes in his apartments despite Lian's denial of knowledge of such activities. "He [Jia Zheng] returned to his apartment, and sat once more silently brooding over Jia Lian and Xifeng's reckless behaviour. Their usury, now that it had come to light, would damage the whole family and he blamed them bitterly for it (*SS* 5.106.131)." Xifeng herself admitted to Patience, "They may not have come here and said so to my face, but I know they blame me for what's happened. It's not true. It was the others outside who started it. But I admit I was foolish to lend money and create trouble for myself (*SS* 5.106.132)."

The text's depiction of Xifeng's financial skills is thereby ambiguous in its reflection of her character. Her talent as a financial manager is at once the reason for her sustained high position in the household but it is also the ultimate cause of her downfall, and thus she loses not only the respect and trust of her elders but also her valued possessions and all her savings. Her usury, while clearly regarded as abhorrent by Jia Zheng and the investigating officials, is extremely successful and also discreet. It is only the indiscretion and excessive wanton behaviour of her father-in-law and uncles that draws her into disgrace as Grandmother Jia says in her attempt to comfort Xifeng "This whole nonsense was started by the men (*SS* 5.107.150)." Xifeng's rise and fall from power symbolizes the Jia clan's rise and fall in a way that no other female character does, with the brief exception of Qin Keqing.

Keqing's connection to sexual immoderation is made evident a number of times in the text despite her early departure, through fatal illness/suicide. Critics have often pointed out that there is an inconsistency between the extant text's description of Keqing's death and Zhiyanzhai's margin comments and the portents of her fate in chapter five.[36] As I mentioned in chapter two, it appears that Cao, on the advice of an elder, amended the text which described Keqing's suicide as a result of the shame she felt at being involved in an incestuous affair with her father-in-law, Jia Zhen. The 'lustful death' (*yin sang*) reading is certainly that taken by almost all critics and as early as the 1830s Wang Xuexiang was writing of Keqing as the leading transgressor in the Ning mansions.[37] Homophones for her name and Jia Zhen's provide fertile grounds for support of this interpretation. Jia Zhen is read as 'false chastity' and both Keqing's names, Qin Keqing and Qinshi (Madame Qin), hint at an excess of '*qing*' or '*qingse*,' love/sex. Xu Decheng and Tian Yuheng argue that her name can be read as meaning "passion can cause decline" while Chen Shujing reads it as "coming to an end."[38]

Keqing's bedroom decor provides additional support for the notion that she is a motif of sexual immoderation. She has displayed in her apartment items belonging to a variety of famous women, many of which have been linked with disrupting social order through transgressive sexual charms. For example she has Wu Zetian's mirror, the quince that was thrown at Yang Guifei, and some silk that had been laundered by Xi Shi (*SS* 1.5.127). Moreover, the text includes this description of her room as prelude to Baoyu's sexual initiation in the Land of Illusion. The previously sexually naive Baoyu takes a nap in Keqing's boudoir and when returning home practises his newly acquired skills on his maid, Aroma.

In Baoyu's dream visit to this fantasy realm of fairies he is married to the Fairy Disenchantment's sister, "Two-in-one" whose pet name is Keqing. The morning after consummating the dream marriage he and Keqing walk out and in their sexual bliss nearly fall into the chasm called "The Ford of

---

[36] See Yu Pingbo, *Honglou meng bian*, pp. 264-72 for the best summary. For more recent analysis see Dai Bufan, "Qin Keqing wan si kao" (Investigating Qin Keqing's late death), *Wenyi yanjiu*, No. 1 (1979), pp. 87-92; and Luo Di, "Guanyu Qin Keqing zhi si" (On Qin Keqing's death), *Honglou meng xuekan*, No. 3 (1980), pp. 251-66.

[37] Wang Xuexiang, "*Honglou meng* zongping," p. 146.

[38] Xu Decheng, Tian Yuheng, "Qin Keqing yu Qin Zhong" (Qin Keqing and Qin Zhong), *Honglou meng xuekan*, No. 1 (1985), pp. 155-56; Chen Shujing, "Jinxiu ronghua qing kejin," p. 224.

Error." As the monsters reach up to drag Baoyu into the chasm he calls out "Keqing! Save me!" Qin Keqing hears him call out and is surprised that he could have found out her childhood name. The novel's attitude to sex is not, however, one of total moral censure and an important part of this dream sequence where Keqing's sexuality is highlighted carries with it the validation of a 'respectable' attitude to sex as opposed to a wanton attitude. Thus Qin Keqing is symbolically 'responsible' for Baoyu's introduction to both the pleasures and dangers of sex, as well as symbolically 'responsible' for the licentious, wanton excess of the elder Jia men.

Significantly Grandmother Jia's opinion of Qin Keqing is at variance with this role. Before Baoyu enters her bedroom for the initiation Grandmother Jia rationalizes the impropriety of the situation saying that Qin Keqing was "a most proper person."[39] She makes a similarly problematic character analysis of Xifeng when she describes her as "a model of wifely behaviour (*SS* 2.44.379)." To the contrary, the two young, sonless daughters-in-law of the Jia mansions are also powerful dual motifs of family decline and as such are extremely problematic characters.

The dualism between Xifeng and Baoyu, one wanting to be male and the other female, can also be read as indicating Xifeng's symbolic role as a motif of decline when one considers the point where the symmetry between the two characters breaks down. Baoyu's feminine activities, such as his predilection for cosmetics and female company and his disdain for the civil service career path, are ultimately less reprehensible than Xifeng's foray into the masculine world. Baoyu ends the novel as a victim who escapes common morality and earthly ties by becoming an immortal. Xifeng on the other hand becomes physically and spiritually destitute and finally is destroyed. The author depicts female transgression of acceptable boundaries as more constricting than male transgression.

The importance of the symmetry between Xifeng and Baoyu is thus heightened when one looks at the points where the symmetry is ruptured. These often emerge through the contradictions and ambiguities in other characters' perceptions of Xifeng. Despite the depiction of a diversity of opinion about Xifeng from characters within the novel, critical appraisal for the last two centuries has been, as we have seen throughout this chapter, rather more consistent in its condemnation of her role. One effective method of elucidating the ideological base for this persistent vision is to invoke the discourse of women's relationship to social power. By so doing it emerges that the text embodies a far more complex vision of Chinese womanhood than can be encapsulated in theories of rigid, hierarchical, dualisms of power which valorize women as the oppressed sex. The success of Xifeng as a character lies precisely in her ability to amplify the social contradictions manifested in her transgression of rigid prescriptions of power, gender and social order.

---

[39] 'Proper' is my translation of *tuodang*. David Hawkes translates this as 'trustworthy.'

CHAPTER SIX

DOMESTICATING THE WOMAN WARRIOR: COMPARISONS WITH
JINGHUA YUAN

Many cultures include in their narrative discourse tales of women who have
gone to war or joined the hunt and indeed Chinese culture has produced a
plethora of tales which relate the deeds of such strong and exceptional
women. The general opinion from Western academics about these women is
that they are rebelling against restraints imposed upon their sex by
patriarchal society and "under the guise of patriotism or wifely devotion
[find] an understandable motive for rejecting hearth and home."[1] That patriarchal discourse should perpetuate through history and literature a subversive
mode of thinking simply because it was duped by the invocations of patriotism and loyalty appears less than convincing. Certainly, if these are the
woman warrior's motives then they have been exceptionally well disguised
by the literary redactions of the deeds of the women warriors in Chinese culture. It is the intention of this chapter to explicate the complexity of the
women warrior in Chinese culture and reveal the multiplicity of discursive
functions she fulfils by using the specific case *Honglou meng* and *Jinghua
yuan*, another text from the mid Qing. The contradictions embodied in the
recurring form of the woman warrior and her Amazonian sisters hold a key to
understanding the complex and ambiguous signifying systems of sexual ideology in mid Qing Chinese culture.

The sustained prevalence of the image of the woman warrior in Chinese
culture suggests that she deserves a more specific analysis than has been
provided in the past. She appears across the broad spectrum of narrative discourse including historical and moral texts as well as popular drama, song
and elite fiction. Hua Mulan, the Yang family women generals, Qin
Liangyu, Liang Hongyu, and Thirteenth Sister are amongst the most well-
known women to have donned military garb and gone to war.[2] More recent

---

[1] Julie Wheelwright, *Amazons and Military Maids: Women Who Dressed as Men in the
Pursuit of Life, Liberty and Happiness* (London: Pandora, 1989), p. 13.

[2] Qin Liangyu (1574-1648) was appointed as general in the Ming forces after the death of
her husband, General Ma Qiancheng and is described as being "talented in both the martial
and cultural arts (*wen wu shuangquan*)." Yuan Shaoying and Yang Guizhen, ed. *Zhongguo
funü mingren cidian* (A dictionary of famous women of China) (Changchun: Beifang funü
ertong chubanshe, 1989), p. 456. Liang Hongyu (circ. 1130), formally a courtesan, became
the wife of the Song general Han Shizhong. At the end of the Northern Song when her husband was locked in a seemingly hopeless battle with the invading Jurched, Liang's courage

historical examples of this tradition are the women of the Red Lantern Brigade and the female battalions of the Taiping forces who are recognized as successful intelligence gathering and fighting forces.[3] Mu Guiying, one of the Yang generals, and Hua Mulan are pre-eminent in narrative discourse among these women warriors.

The various redactions of Hua Mulan's life most readily exemplifies the sustained popularity of the women warrior and its laudation of the Confucian virtue of filial piety.   Mulan, it is said, was born to the Wei family in Anhui.   A late version of her tale describes how during the tumultuous years that led to the fall of the Sui, Mulan's aged, ailing father was called to the army to defend the nation against northern invaders. Mulan, appreciating that her father was too weak to fulfil his duty, dons male attire and takes his place.   She battles as a man, with none suspecting her sex, for twelve years before finally returning home and resuming her female life.   A later version describes how, on hearing of her remarkable deeds, the Emperor requested that she join his palace, but Mulan refused and committed suicide rather than obey his command.[4] From this simple tale of filial devotion and courage many different versions have developed.   An early folk poem, written 1,500 years ago, titled *Mulan shi* narrates her feats in verse and ends with the question "When a pair of rabbits frolic together how can one know if they are male or female?"[5] From here the various renditions of her tale expand in number including the Ming drama *Ci Mulan* (Mulan, a woman), continuing through to Ouyang Yuqian's play, and later movie titled *Mulan cong jun*

---

and battle plans were instrumental in vanquishing their foes. Yuan and Yang, *Zhongguo funü*, p. 530. Her deeds, typified by her fierce beating of the drums which signalled the start of the retaliation, form part of the eighty chapter Qing novel *Shuo Yue quan zhuan* by Qian Cai. This book was reprinted by Shanghai's Guji chubanshe in 1980.   Thirteenth Sister is the heroine of Wen Kang's mid Qing *Ernü yingxiong zhuan* and is renown for her martial arts skills and her defence of justice. She rescues a hapless scholar from bandits and redistributes ill-gotten gains with the aim of righting social wrongs. Hu Shi has written a preface to the novel in which he gives details of the authorship, discusses the extent to which the novel is autobiographical as well as providing a general critique. "Hu Shi zhi kaozheng," in Wen Keng, *Ernü yingxiong zhuan* (Taipei: Xinwenfeng chuban gongsi, 1979), pp. 1-26.
    [3] The Taiping forces had battalions of women amongst their ranks whose peasant origins, unbound feet and trousered legs gave them the reputation of being barbarians. The Red Lantern Brigades emerged during the Boxer Rebellion. Young women, typically between the ages of twelve and eighteen, organized themselves into units which engaged in intelligence and support activities for the local men involved in the rebellion. They adopted a uniform of red shoes, hats, trousers and coats and carried a red lantern. Both the Taiping Women's battalions and the Red Lantern Brigades are discussed in more detail in Ono Kazuko, *Chinese Women in a Century of Revolution, 1850-1950*, edited by Joshua A. Fogel (Stanford: Stanford University Press, 1989), pp. 1-21 and pp. 49-53. Later still, during the Sino-Japanese War Chang-tai Hung has described the development of the women warrior in 'spoken drama' as a method to galvanize people to fight against the invading Japanese. Chang-tai Hung, "Female Symbols of Resistance in Chinese Wartime Spoken Drama," *Modern China*, 15, No. 2 (April, 1989), p. 151.
    [4] Yuan and Yang, *Zhongguo funü*, p. 21.
    [5] This anonymous poem is reprinted in *Yuefu shiji* (Beijing: Zhonghua shuju, 1979), *juan* 25.

(Mulan joins the army) released in 1939.[6] During the struggle against the Qing that culminated in the establishment of the Republic, middle-class women were urged to participate in a women's army established in Wuchang by Wu Shuqing with propaganda that gained inspiration from many literary and historical women warriors. For example, in her praise of the women's army a contemporary of Wu's, Liu Wangli, likened Wu Shuqing to Hua Mulan.[7]

A similar history can be traced for Mu Guiying whose tale exemplifies the virtues of patriotism and loyalty to one's husband. The novel *Yang jia jiang* (Yang family generals), also known as the *Bei Song zhi zhuan*, describes her as being born and raised in Shandong where she gained fame for her wisdom and bravery as well as her skills with the bow and horse.[8] She married Yang Zongbao, grandson of the famous Song general Yang Ye, and returned to the palace with him. The tale describes how during the war between the Khitan Liao and the Northern Song, Mu Guiying and her husband together lead the destruction of the Tianmen battle array. Later after the Yang menfolk, including her husband, are killed, the 100 year old Yang Matriarch, She Taijun, calls on the Yang family's twelve widows to defend the nation. Here Mu Guiying achieves her greatest feat by penetrating enemy territory and successfully driving the Xixia back. This basic historical tale is revised and invigorated in the anonymous Ming novel titled *Yang jia jiang yanyi* (Romance of the Yang Family Generals) and in numerous dramas such as the *Yang men nü jiang* (Women generals of the Yang family).[9]

The Qing dynasty novels *Honglou meng* and *Jinghua yuan* both have Amazons and military women appearing in their texts—*Honglou meng* includes a series of poems written to honour the warrior Fourth Sister Lin and *Jinghua yuan* abounds with women of considerable physical and military skill. While this chapter will focus upon examples drawn from these two fictional Qing texts many of the points discussed could equally apply to the other women warriors mentioned above. The *Jinghua yuan* and *Honglou*

---

[6] Chang-tai Hung notes the resounding success of the movie saying that its songs became popular favourites and its leading actress, Chen Yunsheng, achieved instant stardom. Chang-tai Hung, "Female Symbols of Resistance," p. 164.

[7] Liu Wangli, "Xinhai geming qian de funü yundong" (The women's movement before the 1911 revolution), rpt. in Li Youning and Zhang Yufa, *Jindai Zhongguo nüquan yundong shiliao 1842-1911* (Documents on the modern Chinese women's movement 1842-1911) (Taipei: Zhuanji wenxueshe, 1975), p. 762.

[8] For discussions of the historical origins of the tale see Zhang Tianlin, "Guanyu Yang jia jiang de chuanshuo he lishi" (On the history and legends of the Yang family generals), *Tianjin ribao*, 24.10.1962; Liu Guangsheng, "*Yang jia jiang* de gushi shifou fuhe lishi zhenshi?" (Does the tale of *The Yang family generals* represent the actual history or not?), *Lishi jiaoxue*, 4 (1978); Gu Quanfang, "*Yang jia jiang* zayi" (Miscellany on the *Yang family generals*), *Wenhui bao*, 1.9.1980.

[9] The 1606 Wanli edition of the eight *juan*, fifty-eight chapter *Yang jia jiang yanyi* (also known by its full title *Xinbian quan xiang Yang fu shidai zhongyong tongsu yanyi*) was edited and reprinted by the Zhejiang renmin chubanshe in 1980.

meng are not primarily tales of fighting women, as are *Mulan shi*, *Yang jia jiang* and *Ernü yingxiong zhuan*, but it is the many other similarities between the former two novels, primarily the prominent debate about their sexual ideology, that makes them particularly relevant to my discussion about the complex functions the woman warrior performs within the patriarchal sexual ideology of mid Qing China.

In terms of authorship, period, style and motivation the two novels have much in common and this connection was noted early on by the Qing critic Wang Zhichun. His brief comparison between the two novels also reveals the traditional disdain for *Jinghua yuan*. "The *Jinghua yuan* tries to set itself up as another *Shitou ji* but despite its multifarious contrivances simply emerges as a tiresome tract."[10] C.T. Hsia describes the two authors as belonging to the genre of fiction generated by the scholar-novelist "who wrote in retirement to amuse themselves and their friends as distinct from the professional novelists connected with the book trade." Both Li Ruzhen and Cao Xueqin were from a line of fiction writers who wrote not for financial gain but rather for entertainment and as such included matters of literary, artistic and intellectual merit that may not have been of interest to a mass audience.[11]

Moreover, published in 1828, about fifty years after *Honglou meng*, *Jinghua yuan* reveals a considerable debt to Cao Xueqin. Li Ruizhen appears to have modelled his novel on *Honglou meng* to a certain extent. Frederick Brandauer has noted, "there is a striking similarity in the content of the prologues of the two works. Both refer to women with superior qualities and achievements, and both express concern lest such women sink into oblivion and be forgotten...Li's prologue actually contains whole phrases lifted out of the *Hung-lou meng* prologue."[12] For example "the phrase '*li li you ren*' (clearly there are people) used in reference to talented girls," and the phrase '*yi bing shi zhi min mie*' used in reference to forgetting such talented girls.[13]

Zhang Xun's article of 1988, "*Jinghua yuan* and *Honglou meng*" has also indicated in detail several points of concurrence between the two novels including both construction and ideology. Li's introductory chapters, like Cao Xueqin's, centre upon a mystical world wherein the causative action, that provides the novel with its impetus and implicit ending, is generated. In *Honglou meng*, as in *Jinghua yuan*, immortal beings are sent to earth to experience the suffering of life before being returned to their former mystical positions. Both novels, moreover, are described by Zhang as being similar

---

[10] Wang Zhichun, "Shusheng suibi" (Casual notes of Shusheng), rpt. in *Honglou meng juan*, p. 386.

[11] C.T. Hsia, "The Scholar-Novelist and Chinese Culture: A Study of *Ching Hua Yuan*," *Tamkang Review*, 5, No. 2 (October, 1974), p. 2.

[12] Frederick Brandauer, "Women in the *Ching-hua yüan*: Emancipation toward a Confucian Ideal," *Journal of Asian Studies*, 36, No. 4 (August, 1977), p. 649.

[13] Brandauer, "Women in the *Ching-hua yüan*," p. 649.

in their protestation at the unequal treatment of women. However, Li's ideological position is perceived as surpassing Cao's because Li was able to pro-
pose concrete plans that would improve the position of women whereas Cao
was only able to sympathize while he created tragic fates for his women.[14]
Zhang cites Li's plans for a system of examinations open to women which
would subsequently permit their entrance into administrative and political affairs as evidence of these tangible strategies for sexual equality. On the other
hand, Cao Xueqin was regarded as only being able to write of the frustration
young and capable women like Jia Tanchun felt in their domestic roles as
wives and daughters.[15]

Clearly, Zhang is not alone in describing the novels as treatises in the defence of women's rights or eulogies on the suffering of women in the traditional Chinese social structure. Both novels are perceived to advocate education for women, and reveal opposition to the traditional polygamous marriage system. *Jinghua yuan* also argues against footbinding, and makes important claims for women's welfare. Hu Shi proclaimed that the issue of
central concern to the novel was the treatment of women.[16] Lin Tai-yi says
that Li Ruzhen was a "champion of equal rights for women." Wolfram
Eberhard agrees with Hu Shi that "the greatest importance of this novel lies
in the attack of the author on the treatment of women in his society."[17] As
we have seen in previous chapters many scholars have argued that *Honglou
meng* is sympathetic to women's plight.

Debate about the extent to which these pieces live up to their
'progressive' label has necessarily followed these claims. Brandauer argues
that the ideal of womanhood projected is an enlightened Confucian vision
while Nancy Evans argues that Li's novel continues the sexual inequality of
women in respect to his advocacy of chaste widowhood and parentally arranged marriages.[18] Hsin-sheng C. Kao says that "the world of *Ching-hua
yuan* does not go far beyond the conventional dogma of male superiority."[19]
Wang Pi-twan Huang has summarized the problem as "Basically his [Li
Ruzhen's] sympathy for women stems from a deep belief in the Confucian

---

[14] Zhang Xun, "*Jinghua yuan* he *Honglou meng*" (*Jinghua yuan* and *Honglou meng*),
Huaiyin shizhuan xuebao: zhe she ban, No. 4 (1988), pp. 62-66. Rpt. in *RD*, No. 2 (1989), pp.
47-51.

[15] Zhang Xun, "*Jinghua yuan* he *Honglou meng*," p. 49. Jia Tanchun says in chapter
fifty-six that if she had been born a boy then she would have left home long ago and taken on
a career.

[16] Hu Shi, "*Jinghua yuan* de yin lun" (Introductory discussion of *Jinghua yuan*), in Hu Shi,
Hu Shi wencun di er ji (Taipei: Yuandong tushu gongsi, 1953), pp. 412-33.

[17] Wolfram Eberhard, "Ideas about Social Reforms in the Novel *Ching-hua yuan*," in
Eike Haberland, Meinhard Schuster and Helmut Straube, eds. *Festschrift für Ad.E. Jensen*
(Munisch: Runner, 1964), p. 113; Lin Taiyi, in Li Ju-chen, *Flowers in the Mirror* (Berkeley:
University of California, 1965), p. 7.

[18] Nancy Evans, "Social Criticism in the Ch'ing: The Novel *Ching-hua yuan*," *Papers on
China, Volume 23* (Cambridge, Mass.: East Asia Research Center, 1970), p. 62

[19] Hsin-sheng C. Kao, *Li Ju-chen* (Boston: Twayne, 1981), p. 94.

golden rule, 'What you do not want done to yourself, do not do to others.'"[20] As for the doubt about *Honglou meng*'s 'progressive' sentiment I have argued in the previous chapters that the novel's emphasis on female purity and its eulogy to female suffering suggest a more ambiguous attitude to the position of women than those suggested by earlier critics.

In this chapter I will show that the women warrior succinctly embodies the contradictions perceived in the authors' thinking regarding the position of women noted by the aforementioned scholars. She is threatening to patriarchal power, with its implicit preference for meek and mild women, and yet primarily instrumental in ensuring its continued existence because the deeds she performs are undeniably consolidating of the existing Confucian social and moral order. The disruptive potential encapsulated within her form makes her an enthralling fictional and dramatic figure and this, combined with her consolidating function, ensures her repeated appearance in fiction and drama at both elite and popular levels.

Fourth Sister Lin and the "Jinghua yuan" warriors

The Fourth Sister Lin poems appear in chapter seventy-eight of *Honglou meng*. Jia Zheng is inspired by the story of Fourth Sister Lin and asks his grandson, Jia Lan and his two sons Jia Baoyu and Jia Huan to each compose a poem based upon the events of Fourth Sister Lin's life and death. The poems each have the title *Guihua ci* (Winsome Colonel) with Lan's being in the form of a quatrain, Huan's in regulated verse and Baoyu's a considerably more lengthy ballad. During the Ming dynasty, Jia Zheng narrates, there was a Prince Heng of Qingzhou who, it is told, trained a troop of women in martial arts for his entertainment; simultaneously satisfying his enjoyment of women as well as his love of martial arts.[21] "In the second year of his

---

[20] Wang Pi-twan Huang, "Utopian Imagination in Traditional Chinese Fiction," Unpublished Ph.D. Dissertation. University of Wisconsin-Madison 1980, p. 140. Many of Li Ruzhen's most humorous satires on the treatment of women in his time are found in his chapter on the Women's Kingdom where a male protagonist is captured and subjected to the many painful beautification processes, such as foot-binding and hair plucking that women in the Qing were subjected to. Wang notes Li's debt to books such as the *Shanhai jing* which contains a women's kingdom that has no male citizens. Wang, "Utopian Imagination in Traditional Chinese Fiction," pp. 120-21. The poem titled the "Land of Women" appears in the "Haiwai xijing" section of the *Shanhai jing* and proceeds as follows: "Chien Ti swallowed, and/ Chiang Yüan walked;/ In the Land of Women/ They bathe in the Huang River,/ Then are pregnant and give birth;/ If a boy, he dies." The first two lines refer to the legends of conception wherein two concubines of the Emperor Ku, the aforementioned Jian Di and Jiang Yuan conceive by asexual means: Jian Di while bathing in the Xuan Qiu river, swallows a colourful egg dropped by a crow and Jiang Yuan after treading in the footprint of a giant. *Shan Hai Ching: Legendary Geography and Wonders of Ancient China*, Commentary by Kuo P'u—Chin dynasty, Explanatory notes by Hao Yi-hsing—Ch'ing dynasty. Translated by Hsiao-Chieh Cheng, Hui-Chen Pai Cheng and Kenneth Lawrence Thern (Taipei: National Institute for Compilation and Translation, 1985), p. 345.

[21] The first Prince Heng is recorded as being responsible for the security of Qingzhou starting in the twelfth year of Hongzhi (1499). He died in the seventeenth year of Jiajing

governorship a horde of bandits, latter-day descendants of the Yellow Turbans and Red Eyebrows of the Han period, swept over the whole of Shantung Province, looting and pillaging as they went. The Prince, scorning to mobilize fully against an enemy whom he regarded as a mere rabblement of sheep and curs, took the field against them himself at the head of only a light force of cavalry (*SS* 3.78.566)." The Prince was defeated and in the process lost his life. This caused panic amongst the civil and military authorities of Qingzhou and they decided to prepare to surrender to the rebels. Upon hearing this news Fourth Sister Lin called her troop of women warriors to fight and avenge the Prince's death. Her foray was successful in that it decapitated a number of the enemy's leaders but it cost the lives of her entire troop. The rebel forces were later defeated by a larger Imperial army which was mobilized after being inspired by the heroic deeds of the women warriors. To Jia Zheng this story exemplified "the romantic, the edifying, the heroic and the pathetic (*SS* 3.78.565)."

There are other texts that have related the tale of Fourth Sister Lin and Cao's particular version of her life and death emerges as being quite unique to *Honglou meng*. For example Wang Shizhen's (1634-1711) *Chi bei ou tan*, Pu Songling's *Liaozhai zhiyi* (1640-1715) and Chen Weisong's (1626-1682) *Furen ji* each mention Prince Heng of Qingzhou and his concubine Fourth Sister Lin. In details however, they are quite different from the Fourth Sister Lin of Cao Xueqin's version. Wang's tale narrates the relationship between a man called Chen Baoyao and the ghost of Fourth Sister Lin who had died at a young age and was buried in the palace. After the palace is destroyed by the invaders she wanders around as a displaced ghost. Pu Songling's tale also discusses Chen's love for the ghost of the dead concubine although his tale enters into more romantic and seductive detail. Both these tales include the beauty and sadness of her singing when she remembers the destruction of the palace. Chen Weisong's Fourth Sister Lin enters the narrative after a ghostly re-enactment of the downfall of the palace has been performed before the bewildered Chen. She too wines and feasts with Chen Baoyao.[22] Both Chen's and Wang's tales describe a woman dressed in swordswoman's clothing while Pu Songling's romance describes her as being dressed in palace gowns. Cao Xueqin has adapted this tradition of romance and lament and created a unique, loyal, self-sacrificing and beautiful warrior in Fourth Sister Lin. Cao chose to write of her deeds while she

---

(1538). Li Xifan and Feng Qiyong, *Honglou meng da cidian* (A comprehensive *Honglou meng* dictionary) (Beijing: Wenhua yishu chubanshe, 1990), p. 800. Lin Siniang's Prince was the sixth Prince Heng.

[22] Pu Songling, "Lin Siniang" in *Liaozhai zhiyi: di yi ce* (Tales of Liaozhai—volume one) (Jinan: Jilu shu she chuban faxing, 1981), pp. 437-42; Wang Shizhen, *Chi bei ou tan—xia ce* (Casual chats north of the pond—volume two) (Taipei: Shangwuyin shuguan, 1976), *juan* 21; Chen Weisong, *Furen ji* (Collections on women) reprinted in *Congshu jicheng xinbian*, No. 101 (Taipei: Xinwen feng chubangongsi, 1986), p. 712.

was alive rather than her emotive displays of loyalty to her prince as a ghost. Moreover, neither does Cao's heroine become romantically attached to the recurring figure of Chen Baoyao. She is loyal through her life and death.[23] While Cao's "Winsome Colonel" is unique in the historiography of Fourth Sister Lin tales her image is strikingly similar to other women warriors, particularly those in the *Jinghua yuan*. These similarities, which will become apparent throughout the course of the chapter, indicate the typicality of Fourth Sister Lin amongst the host of other women warriors.

These similarities do not necessarily ensure identical treatment by post 1949 Chinese critics. Until the last decade, the analyses of *Honglou meng*'s *Guihua ci* written in the People's Republic of China have been negative. In contrast, Hua Mulan has received considerable positive appraisal since 1949 as an example of "the bravery of the labouring women in traditional China" embodying their spirit of self-sacrifice and resolution of spirit, or alternatively by challenging patriarchal society by asserting that men and women are the same.[24] The Fourth Sister Lin poem by Baoyu on the other hand, was regarded as a flaw in both Cao and Baoyu's ideology. By eulogizing the opponent of a peasant rebellion, that is Fourth Sister Lin, Baoyu is regarded as having revealed his feudal ruling class origins. Recent work by Zhu Meishu has attempted to redeem Cao and Baoyu for this lapse in political ideology by arguing that the poem was really about Baoyu's own relationship with Skybright, his personal maid who had died in the previous chapter. Baoyu thought of himself as Prince Heng and took Fourth Sister Lin to be Skybright. Skybright was regarded by post 1949 *Hongxue* scholars as being an anti-feudal character for her rebellious and forthright behaviour. Linking the *Guihua ci* with this rebellious character is an attempt to redeem by association.[25] Similarly, Zhu Danwen attempted to redeem Cao by saying that

---

[23] See my article "Historiography of Lin Siniang: Desirability and Virtue," *New Zealand Journal of East Asian Studies*, 1, No. 2 (December, 1993), pp. 63-75 for a discussion of the various works relating to Fourth Sister Lin.

[24] Bai Yun, "Gudai funü de yingxiong xingxiang" (Images of ancient heroines), *Jiefang junbao*, 7.3.1951. See also Zhang Rufa, "*Mulan shi* de zhuti shi shenme?" (What is the main theme of the *Poem of Mulan*?), *Yuwen xuexi*, No. 11 (1981), pp. 14-15. The latter article argues that *Mulan shi*'s main theme is not the call for sexual equality because, among other things, Mulan assumes a domestic role as soon as her filial duties are accomplished. Zhang argues instead, like Bai Yun above, that the poem tells of the devotion to the nation and the bravery of the labouring women in traditional China and how hard they worked for peace. His argument is framed against a comment in the Zhongguo wenxue yanjiusuo's *Zhongguo wenxue shi*, where the idea that *Mulan shi* was in opposition to the discriminatory treatment women received in traditional China and was supportive of women's equal access to social power was promoted. Zhongguo shehui kexueyuan wenxue yanjiusuo, ed., *Zhongguo wenxueshi* (A history of Chinese fiction) (Beijing: Renmin wenxue chubanshe, 1985), pp. 324-27.

[25] Zhu Meishu, "*Gui hua ci* xin jie" (A new understanding of *The winsome colonel*), *Liaoning daxue xuebao*, No. 3 (1980), pp. 71-75. See also Zhou Jianyin, "Guanyu *Guihua ci*" (On *The winsome colonel*), *Honglou meng xuekan*, No. 1 (1983), pp. 187-90; Mao Yizhao, "*Guihua ci* shi shuo?" (What does *The winsome colonel* say?), *Honglou meng xuekan*, No. 2 (1980), pp. 232-33.

the poem was another example of Baoyu's opposition to the notion of loyalty expressed in the phrase "Scholars die making memorials, warriors die in
battle," whereby expressions of loyalty are praised if they take the servant to
his or her death.[26]

The women warriors and Amazons in the *Jinghua yuan* are more difficult
to focus upon since they occur throughout the novel. Initially they appear
in the course of Tang Ao's adventures overseas but their warriors' roles are
subsequently expanded to include descriptions of their participation in the rebellion against Empress Wu's armies. Amongst the one hundred flower-
fairies, around whose journey to the 'Sea of Transmigration' the plot re-
volves, the Amazons include the following ten characters whose masculine
attire and heroic deeds are described in detail by Li Ruzhen. Three of the
women are involved in rescuing the adventurers Tang Ao, Merchant Lin and
Grandad Duo from a variety of hazards. In chapter ten Luo Hongqu (Red
Lotus) rescues them from an attacking tiger by shooting her poisoned arrow
straight into its eye where the poison would more quickly penetrate the
blood stream ensuring instant death. She disguised herself in tiger skin beneath which she wore a white archer's suit with a white fisherwoman's scarf
around her head. Around her shoulders she carried her bow (*JHY* 10.51).[27]
Ziying (Purple Cherry) rescues Lin and Duo from a pack of wild animals
with her expert shooting in chapter twenty-one. The men are aghast at the
expertise of their rescuer and while praising 'his' skill they walk over to be
confronted by a young lad of about fourteen or fifteen years. It is only in the
course of their discussion that Ziying reveals her female identity and explains
why she is using a male disguise (*JHY* 21.134). In chapter twenty-six
Lirong (Beautiful Hibiscus) single-handedly rescues the junk, in which Lin,
and Tang Ao are travelling, from a hoard of bandits with pellets shot from
her bow and arrow (*JHY* 26.163).

There are two women of considerable fighting skills who are rescued at
the last minute from certain ill-fate. Jinfeng (Flowering Maple), a young
sea slug diver who was captured by a fisherman, is bought out of bondage by
Tang Ao and she repays his kindness with a pearl that she gained by fighting
and killing a giant oyster with her sword in chapter thirteen. Yuchan (Jade
Moonlight) was travelling with her sisters and mother to the capital for the
examinations in chapter fifty-eight and was on the lookout for wild animals
when she was mistaken for an Imperial spy by members of the anti-Zhou re-

---

[26] Zhu Danwei, *Honglou meng yanjiu* (Research into *Honglou meng*) (Taipei: Guiya
wenhua, 1990), pp. 166. This is originally published in the PRC and was reprinted in Taipei.

[27] I have abbreviated the title to *JHY* and accompanied it by the chapter and page number. I have used the following edition of *Jinghua yuan* and all translations are my own. Li
Ruzhen, *Jinghua yuan* (1828; Taipei: Xuehai chubanshe, 1985), p. 51. An abridged translation has been completed by Lin Taiyi (see earlier note). I have included Lin's translations of
the characters' names in parentheses next to the first mention of a character's name for those
readers who are familiar with the novel in this translation only.

bellion.[28] On being attacked it soon became apparent that she was clearly "skilled in the art of battle." However Yuchan could not withstand the onslaught of the battle trained men. Fortunately she was rescued by a brother-in-law who happened to be an ally of the anti-Zhou rebels. In chapter ninety-seven Yuchan rides into the enemy's magic battle array on a surveillance mission after some of the rebel forces were trapped inside. Unfortunately she was overcome by the magic alcoholic fumes and was unable to continue.

Magical swordswomen in the form of Thirteenth Sister from the *Ernü yingxiong zhuan* appear later in the novel to aid in the anti-Zhou rebellion.[29] Zixiao (Purple Silk), typified by her red attire and deep red face, a skilled swordswoman who could cover miles in a few minutes, appears in chapter fifty-four. She is latter responsible for the rescue of the Prince of the anti-Zhou rebellion, Songsu (White Prince). Songsu's fiance, Yan Ziqiong (Purple Jade), is also trained as a swordswoman and she accompanies Zixiao on the rescue mission and facilitated the establishment of a safe house for her fiance (*JHY* 60.394). After the rescue the women's discussions are interrupted by a third magical swordswoman who "flew into the room" armed with a dagger demanding to know who was responsible for kidnapping Songsu. (*JHY* 60.397) The swordswoman is Ziling (Purple Caltrop) and she proceeds to query the rescuers about their mission as follows; "I thought it must have been someone with three heads and six arms [who released the Prince] and yet it wasn't at all. However, I can see that you are both bearing precious swords so I assume you must be skilled swordswomen (*JHY* 60.397)."

Some of these trained warriors and swordswomen participate in the battle of the four passes when their earth bound male companions are at a loss for a battle plan. The magical swordswomen, through their contacts with the immortals often provide the vital antidote to the evil spells cast over the area of the four battle arrays through which the anti-Zhou forces must penetrate. Ziqiong flies to Mount Penglai to seek help and is told by a nun that "These four battle arrays, although they are individually called names like 'water of the earthly branch,' or 'knife of *ba*,' together they have the name 'The self destruction formation.' Although there are presently several men trapped inside they won't come to any harm because as soon as one of them is attacked then the spell would break... If they do come to harm inside the battle array then it is because they themselves were unable to be morally resolute (*JHY* 97.675)." Indeed only those soldiers who lacked self-discipline in relation to

---

[28] The anti-Zhou rebels were the opponents of the Empress Wu whose reign (684-704) was called the Zhou Dynasty.

[29] The novel is ironic on this point. Many of the women who participate in the first examinations open to women, organized by the Empress Wu, are members of the anti-Zhou rebel families and despite having received this benefit from the Empress participate in the battle against her forces at the close of the novel.

wine, wrath, women and wealth are killed. On a subsequent journey Ziqiong is told of the antidote to the spell of the third battle array where the soldiers are falling prey to lustful desires. The potion she is given invokes the spirit of Liu Xiahui, a scholar of the Spring and Autumn Period, who was well-known for his indifference to the pleasures of the flesh (*JHY* 99.685). Even women less-practised in the martial arts such as Shunying (Peaceful Blossom) and Xiuying (Fair Heroine) also assume a military role at the end during the height of the rebellion by successfully killing one of the leaders of the Imperial forces, Wu Number Five in revenge for the deaths of their husbands (*JHY* 98.683).

Filial piety, loyalty and the Amazons

In each case where women assume a fighting function noted in these two novels the causative and rationalizing moral principles are either filial piety (*xiao*) or loyalty (*zhong*). Each of the women assumes the role of an aggressor, not in response to her own particular goals and ambitions in life, except in so far as the goals and ambitions are to become a filial and loyal. This is not such an uncommon rationale within the Qing social order and neither is it particularly associated with women because men also often justify extreme behaviour in terms of filial piety or loyalty. However, as we shall see, men also use the Confucian concept of *yi* or brotherly loyalty as justification whereas women warriors do not.

That loyalty or filial piety are upheld in the depiction of the Amazons in *Guihua ci* and *Jinghua yuan* lies in dramatic contrast to the 'military maids and Amazons' of the Western narrative discourse described by Julie Wheelwright and Dianne Dugaw. Wheelwright argues that in Western narrative from the eighteenth through to the twentieth centuries women dressed as men to embark upon adventures as an escape from domestic boredom or gain employment in spheres normally denied women. "The thread that pulls these stories [of women warriors] together is women's desire for male privilege and a longing for escape from domestic confines and powerlessness." Dugaw on the other hand shows how the women warriors of popular balladry were initially inspired by heterosexual love and at the close of the novel realize this love with marriage.[30] This self-indulgent realization of fantasy lifestyles or attainment of romantic desires is absent in the women warriors of the Chinese tradition. In each of the Chinese cases the aberrant behaviour of the Amazon is rationalized as either having some significant social purpose or alternatively as being the result of the initiative of the controlling patriarch.

In Baoyu's *Guihua ci* for example the first stanza reveals the troop of warriors depend for their inception upon Prince Heng's whims.

---

[30] Julie Wheelwright, *Amazons and Military Maids*, p. 19; Dianne Dugaw, *Warrior Women and Popular Balladry, 1650-1850* (Cambridge: Cambridge University Press, 1989).

> Prince Heng was fond of a pretty face and of martial arts also
> So he trained the ladies of his court to ride and draw the bow.
> In ravishing songs and beguiling dances the Prince took no delight,
> But to watch the pike-drill he was fain of fair maidens in a row (*S S* 3.78.570).[31]

An aristocratic man's desire was sated by the establishment of a troop of women warriors and the women's participation was simply an extension of their duties as concubines and handmaidens to the prince. Their performance of military drills was an extension of their aesthetic and sexual functions within the palace in a fashion more akin to dance than war. In the process of training the women in the art of horse riding and archery Prince Heng was also able to generate a spirit of loyalty and fidelity in his fair maidens that was to be given an opportunity to manifest itself in the middle five stanzas.

> Next year the whole North-east land with rebels was a-run,
> Like ravening beasts, or swarming bees after the queen has flown.
> The Prince led forth the Emperor's men the rebel hordes to quell.
> He fought them once and he fought them twice, but his army was over-thrown.
> A stench of blood upon the wind blighted the standing corn,
> And on empty tents and an empty camp the setting sun went down.
>
> 'Twas the rainy time, and sounding rills down the lone green hillsides sped
> When Prince Heng, his fighting ended, on the battlefield lay dead.
> Now rain has washed the white bones clean, but not the blood-soaked grass,
> And as the moon rises, shivering ghosts stand at each corpse's head.
>
> The officers refused to fight for fear they might be killed,
> And with no defenders, Qingzhou's fate seemed already to be sealed.
> But though the men were all afraid, the girls were loyal and true:
> And among them Prince Heng's favourite with especial zeal was filled.
>
> Now who the Prince's favourite was to you shall be revealed:
> Fourth Sister Lin she was by name, the Winsome Colonel called.
> She rallied her companions fair and issued a command,
> And like a troop of lovely flowers they rode into the field.
>
> Their heavy saddle-cloths are wet with tears of the spring sky's woe,
> And the iron of their armour chills them, as through the cold night they go.
> Though the outcome may be uncertain, they have taken a solemn vow,
> Whate'er befall, before they die, for the Prince to strike a blow (*S S* 3.78.573-74).

Jia Huan's poem similarly draws out the importance of loyalty, fidelity and self sacrifice to the image of Fourth Sister Lin. The last four lines are as follows,

---

[31] A good linguistic explanation of the poems is provided by Xie Yafei et al ed, *Honglou meng zhuping* (Critical comments on *Honglou meng*) (Nanning: Guangxi renmin chubanshe, 1982), pp. 390-95.

"However great the odds," she said, "I can
"My debt repay, if not avenge this ill."
The inscription graved upon her tomb shall be:
"Here buried lies the world's fidelity (*SS* 3.78.568-69)."

In the *Jinghua yuan* the importance of the existence of an initial filial or
loyal motive is used as justification of warlike aggressive behaviour in almost every instance. Unlike Fourth Sister Lin, however, the women warriors of the *Jinghua yuan* usually take up the bow and sword of their own
initiative. Moreover, the significance of the colours purple and red in the
names, clothing and skin of the Amazons created by Li Ruzhen becomes apparent in the light of broader overriding moral principles. That purple (*zi*)
and red (*hong*) appear so often in the descriptions of the women warriors is
not incidental nor singularly for aesthetic purposes. Rather the repeated reference to shades of purple and red is part of a rich fabric of symbolism
within the novel that has resonances with a broader cultural tradition.
Wolfram Eberhard has noted these are the colours that symbolize loyalty and
imperturbable spirit in a character.[32] These are features that both Hongqu,
Ziqiong, Zixiao, Ziling, Qinfeng, and Ziying have in common either in
clothing colour or name.

Hongqu is avenging her mother's death by killing all the tigers on the
mountain and while on one of these missions she rescues the adventurers.
Her mother was crushed to death when their temple refuge collapsed under
the weight of rampaging tigers who were in pursuit of other wild beasts.
"To avenge my mother's death I have sworn to kill all the tigers on this
mountain. I used a poisoned arrow to kill the tiger and have just taken its
heart out to make an offering to my mother's spirit (*JHY* 10.52)." Her own
clothing, a white hunter's suit, also carries symbolic reference to her loyalty
and filial piety because, as her grandfather later tells Tang Ao, she has sworn
to remove her mourning clothes only after she has slaughtered every tiger on
the mountain (*JHY* 10.52-53). So steadfast is her desire to eradicate the
tigers from the mountain, and so certain is her resolve to serve her grandfather that she refuses to leave the mountain and return to China on Merchant
Lin's boat as her grandfather and Tang Ao had arranged. "Firstly, my grandfather is old and there would be nobody to look after him out here in the
wilderness and secondly, there are still two more tigers on this mountain that
I will seek revenge on (*JHY* 10.54)."

In chapter thirteen Jinfeng dives for sea slugs because her ailing mother
depends upon these rare creatures for her nutrition. Being too poor to purchase these expensive items Jinfeng decides to dive for them herself. In order
to reach the depth required to retrieve the sea slugs Jinfeng practises holding
her breath by submerging herself in a large urn for increasingly longer peri-

---

[32] Wolfram Eberhard, *Dictionary of Chinese Symbols* (Singapore: Federal Publications,
1990), p. 243.

ods until she had reached the point where she is able to be submerged for considerable lengths of time. It was while she was on one of these filial missions that she was caught up in a fisherman's net. The fisherman decided that she, like the fish in the net, was part of his catch and thereby his to sell. Jinfeng pleads with the adventurers saying "My own life is as worthless as the weeds on the riverbank [*gao cao*] but there is still my widowed mother who will be left with nobody to serve her (*JHY* 13.75)." Jinfeng then swears that if the adventurers help free her she will become a dog or a horse in a future reincarnation to serve them. She too is wearing "a silvery red [*yin hong*] vest...and slipped in next to her chest was a precious sword (*JHY* 13.74)."

Ziying is introduced in chapter twenty-one as a formidable marksman for she kills a lion that is descending with great speed upon the hapless adventurers. Dressed as a boy she explains that she is a substitute for her ailing brother who, along with her now deceased father, was commissioned by local villagers to kill the wild beasts on the area. Her brother is weak and troubled by recurring illness and "is not able to withstand hardship" and so Ziying taught herself to shoot and carries out the task herself, thereby supporting her widowed mother (*JHY* 21.134).

Purple clothing appears in relation to another of the women warriors of the *Jinghua yuan* despite her name not containing any direct purple/red reference. In chapter twenty-six Lirong rescues the adventurers from bandits by shooting pellets from her bow. Wearing a blue turban on her head and purple trousers Lirong is described as being a beautiful girl (*JHY* 26.163). Her fighting skill and indomitable spirit are such that she is powerful enough to repel two attacks from the bandits and one of these single-handedly.

Once the tale switches from narrating Tang Ao's search for immortality towards the resolution of the fates of the young women the continuity in themes of loyalty and filial piety continue with the use of the colours red and purple. Zixiao disturbs Tang Guichen (Tang Xiaoshan's scholarly name) and Hongju in their readings: "Suddenly a red girl leapt in through the window. She wore a red silk shirt, beneath which was a pair of red silk trousers. Her head bore a red silk fisherwoman's scarf and on her feet were a pair of three inch red slippers. Around her waist she had tied a red silk cummerbund and slipped into her chest was a precious sword in a red scabbard. Her face was also a deep red colour (*JHY* 54.364)." It is after this meeting that Li Ruzhen directly draws our attention to the importance of red and purple through the naive questioning of Xiaochun who asks "Why doesn't this red person have red in her name instead of purple? Whereas Honghong (Red Rose) has a purple face and yet she has red in her name. From my way of looking at it these two girls should swap names (*JHY* 55.367)."

Zixiao enters the narrative to enquire about the magic Gibbon who had just flown from Tang Guichen's room with the book of names foretelling the young women's fortunes.[33] Zixiao then agrees to help them rescue the leader of the rebellion, Songsu who had been captured by the Empress' troops. It is through Zixiao that the girls are introduced to Ziqiong, the fiance of Songsu. She was wearing a purple outfit (complete with purple jacket, trousers, scarf, cummerbund and shoes and scabbard in the pattern of Zixiao above) and had a peach complexion (*JHY* 59.393). Like Zixiao she was an expert swordswoman and she had been instrumental in aiding in the rescue of Prince Songsu and in finding a temporary safe house for him. After the rescue, the swordswoman Ziling enters the scene and in similar fashion is wearing a peach red (*tao hong*) outfit (complete with peach red jacket, trousers, scarf, cummerbund, shoes and scabbard as well) (*JHY* 60.397). Similarly she is also performing an act of loyalty but this time to her cousin who had captured the Prince and since lost him to the two swordswomen, Zixiao and Ziqiong. At first she demands that they return her cousin's prisoner but upon discovering that the Prince was from the House of Tang, and thereby had a legitimate claim to the throne, she gives up her mission. Ziling agrees to tell her cousin that she was unable to find the swordswomen and their anti-Zhou party.

In both *Jinghua yuan* and the *Guihua ci* the pivotal position of men or elders within the Amazon's moral code, where loyalty and filial piety are upheld, is exemplified by the absence of the equally Confucian concept of *yi*. The latter, *yi*, focuses upon a non-hierarchical notion of loyalty between comrades whereas the former *xiao* and *zhong*, are implicitly hierarchical in their explication of the desired behaviour of a subordinate to a superior. Stephan Roddy has noted that "unlike their brothers, fathers, and husbands, then, the hundred girls are portrayed as unencumbered by male prescriptions regarding loyalty."[34] None of the women warriors in the *Jinghua yuan* work

---

[33] Herein lies another similarity with *Honglou meng*. With the existence of a book that gives the protagonist Tang Xiaoshan/Jia Baoyu a cryptic preview of the events about to occur in the novel the parameters of plot development are neatly outlined. In *Honglou meng* the Registers are viewed as part of Baoyu's dream and can not thereby be studied carefully by the puzzled Baoyu. Whereas in the case of *Jinghua yuan* Xiaoshan actually copies the text and carries it with her for many months until the Gibbon flies off with it.

[34] Stephan John Roddy, "'Rulin waishi' and the representation of literati in Qing fiction." Unpublished Ph.D. dissertation. Princeton University, 1990, p. 285. Wu Qingyun argues that a sisterhood is developed amongst the women who come together to take the examinations saying "For the first time in Chinese history, women strive for the same goal and share the same fears and joys." However, Wu forgets that the women are competing against each other for recognition and their sisterhood is based upon a mutual competitiveness rather than mutual devotion. Wu Qingyun, "Transformations of female rule: Feminist utopias in Chinese and English literature." Unpublished Ph.D. dissertation. Pennsylvania State University, 1991, p. 170. Moreover, as Stephan Roddy as pointed out *Jinghua yuan*'s "feminization of the literati experience" through the examination success of the hundred girls is "devoid of any serious moral content...and [is] notable precisely for the conspicuous absence of any concern

together for extended periods and in the occasional instance when they co-operate the prime motivation is their separate loyalty to the same male figure, as in the aforementioned case of Zixiao and Ziqiong in their co-operation in the rescue of Songsu. Similarly the troops under Fourth Sister Lin are not described as banding together in a mutual comraderie and devotion to each other, as with the bandits of the *Shuihu zhuan*, but rather they are described as joining together to show their devotion to their patriarch. Thus, the particular Confucian values the women warriors adhere to are those of the subordinate sex as indicated by their hierarchical nature.

While the women warriors described above do transgress the gender boundaries expected during their time they do so to reflect the Confucian moral principles of *xiao* and *zhong* such as rescuing the rightful heir to the throne, avenging the death of a parent, maintaining the health of a parent or satisfying the desires of her patriarch. Judith Zeitlin has juxtaposed this type of 'hero among women' with 'the shrew' in an instructive manner. She argues that both were favoured images in Ming and Qing fiction revealing the depth of the perceived 'essential' divisions between the sexes. The women warrior fits into Zeitlin's category of the 'hero among women' in her adoption of masculine traits and yet "although she transgresses boundaries, she does not pose a threat to the greater social order. Her exploits demand a greater respect for the female sex, but as such she can be contained under the old rubric of 'exemplary women'." However, as we saw above the masculine traits she adopts exclude the non-hierarchical *yi* leaving her always in a subordinate position within the rubric of an exemplary woman. In Zeitlin's categorization the shrew, on the other hand, is quintessentially feminine or 'hyper feminine' in her jealous, stingy, tyrannical behaviour.[35] Despite her perceived dominance over her husband the shrew has none of the manly qualities of loyalty, bravery and filial piety. The shrew too then forms an important part of the Qing sexual ideology in complementary opposition to the female warriors and Amazons. Her tyrannical behaviour, with its implicit potential to destabilize existing social norms is perceived as being 'typical' of a woman. Empress Wu, as described in the *Jinghua yuan*, is indeed this archetypal shrew. She actually achieves dominance over all men. The women warriors, on the other hand, are considered atypical. Their mimicking of manly physical skills makes them highly laudable characters, as does their consolidation of values that perpetuate male interests. The importance of Zeitlin's juxtaposition of the shrew and the 'hero among women' to this current chapter will continue to become evident below when we analyse the manner in which Amazons become moral mirrors for patriarchal discourse.

---

with the larger moral order" of the political world. Roddy, "'Rulin waishi' and the representation of literati in Qing fiction," p. 283.

[35] Judith T. Zeitlin, "Pu Songling's (1640-1715) *Liaozhai zhiyi* and the Chinese Discourse on the Strange." Unpublished Ph.D. dissertation. Harvard University, 1988.

Moral mirrors for society

In the tale of Fourth Sister Lin another important feature of the women warrior emerges. She shames the menfolk by her depth of loyalty and devotion to her patriarch. The women warrior is thereby a moral mirror for the degenerating menfolk. When the women are more moral than the men a strong condemnation of the depths of depravity into which society has sunk is implied. The same condemnation of men emerges within the discussion of excellent women scholars. Pu Songling's 'Historian of the Strange' comments of the character Yanshi, who dresses as a man and takes her husband's place in the examination and in officialdom, that "All those wearing scholar's hats should die of shame [before such a woman]."[36] In *Jinghua yuan* Tang Ao is similarly shamed when he is confronted by two young women scholars, Hongwei (Honghong's scholarly name) and Zixuan (Tingting's scholarly name, translated as Purple Lily), whose knowledge rivals his own (*JHY* 19.122) In the same way 'masculine' acts by military women were used as moral mirrors for a patriarchal society. The final two stanza's of Baoyu's *Guihua ci* reveal this motive well.[37]

> A courier riding through the night to the Emperor's city came,
> And all who heard his heavy news with sadness did exclaim.
> The Son of Heaven looked aghast when he learned of Qingzhou's fall,
> And his captains and his counsellors all hung their heads for shame.
>
> The captains and the counsellors and men of high degree
> Were put to shame by Fourth Sister Lin's fidelity.
> For Fourth Sister Lin my heart with grief doth swell,
> And though my song is ended now, my thoughts on her still dwell (*SS* 3.78.574).

As mentioned above, in Jia Zheng's narration of the tale such a loyal and heroic death by women then shames the menfolk into action and the Imperial troops then go on to defeat the rebels.

The swordswomen of the *Jinghua yuan* serve a similar although not identical purpose. While not depicted as shaming men into action through their deeds, they do represent the attempt to achieve social order and in this respect they serve as models for correct behaviour. Their fundamental loyalty, filiality and incessant search for righteousness are the qualities that are upheld. The largely unproblematized depiction of their 'manly' virtues would make

---

[36] Pu Songling, translated and cited in Zeitlin, "Pu Songling's (1640-1715) *Liaozhai zhiyi* and the Chinese Discourse on the Strange," p. 119.

[37] The use of female virtue as a moral mirror to degenerating menfolk is not unique to this particular section of *Honglou meng*. Rather throughout the novel, female competence in almost every aspect is emphasized as being better than men's. As I argued in the previous chapter this is not only praise to the talents of these women but also a symbol of social decline and disorder.

them one dimensional, uninteresting fictional characters if it were not for the drama that emerges from their rupturing of sexual boundaries. Indeed, all of the women warriors mentioned earlier, Hua Mulan, Mu Guiying, Qin Liangyu perform deeds that many men before them have performed without achieving the same degree of fame and recognition. Their exception from the normal female roles ensures their fame but this fame is always written against the unstated signifier, that is the domestic woman. Both visions of womanhood thereby interact in the search for moral and social rectitude.

The two magical swordswomen, Zixiao and Ziling, both determine the righteousness of the cause before proceeding with any action and the overriding principle of judgement appears to be adherence to an unquestioned Confucian order. These women then attempt to create order out of chaos within the limits of notions of order expected by a Confucian society. Tang Ao's daughter explains to her friends, "The swordswomen of ancient times like Nie Yinniang and Hongxian[38] were capable of performing an extraordinary array of feats in order to save people. They would always make sure that they were acting morally and if asked to serve a disruptive or illegal cause then they would refuse. You would have noticed how she [Zixiao] ensured that Songsu had committed no crimes before agreeing to help him (*JHY* 59.392)." The magical swordswomen then intervene when a wrongdoing has occurred and would never aid a criminal. In the words of Ziling,

---

[38] Hongxian and Nie Yinniang are two swordswomen of the Tang. Hongxian appears in Yuan Jiao's (circ. 853) Tang *chuanqi* "Hongxian zhuan" (The tale of Red Thread). See Xu Shinian. ed., *Tangdai xiaoshuo xuan* (Changchou: Changchou shuhua, 1982), pp. 378-89. A servant to the Luzhou Military Governor Xie Song, Hongxian proved herself to be invaluable in her advice to her master. Through her magical talents she ensures that Tian Chengsi, the rebellious military governor of Weibo, is supportive and loyal to her master by stealing a precious golden casket from his pillow while he slept. The casket was then sent back to Tian by Xie to symbolize the latter's might and generosity. It is explained at the end of the tale that Hongxian was formally a male healer who accidentally killed a woman who was pregnant with twins by providing the incorrect prescription. As punishment for this error he was reborn as the servant girl Hongxian. The tale of her deeds reappears in Liang Chenyu's Ming *zaju* titled *Hongxian nü ye qie huang jin he* (Hongxian steals the golden casket at night). Nie Yinniang is the central character of Pei Xing's (825-880) *chuanqi* of the same name. This tale forms part of Pei's collection of wondrous tales titled *Jian xia zhuan* and can be found in Zhou Lengqie, ed., *Pei Xing chuanqi* (Shanghai: Guji chubanshe, 1980), pp. 22-25. The daughter of the General Nie Feng, Yinniang was kidnapped by a nun at the age of ten and for five years was trained in magical transformations and sword-skills. After returning home she marries and on the death of her father she and her husband join the Weibo Commanding Generals' household. Sent on a mission to kill, Liu Changyi, the Chief general of the neighbouring province, Nie Yinniang instead decides to stay in Liu's service as she discovers him to be a man of greater talent and wisdom than her original master. Here she protects him from two assassination attempts with her magic power. Yinniang's tale is the basis of Yu Tong's (1618-1704) play *Hei bai wei* (The Black and White Donkeys). English translations of both these tales are found in Karl S.Y. Kao, *Classical Chinese Tales of the Supernatural and the Fantastic: Selections from the Third to the Tenth Century* (Bloomington: Indiana University Press, 1985), pp. 357-62 and pp. 363-70. Christopher Levenson's translation of Wolfgang Bauer's and Herbert Franke's *The Golden Casket: Chinese Novellas of Two Millennia* (London: George Allen and Unwin, 1965) includes the story of Hongxian on pp. 136-42.

"Among the well-known swordswomen there was not one who was not ex-tremely just and selfless. If one was biased and partial then she would be sure to encounter retribution. So it is particularly important to support good and honest people and eradicate tyrannical and brutal people (*JHY* 60.397)."

The moral codes that one of the swordswomen, Zixiao, adopts in this story reflect an unproblematized anti-Zhou position. Right and wrong are clearly linked with anti-Zhou and Zhou respectively. In the rescue of Songsu for example, Zixiao ascertains that he committed no crimes and then agrees that she would rescue him. According to the Empress Wu's notions of right and wrong however, Songsu is a treacherous rebel who threatens the stability of the nation. Li Ruzhen has provided a scene where the conflict between contradictory notions of right and wrong are revealed in the case of Ziling who acts on her cousin's behalf in agreeing to search for the escapee Songsu and who then discovers that Songsu has committed no crime. In re-treating from her demand for the return of the prisoner she rationalizes her paradoxical position by saying "If I was serving the Zhou dynasty, then I would of course loyally act on their behalf and help solve their problems without bothering to concern myself with the affairs of others. Fortunately I came on behalf of my cousin and not the government. You rescued him with a righteous motive so how dare I challenge this intent (*JHY* 60.398)." Here Ziling presents the conflict as being that between a servant's loyalty to her superiors and a swordswoman's loyalty to the moral code that defends righteous causes. Her loyalty to her cousin is not a problem and his cause is implicitly deemed as being unrighteous by Ziling's refusal to carry out his wishes. He is working for the Zhou dynasty but by deputizing his cousin to perform his task the authority of the Zhou dynasty, and the loyalty of a ser-vant to his/her superior is lost. The remaining moral code is the swordswoman's honour and, as with the case of Zixian above, this is an un-problematized anti-Zhou position with the goal of restoring the Tang house to the throne.

In both cases the swordswomen are serving to re-establish social order in the face of supposed disorder. The overriding principle being loyalty to an unquestioned Confucian order. Ironically it is the very existence of women in men's clothing or women in men's roles, such as we find in the women warriors, that is simultaneously symbolic of social disorder. Women would not dress as men and perform manly deeds were it not for the fact that there was some major disharmony within the broad social fabric of China. Ann Waltner draws this point out in her discussion of the wife of Wang Xijue. Wang's son, in writing of his deceased mother, lamented the fact that she lived during times of peace and order because this meant that she was not given the opportunity to reveal her true mettle.[39]

That Li Ruzhen set his tale during the reign of Empress Wu is significant in this respect because her reign in itself is considered to be an aberration in the normal pattern of social order. Empress Wu is depicted as being the reincarnated spirit of the Heart Moon Fox (*xinyue hu*) who is sent to earth to "render chaos between the principles of yin and yang and thereby settle the case between the Sui and Tang dynasties (*JHY* 3.12)."[40] The rupture to social order represented by Empress Wu, and her overthrowing of the house of Tang, generates a broader social imbalance that then in turn generates the need for the existence of the women warriors. When the Empress Wu's forces are defeated and a man returns to the throne, correcting the historical and metaphysical imbalance between the principles of yin and yang, the women warriors and the exceptional female scholars are dead, have returned overseas, or ascended to the realm of the immortals. These exceptional women then, perform a complementary, albeit superficially contradictory role. They represent both the struggle for values of social order and yet they are also symbols of social chaos. That they serve to create order from the disorder then places them into the realm of the 'hero among women' or honorary men.

The dramatic and ideological success of the loyal woman warrior depended upon the transitory nature of her Amazonian behaviour because once order is restored the women warrior should no longer exist. The requirement that she be a temporary 'honorary man' could either be achieved by her death or her assumption of wifely duties. One of the dominant features of the woman warrior is her unflinching resolve in the face of certain death. The romanticization of the deaths/suicides of these women provides the matrix that establishes the link between the expectations of an audience who has become attached to the characters as Amazons, and the ideological requirements of a patriarchal discourse that perceives that women can only be men during temporary periods of social disorder. A loyal death is the tidiest way to resolve such a contradiction. This is typified best by Fourth Sister Lin's suicidal foray into the night. Jia Lan's poem includes the line "In Qingzhou where, her Prince to avenge, she threw her life away" and Jia Huan's "She dried her woman's tears and fearless rode/ Through Qingzhou's gates to be killed and kill (*SS* 78.568)" and both these lines aptly summarize the conscious self-sacrifice imbued in her warrior's death.

---

[39] Ann Waltner, "The Grand Secretary's Family: Three Generations of Women in the Family of Wang Hsi-chüeh," *Family Process and Political Process in Modern Chinese History: Part I* (Taipei: Zhongyang yanjiu yuan jindai shi yanjiu suo, 1992), pp. 543-77.

[40] The disruption of her reign to notions of social order is supposed to atone Emperor Yang of the Sui for the overthrow of his dynasty by Tang in the judgement of the heavenly court of justice.

In the *Jinghua yuan* the magical swordswoman Ziqiong dies in the spell of wealth as does the fighter Yuchan. Both show fearless resolve in the face of the spells cast by the Wu Brothers and perform several dangerous tasks before dying. Zixiao becomes a Daoist immortal and lives overseas in the island of Penglai with Tang Guichen. Hongqu marries Tang Guichen's brother, Tang Xiaofeng, and becomes a dutiful filial daughter-in-law to Mistress Lin. Guichen says as they part "For all those years you single-mindedly sought revenge for your mother without concern for your own safety. Moreover, without indulging in melancholy you served your grandfather in the last years of his life. In these respects you are extremely filial. In the future if our mother has need of some special treats you will of course provide these for her. It's not necessary for me to leave specific instructions for you. But, because I am now going far away, I will be unable to fulfil such filial duties so I will gratefully place the responsibility on your shoulders (*JHY* 94.657)."[41] Upon her assumption of these duties she does not participate in the battles in any way. Lirong marries Kabi (Badge) and no longer uses her magical pellets and bow. Jinfeng marries Junyu (Jade) in a match arranged early on by Tang Ao and she lives in the women's camp throughout the battle with Junyu's mother Mistress Liang. Thus the honorary men are neutralized as the novel proceeds towards a state of social order.

The sexualized women warrior

Part of the fictional and dramatic success of the woman warrior lies in her power to titillate the reader is a subtle sexual sense. The language of war has long featured in sexual discourses and the woman warrior, with her temporary rejection of feminine modesty, neatly draws together the martial and sexual themes. In his work *Sexual Life in Ancient China* Van Gulik states "Chinese literature often refers to sexual congress as a 'battle,' and… later sexological and erotic books worked out the details of the coitus as military moves on the battlefield."[42] Significantly, a triangular link between battles, flowers and sexual titillation has evolved within the literary discourse of China. One of the Ming erotic albums was titled *Variegated Battle Arrays of the Flowery Camp* (*Huaying jinzhen*) and in Sima Qian's *Shiji* further evidence of the triangular link is given. In chapter sixty-five it is noted that the great master of military strategy, Sunzi, was ordered to demonstrate his principles of war using the ladies of the court. Sunzi divided the women into two camps and appointed a general within each. When the women giggled

---

[41] The lead character Tang Xiaoshan, although not a woman warrior, is also depicted as being the epitome of virtue in the traditional Chinese sense. Hsin-sheng C. Kao states that "Tang Kuei-chen's progress toward the immortal planet…depends upon the success of her earthly fulfilment of female loyalty, piety, and chastity." Kao, *Li Ju-chen*, p. 95.

[42] R.H. Van Gulik, *Sexual Life in Ancient China*, p. 76.

and refused to obey Sunzi's commands he had the 'generals' summarily decapitated despite the Prince's protests. Thus the Prince came to understand
the importance of discipline in an army. Van Gulik notes that playful sexual expression such as *hua zhen* 'the flowery battle-array' and *wu ying*
'Camp of Wu' are borrowed from this anecdote.[43]

The sexualization of the woman warrior is achieved in part by the
trivialization of her deeds. For example the exertions of training are
trivialized in Baoyu's *Guihua ci*. The second and third stanzas draws out the
juxtaposition between feminine traits and the masculine art of war that they
are being trained in a manner that heightens sexual interest.

> As he watched them drill, he scarcely saw the clouds of dust arise;
> 'Twas the lovely Colonel's lamplit face that swam before his eyes.
> When the rosy lips framed their harsh commands he could smell the
> mouth's sweet breath;
> But the weapons oft shook in the fair white hands, too weak for such exer-
> cize.
>
> The lotus belt round the Colonel's waist in a clove-shaped knot was tied
> Yet it was not strung pearls that hung from it, but the good sword at her
> side.
> When late at night the jousting ended, her courage was quite spent,
> And her handkerchief with carmine sweat from her streaming face was dyed
> (*SS* 3.78.571-72).

The physical attributes of Fourth Sister Lin that are invoked in this poem
promote a sexual and not a warlike vision. Sweet breath, rosy lips, fair
hands, and carmine sweat are juxtaposed with harsh commands, jousting,
dust and weapons in a titillating and patronizing description of the warrior.

The trivialization and sexualization of the 'Winsome Colonel' is moreover an integral part of the poems' title *Guihua ci*. *Guihua* is an ancient
word for leisured beauty and the phrase *guihua jiangjun*, used to refer to
Fourth Sister Lin in both Baoyu's and Jia Lan's verse literally means 'a
Colonel of leisured beauty.'[44] Trivial, temporary and always physically attractive the notion of Fourth Sister Lin as a *guihua jiangjun* has been aptly
captured by David Hawkes' use of the word 'winsome.' Imbued with sexual
rather than warrior-like overtones the Winsome Colonel can not be taken as
a serious threat to social order but rather more as a rather titillating aberration. Jia Lan's opening couplet makes the contradiction between *guihua* and
jiangjun apparent.

> Fourth Sister Lin was the Winsome Colonel's name:
> She was beautiful and gentle, yet her valour none could tame (*SS* 3.78.568).

---

[43] R.H. Van Gulik, *Sexual Life in Ancient China*, p. 157.
[44] Li Xifan and Feng Qiyong, eds, *Honglou meng da cidian*, p. 800.

A literal translation for the second line would be that "her bones and muscles were of jade but her guts were made of steel." Similarly, Jia Huan's opening lines contrast the female's passive beauty with qualities of active aggression.

> The lovely lady would not sit and grieve;
> For sterner thoughts her warlike breast did fill.
> She dried her woman's tears and fearless rode...(*SS* 3.78.568).

A literal translation of the first line amplifies the sexual nature of the juxtaposition between passive femininity and active femininity. "The red powder didn't know grief, with a colonel's thoughts she resolved to go to battle. She covered her tears and left the embroidered curtains." Here references to cosmetics, tears and embroidered curtains is juxtaposed with battle terminology. Ultimately, Fourth Sister Lin is an exemplary beauty who nobly commits suicide after her husband's death.

Such trivialization of female physical action appears only once in the *Jinghua yuan* and not in connection to the swordswomen or female archers who are almost always respected by men for their skill. Often this respect for the physical skill is revealed before the narrator realizes the sex of the archer or warrior. Early in the novel Li Ruzhen plays upon such 'unlikely' events, women being excellent archers or fighters, to realize his ironic and humorous intent. Later in the novel when the reader is already accustomed to the ploy where there is juxtaposition between the readers/characters' expectations of male warriors and the reality of the female warriors, the mystical swordswomen are the predominant female warriors described. That they are intended to be magical takes the description of female warriors into another level of literary fantasy. The notion that the female swordswomen are fantastic and supernatural provides both new fictional excitement to an audience already well prepared for the female warriors. It also permits some of these Amazons to take part in the novel on 'earth,' that is, in China and not in the non-world where the previous women had existed as part of Merchant Lin's travels abroad.

Two women who have not trained in the art of battle assume the role of warriors to avenge their husbands' deaths later in the novel and, in this instance, Li Ruzhen trivializes their efforts. Once the deaths of their husbands are reported back to the women's camp Xiuying and Shunying decide to seek revenge. They secretly ride into the enemy's spell and take on the leader Wu Number Five.

> When he saw Xiuying and Shunying in the distance he couldn't help but laugh to himself 'There I was lonely in my home and now heaven has sent a couple of beauties down to accompany me!'... Just as he was ruminating, Xiuying and Shunying came galloping towards him with their swords in their right hands and their reins in their left. When Wu saw the two coming towards him, looking so awkward and amateurish in their battle mode, they were an unadulterated vision of feminine weakness and softness. They looked ridiculous and yet pitiful and although Wu wanted to take them both

alive he saw that this would not be possible and so he stiffened his resolve and said 'It seems I can only take one beauty so I'll kill the least beautiful one' (*JHY* 98.683).

In the process of slaughtering Shunying, Wu Number Five is fatally stabbed by Xiuying. During her retreat she is shot and killed by arrows from the shocked troops under Wu Number Five's command.

This trivialization is a form of sexualization in the cases of Fourth Sister Lin, Shunying and Xiuying. The women are desired as sexual objects for their 'pitiful' and 'helpless' attempts to ape warlike actions. *Jinghua yuan*, in typically ironic fashion, skews the sexualization so that it leads to Wu's death. Wu loses his guard because he is is fantasizing about the anticipated sexual pleasures and thereby does not take the attack seriously. Such irony is missing in Baoyu's *Guihua ci* where the women warriors' mission is described as pitiful and pathetic and their deaths as tragic and noble. The description of Fourth Sister Lin's death draws this point out.

> But what chance against their savage foe had that gallant band?
> Like gentle flowers they perished, crushed by a brutal hand.
> The horses' hooves are fragrant yet that trod them in the mud;
> Near the city walls their poor ghosts flit, where they made their final stand
> (*SS* 3.78.574).

This romanticization of her death is, moreover, sexualized. We are invited to picture the trampled flowers and smell their fragrance where, as we noted above flowers, battle and sex are closely linked symbols. As trampled flowers the women are metaphorically raped and then murdered. Jia Lan's poem makes a similar, although less direct reference to female fragrance in his closing line. "The very ground on which she fell is fragrant to this day (*SS* 3.78.568)." 'Ground' or *ni tu* could also be translated as 'mud' in which case it would generate a stronger impression of the degradation of her body.

An alternative form of narrative sexualization of the Amazons occurs in Li Ruzhen's tale through the repeated invocation of male sexual interest in female virgins. In the *Jinghua yuan* the warriors' ages are drawn out in almost each description of the Amazons and each of the heroic women is described as being roughly fourteen or fifteen. This particular age is an important point in a young woman's sexual life cycle. She is just on the verge of, or has just reached, physical maturity and, as described in the novel, also marriage. The numerous special phrases that developed to describe this age group reinforce my point. The term *ji ji* (to reach the hairpin) is used to describe a girl who has reached the marriageable age of fifteen. Similarly the term *po gua zhi nian* (the year to split the melon) refers to the year when a girl turns sixteen and metaphorically refers to the loss of virginity.[45]

---

[45] Zhai Hao of the Qing dynasty wrote in his *Tong su bian: Funü* that although the coarse interpretation of this phrase takes *po gua* to mean *po shen* (to deflower) the actual meaning is derived for the structure of the character for melon (*gua*). *Gua* can be broken down to form

It is here that the sexualization of the women warrior in her mid-teens occurs. This virginal girl is at the point of becoming a sexual woman and the convergence of these two features, sexual innocence and sexual awareness, makes her an ideal figure for romanticization. It is the time in a woman's life when her sexual power has yet to be realized through pregnancy and childbirth, and her sexual knowledge is limited. Virginity as a temporary state in these young women's lives adds the promise of sex to further titillate the reader. The temporariness of her lifestyle is therein also linked to her age. Once she has become a married woman her Amazon lifestyle must be forfeited or she pays the penalty of death. The Amazon is thereby tamed by sexual contact with men or death.[46]

The virginal Amazon is moreover juxtaposed in *Jinghua yuan* with the symbol of excessive sexuality, Wu Zetian. Depicted as the reincarnation of a fox spirit, Li Ruzhen's Wu Zetian follows the pattern of centuries of historiography which has vilified Empress Wu as being licentious and insatiable in her sexual desires. Fox spirits are understood to be particularly licentious beings because it is through the absorption of human essence that they further their chances to attain immortality and, as Fatima Wu has described, "To have sexual intercourse with a man is probably the surest way to immortality."[47] In the symbolic battle between the virginal Amazons and the nymphomaniac Empress the latter is deposed and the former eradicated in the attainment of the reordering of Confucian society. In chapter one hundred we read of the slaughter of Wu Zetian's male concubines Zhang Zhangzong and Zhang Yizhi whose decapitation likewise symbolizes the end of excessive female sensuality/power.

Disruptive potential

The woman warrior's potential to disrupt the gender order of Chinese society, as we saw above, is neutralized by the literary redactors of her tale. She is granted the task of upholding patriarchal moral codes, she begins her temporary Amazonian behaviour only as the result of Confucian values and she is trivialized and sexualized even as she performs her deeds. However, the woman warrior is not completely devoid of the revolutionary or subversive

---

two characters for the number eight (*ba*) and two lots of eight make sixteen. That Zhai was forced to discredit the coarse interpretation shows the extent to which it was prevalent. Xiang Guanzhong et al, *Zhonghua chengyu da cidian* (A comprehensive dictionary of Chinese proverbs) (Changchun: Jinlin wenshi chubanshe, 1986), p. 169.

[46] Cao Xueqin's *Honglou meng* eulogizes the innocence and purity of girls/women in this particular age group as well although this theme is not elaborated in the *Guihua ci*. Lucien Miller presents a thorough survey of notions of childhood and adolescence in *Honglou meng* in his conference paper "Children of the Dream: The Adolescent World in Cao Xueqin's *Honglou meng*." Paper presented to the Symposium on Children in Pre-Modern China. May 25-27, 1990 at the Center for Advanced Studies, University of Virginia, Charlottesville.

[47] Fatima Wu, "Foxes in Chinese Supernatural Tales (Part I)," *Tamkang Review*, 17, No. 2 (Winter, 1986), p. 123.

potential noted by previous scholars. While it is rather unlikely that Amazons were invoked as part of a specifically focussed anti-patriarchal movement during the Late Imperial period it is possible that these symbols of female strength, performing exemplary deeds, served to support women who felt constrained by prescriptions of femininity. The revolutionary changes to women's social circumstances that developed within the Republican movement were indeed promoted by invocations of Hua Mulan and Qin Liangyu as models for emulation. Education outside the family, employment and political rights were each championed in the name of Hua Mulan just as was the encouragement for middle class women to join the military in Wuchang.[48]

The 'domesticated' women warriors of fiction and history also provide a fertile base from which more subversive versions may emerge. For example, during the radical years of the Cultural Revolution the revolutionary ballet *The Red Detachment of Women* redrew the boundaries for women warriors. In this ballet the leading female soldier joins the army to seek revenge for the suffering she experienced as a bondmaid. Motivation for her extreme behaviour does not develop through loyalty to a husband or filial piety to a parent and neither do we read of her death or resumption of wifely duties at the end of the ballet. Instead she continues the struggle and continues to seek the liberation of more bondmaids with her newly acquired military and political weaponry.[49] Her position liberates the women warrior from the almost robotic adherence to the Confucian morality typical of Mulan, Fourth Sister Lin and the *Jinghua yuan* Amazons. Her struggle is self-serving from the outset and then proceeds to a more altruistic plane once she has mastered Communist morality.

The persistent reappearance of the women warrior in popular *gongfu* movies throughout the Chinese speaking world reveal that the contradictions and ambiguities her form generates, the virtues and morals she embodies, still hold resonances with contemporary Chinese. The women warrior then, can be seen to maintain a much more complex discursive position than one of simple opposition or support of patriarchal society. Certainly, mid-Qing sexual ideology, as represented in *Honglou meng* and *Jinghua yuan*, successfully contained the disruptive potential of the women warrior and her Amazonian sister within its matrix.

---

[48] See for example Liu Shurong, "Sichuan nüxuetang kaixue zhi yanshuo" (Lecture at the opening of the women's school in Sichuan), rpt. in Li Youning and Zhang Yufa, *Jindai Zhongguo nüquan yundong shiliao 1842-1911*, p. 619; Liu Wangli, "Xinhai geming qian de funü yundong," p. 762.

[49] An English translation of this text can be found in *Red Detachment of Women: A Modern Revolutionary Ballet* (Beijing: Foreign Languages Press, 1972).

CHAPTER SEVEN

JIA FAMILY WOMEN: UNRESTRAINED 'INDULGENT MOTHERS'

In earlier chapters I discussed Baoyu's view that upon marriage women became infected by 'something' in the man. These comments are juxtaposed
with his eulogies to the young, pure unmarried female cousins and servant
girls. His predilection for the female sex does not, thereby, include the
women who have lost their virginity and assumed family responsibility.[1] I
argued that this position effectively undermined the legitimacy of women
who hold power. Here I would like to refine this general paradigm by examining the discourse of motherhood in *Honglou meng* to make evident the
manner in which mid Qing discourses of maternal value perpetuate and indeed generate this distrust of women in power. In chapter fifty-eight Baoyu
ponders the dismal fate of women once they become mothers in his reminis-
cence on a Du Mu poem. Du Mu visited Huizhou and met up with a dancer
he had known some years before. The beautiful dancer was married and had a
brood of children. Baoyu ponders "People had to marry, of course: they had
to reproduce their kind. But what a way for a lovely young girl to end! (*SS*
3.58.123)." To Baoyu motherhood is some form of inevitable disaster.
Here I will be elucidating the important way in which *Honglou meng*'s ideologies of motherhood serve to subdue women rather than empower them.
Margery Wolf's notion that women create uterine families within which
their power is predominant must thereby be negotiated against other ideologies of mothering.[2]

The thematic basis for this analysis derives from the phrase often used in
conjunction to the parenting of the Jia children, *yan fu ci mu* (Stern father
and compassionate mother). The contrast between the two is accepted as inseparable, with qualities of strictness being associated with father and loving
kindness with mother, as is clear from the fact that *ci* is an epithet for
'mother' and *jia ci* (the loving one of the family) a way of saying 'my
mother.' Similarly, *yan* is an epithet for 'father' and *jia yan* a synonym for
'my father.' The familial balance and harmony implied within these phrases

---

[1] The PRC critic Fu Ying also noted this in the 1990 article, "Guangcai minmie de 'yu mu'
shijie ji qi beiju—*Honglou meng* gui furen qunxiang fenxi" (The tragedy of the vanishing
splendour of the 'fish eyes' world—an analysis of the images of the aristocratic women in
Honglou meng), *Guangdong shehui kexue*, No. 3 (1990), pp. 91-96, rpt. in *RD*, No. 4 (1990),
p. 52.
[2] Margery Wolf, *Women and the Family in Rural Taiwan* (Stanford: Stanford University
Press, 1972), pp. 32-41.

is undermined by the implicit praise of the *yan* and censure of *ci* evident in phrases such as "love is revealed in severity and harm comes from laxity" (*yan shi ai, song shi hai*) and "a kind mother spoils her son" (*ci mu bai zi*). It will become clear in this chapter how the notion of a *ci mu* serves as a form of censure of married women in *Honglou meng*. The underlying misogyny of the notion of a *ci mu*, in contrast to her opposite, the *yan fu*, will also emerge.

The *ci mu* is someone whose devotion to her children surpasses her self interest. She is forgiving, caring and generous. This notion of a *ci mu* idealizes and romanticizes mothers and motherhood as all-loving and self-sacrificing. This idealized form generates its supposed opposite, the bad mother. The creator of children turns destroyer of children. The integral unity of the two aspects 'bad mother' and *ci mu* is apparent in the *ci mu*'s tendency to spoil her children. The *ci mu*'s transformation into the 'bad mother' is a straightforward progression along the same trajectory. The *ci mu* often indulges the children's whims to the point where it is positively harmful to their development and future social position.

Women are often perceived as being victims of 'maternal instinct' and unable to be anything other than an all-loving all-forgiving person because of a mother's 'natural' passivity in relation to her 'instincts.'[3] On the other hand a virtuous mother is also one who is self-trained and self-disciplined in conscious acts of sacrifice and loyalty. The mother's level of devotion to her child's welfare should surpass every personal need she may feel. It is linked in these respects to the romanticized notion of female long-sufferance of hardship which serve the male order well. The failure to become such a mother is thereby indicative of failure to learn and practise, indeed it is a failure in personal morality. As will become evident throughout this chapter, critical reception of the various mothers in *Honglou meng* over the past two centuries reveals that even if a woman performs the emotional deeds of a *ci mu* she risks censure as over-indulgent and over-feminizing. Moreover, the whole notion of a compassionate mother is written upon the assumption that it is accompanied by a *yan fu*. One without the other is not the perceived ideal upbringing of a child, particularly a son. The ideal balance between the two, as will become clear, is not achieved in the Jia family of *Honglou meng*.

This balance also impinges on my discussion of men in the novel in this and the next chapter, who are 'over-feminized' in their social relations. As uncontrollable victims of their own desires for pleasure the Jia men are suffering from dominance of the feminine because they are unable to be strict with themselves. Even the moral upstanding Jia Zheng, the *yan fu*, is depicted as being dominated by the excessive indulgence of his mother, Grandmother Jia. In this chapter then, I will discuss the ways in which the

---

[3] Mary Ellman, *Thinking About Women* (London: McMillan and Co., 1968), pp. 131-36.

images of Grandmother Jia, Lady Wang, Lady Xing, Aunt Xue and Aunt Zhao evolve within this discourse of the *ci mu*.

'Ci mu' as destroyer of children

Baoyu and Daiyu are depicted as having an especially close relationship with the Jia matriarch, Grandmother Jia. The perceived effects of this partiality, particularly on Baoyu, are depicted as being problematic for his childhood education because of the elder woman's indulgence of Baoyu's whims.[4] It is in her apartments that Baoyu lives as a young boy and it is into her apartments that Daiyu is placed on her arrival in the mansions. These two are the prime objects of Grandmother Jia's affection and this is repeatedly mentioned in the novel. For example, each are given one of Grandmother Jia's personal maids because their own servants are regarded as inadequate. "Like Nightingale [Daiyu's principle maid], Aroma [Baoyu's principle maid] had previously been one of Grandmother Jia's own maids. Her real name was Pearl. Baoyu's grandmother, fearful that the maids who already waited on her darling boy could not be trusted to look after him properly, had picked out Pearl as a girl of tried and conspicuous fidelity and put her in charge over them (*SS* 1.3.105-106)."

Once again in chapter five the narrator amplifies Grandmother Jia's partiality towards Baoyu and Daiyu.

> From the moment Lin Daiyu entered the Rong mansion, Grandmother Jia's solicitude for her had manifested itself in a hundred different ways. The arrangements made for the meals and accommodation were exactly the same as for Baoyu. The other three granddaughters, Yingchun, Tanchun and Xichun, were relegated to a secondary place in the old lady's affections, and the objects of her partiality themselves began to feel an affection for each other which far exceeded what they felt for any of the rest (*SS* 1.5.124).

Grandmother Jia's tendency towards partiality in her affections is described as being a long-term feature of her mothering and not simply something that emerged when her exceptional grandson was born with a piece of jade in his mouth. Daiyu's arrival in the mansions occurs after the death of her mother, Jia Min, Grandmother Jia's daughter. In chapter three when Grandmother Jia greets Daiyu she says, "Of all my girls your mother was the one I loved the best," she said "and now she's been the first to go, and without my even being able to see her again before the end. I can't help being upset (*SS* 1.3.90)."

Grandmother Jia's repeatedly mentioned tendency towards partiality and excessive favouritism is described as being a rather quaint feature of the fam-

---

[4] The novel remains ironic on this point since Baoyu's 'bad' upbringing is clearly also that which enables him to transcend normal social strictures at the close of the novel. However, the view that this upbringing is 'bad,' reflects one vision of good/bad parenting that has been reiterated by subsequent critics.

ily since it alters, among other things, the normally expected pattern of strict division between the sexes. The filial respect shown her as the eldest surviving Jia permits her a great degree of influence over family customs and so, at her wish, Baoyu is permitted to live with the women and girls past the accepted age. This privilege extends into adulthood for as the narrator assures the reader near the close of the novel, "Though Baoyu was a married man, as Grannie's favourite he was allowed to join in the fun (*SS* 5.108.162)." This aberration was queried by the Qing critic "Er zhi dao ren" as being a challenge to Confucian ethics.

> Concubine Yuan (Yuanchun) ordered that Baoyu should live with his sisters and female cousins in the Garden. The *Book of Rights* says 'Males and females should not mix together, and should have separate clothes racks, and separate servants' and it also says 'Male and females should have separate wardrobes.' Confucius thought this would nip the problem in the bud. How can he heed the sage's words?[5]

However, this Jia family quirk, whereby a rapidly maturing boy continues to live with the women is noted by other characters as being problematic in both the moral and social senses. Lady Wang, Baoyu's mother, describes her son to Daiyu as follows: "There is only one thing that worries me. I have a little monster of a son who tyrannizes over all the rest of this household...the thing to do is never to take any notice of him. None of your cousins dare provoke him (*SS* 1.3.97)." The reason for this "exceptionally wild and naughty" behaviour, his loathing of study and his predilection to "spend all his time in the women's apartments with the girls" is that "Grandmother Jia doted on him so much, no one ever dared to correct him (*SS* 1.3.98)." Later on she reiterates this sentiment saying, "Baoyu is a law unto himself. Because your grandmother is so fond of him she has thoroughly spoiled him. When he was little he lived with the girls, so with the girls he remains now (*SS* 1.3.98)." Aroma later confirms this by saying: "Recently he had taken advantage of the comparative immunity from parental control, afforded him by the all-encompassing protection of his doting grandmother, to become even more wild and self-indulgent and even more confirmed in his aversion to serious pursuits than in previous years (*SS* 1.19.389-90)."

The significance of Grandmother Jia's partiality in sheer financial terms is not lost on others in the household either, as we see from Xifeng's joking harassment of the Matriarch in chapter twenty-two. "You forget, Grannie, when you go to heaven young Baoyu won't be the only one who'll walk ahead of the hearse. You've got other grandchildren too, don't forget! You don't have to leave *everything* to him. ...Mother-in-law is just as soppy about Baoyu as you are...(*SS* 1.22.433)." While Xifeng sees their relationship as a financial threat, for Grandmother Jia's son, Jia Zheng it assumes

---

[5] "Er zhi dao ren," "*Honglou meng* shuo meng," rpt. in *Honglou meng juan*, p. 86.

more a subtle emotional significance as he perceives that he is a low priority in his mother's affections. During a family gathering he says, "You have so much affection for your grandchildren, Mama. Can you not spare just a tiny bit for your son (*SS* 1.22.447)?"

Jia She, Grandmother Jia's eldest son appears acutely aware of his low place in his mother's affections. Indeed, he is regarded with even more disdain by Grandmother Jia than his younger brother, Jia Zheng. During the Mid-Autumn celebrations Jia She is asked to tell a joke to amuse the family.

> This one is about a dutiful son whose mother was ill. He tried everywhere to get a doctor for her, but couldn't find one, so in the end he was reduced to calling in an old woman who practised acupuncture. Now this old dame knew nothing of physiology, nevertheless she assured the son that it was inflammation of the heart that his mother was suffering from and that she could cure it instantly with her needle. The son became very alarmed. "If metal in any form comes into contact with the heart," he said, "it means death. Surely you're not going to put a needle in her heart?" "No, no, I shan't put it in the heart," said the old woman. "I mean to put it in here, over the ribs." "But that's too *far* from the heart," said the son. "Surely if you put it in there, it won't do any good?" "Oh yes it will," said the old woman. "A mother's heart always inclines towards one side (*SS* 3.75.504-505)."

Grandmother Jia comments wryly, "Perhaps I could do with a bit of the old dame's acupuncture myself" and it is only then that Jia She realizes that his joke could be interpreted as a criticism of his own mother. References to Jia She's gaffe continue through the night revealing that Grandmother Jia had indeed recognized the applicability of the joke to her relationship with Jia She and Jia Zheng.

That the indulgent grandmother is blamed for the wild behaviour of her grandson is regarded as being a personal and harmless indulgence by the women around. However, as is clear from the history of *Hongxue*, critics perceived this 'quirk' as signifying far more serious family disruptions. For example Tu Ying's Qing critique goes as far as connecting excessive fondness with the destruction of the objects of this affection. In his discussion of Grandmother Jia, Tu Ying says, "Human sympathies and emotions are endless and the wise one could not restrain her's so she developed a doting affection! ...Did not Grandmother Jia have great plans for Daiyu and even greater ones for Baoyu? But she lived in a fool's paradise and lacked foresight. It was Grandmother Jia who killed Daiyu and not Aroma. It was Grandmother Jia who drove Baoyu from home and not Daiyu."[6] Just as in the previous generation, the person upon whom her affection was focussed, Jia Min, dies an early death. Thus the discourse of motherhood shows an unrestrained *ci mu* transformed into the destroyer of her children. The counterbalance to this potentially destructive influence is the *yan fu*. As

---

[6] Tu Ying, "*Honglou meng* lunzan," rpt. in *Honglou meng juan*, p. 153.

Xifeng says to Baoyu after he had resumed his normal bouncing, leaping and incessant chatter on the departure of his father from the lantern riddle party, "You ought to have Uncle Zheng with you every day and never budge an inch from his side (*SS* 1.22.450)!"

The detrimental effects of Grandmother Jia's indulgence are roundly recognized, by critics, the narrator, and other characters yet it is unchallenged throughout the novel. Indeed, this practice is part of the carefully constructed ministering to each and every one of Grandmother Jia's wishes. All the characters, from elder men to youngest servant are consistently careful to ensure that Grandmother Jia's wishes take first precedence. As the oldest member of the clan, although in the junior Rong branch, Grandmother Jia is placed in an honoured position. She is also depicted as demanding this honour and expecting her children and grandchildren to perform their deeds of devotion with a regularity which should be anathema to the self-effacing, self-sacrificing mother. Thus, the young generations indulge and pander their eldest member and ultimately, this leads to the destruction of clan stability. In chapter twenty-two we see that Baoyu is quietly instructed to tell the matriarch the answers to Jia Zheng's riddle to ensure that she answers correctly. On her pronouncement of Baoyu's answer she receives false praise from her son who was party to the ruse. "'Bravo, Mamma! Right first time!' said Jia Zheng, and turning round to address the servants, he asked them to bring in the presents for Lady Jia (*SS* 1.22.447)." The trinkets are depicted as being trifles chosen to please the 'child-like' matriarch. Similarly, Baochai chooses plays Grandmother Jia enjoys despite her personal disdain of noisy, acrobatic pieces. Xifeng regularly lets Grandmother Jia win at cards (*SS* 2.47.431). Lady Wang refuses an invitation to visit her brother's wife because "she could see that Grandmother Jia did not want to (*SS* 1.25.489)." The whole family system is set up to flatter and pander to the wishes of the old matriarch. Indeed, Grandmother Jia demands that these rituals are performed. She selfishly perpetuates a destructive fantasy world by repeatedly invoking notions of filial piety.

The linkage of Grandmother Jia's happiness to all decisions regarding Baoyu is instrumental in his inclusion in the all-female party allowed to dwell in Prospect Garden. This episode shows that the Imperial Concubine, Yuanchun, is similarly careful to sacrifice the 'good' of the family heir's development for Grandmother Jia's happiness. After her brief Visitation she decides that the garden built for her pleasure should not remain closed but should be handed to the young female cousins as their personal apartments.

> Assuredly, the girls must be allowed into the garden. It should become their home. And if the girls, why not Baoyu? He had grown up in their midst. He was different from other boys. If he were not allowed into the garden as well, he would consider himself left out in the cold, and his distress would cause Lady Wang and Grandmother Jia to feel unhappy too. Unquestionably she should ask for him to be admitted along with the girls (*SS* 1.23.455).

The women all want to indulge and 'mother' Baoyu and Yuanchun is described, at one point, as being more of a mother to Baoyu than a sister (*SS* 1.18.358). Publicly rationalized as action that will please Grandmother Jia, the pampering of Baoyu ultimately fulfils these elder women's own desires to win favour with and thus control over the most promising male of the clan. Grandmother Jia's wishes serve as a sanction.

The authority wielded by Grandmother Jia over other people's dealings with Baoyu easily overrides that of Baoyu's mother Lady Wang who has shown little resistance to her mother-in-law's whims. When Baoyu is burned by candle wax by his half-brother Huan, Lady Wang's emotions are described as follows, "When Lady Wang saw it [the burn], she was both full of anguish for her son and at the same time, when she thought of the questioning to which she would inevitably be subjected by Grandmother Jia and wondered what she would say, terrified on her own account (*SS* 1.25.492)."

From this we see the pivotal role Grandmother Jia plays in the perpetuation of and legitimization of the indulgent mothers of the Jia clan. She sets the tone by linking her own happiness and health to continued special treatment of Baoyu, thereby linking indulgence of Baoyu with filial piety and obedience of juniors. Simultaneously, she gives the other women in the clan, particularly Lady Wang, the excuse to relax any maternal notions of 'educating' and give in to their 'natural' maternal instincts of pampering their son.

Decline of the 'yan fu'

Grandmother Jia was well aware of the power she exerted and so she continued to perpetuate the system whereby her juniors pander to her whims and desires. This awareness of her power is clear in her assurance to Baoyu, who is clinging fearfully to her after being summonsed by his father, "There, there, my little lamb! You'd better go and see him. Grannie will see to it that he doesn't hurt you. He wouldn't dare." Her instructions to the nannies who will accompany him are "See that his Pa doesn't frighten him! (*SS* 1.23.456)." Careless in her undermining of Jia Zheng's authority, Grandmother Jia dominates the household demanding that all pay court to her wishes.

Grandmother Jia perpetuates the notion that Jia Zheng's demands on Baoyu to study are causing him to be ill. When Baoyu was near death as a victim of Mother Ma's magic, Grandmother Jia links the machinations of Aunt Zhao with Jia Zheng's repeated insistence that Baoyu improve himself through study. She wrongly assumes that Baoyu has been driven to this state of ill health through his father's efforts to make him study. Although the reader knows it to be black magic, and not Jia Zheng, which has driven Baoyu to his death bed, Zheng has been accused and publicly rebuked.

Grandmother Jia shouts accusingly at Aunt Zhao "It's your spiteful meddling that has forced him to do all this studying. You have reduced the poor child to such a state that the mere sight of his father makes him more scared than a mouse with a cat after it (*SS* 1.25.503)."[7]

Indeed, at no stage in the novel is Baoyu's supposed sickly constitution revealed. Lady Wang and Grandmother Jia insist that he is not very strong but the readers are witness to this physical susceptibility only when 'magic' is involved as in the above mentioned case or at the end of the novel when he loses his mind before leaving to join the immortals. Indeed, Abbot Zhang comments on Baoyu's healthy appearance only to be contradicted by Grandmother Jia, "He looks well enough on the outside, but underneath he's delicate. And his Pa doesn't improve matters by forcing him to study all the time. I'm afraid he'll end up by making the child ill (*SS* 2.29.76)." Ultimately, of course, Baoyu's mental illness is not related to studying excessively but rather to the mysterious loss of his jade in chapter ninety-four. This in turn leads to his being tricked into marrying Baochai (to turn his luck) which in turn precipitates Daiyu's death. Grandmother Jia's insistence that study is harmful to Baoyu is then depicted as being unreliable and fictitious, designed primarily to ensure that Baoyu remains under her control and away from Jia Zheng's influence.

The situation is similar, although not as extreme, when one examines Lady Wang's attitude to Jia Zheng's authority. In her indulgence of Baoyu's faults she subtly undermines the power of her husband and his efforts to discipline the boy. In the discussion over Aroma's name, Jia Zheng asks which of the maids has such a frivolous name so "Lady Wang could see that he was displeased and did her best to cover up for Baoyu: 'I think it was Lady Jia who gave her the name' (*SS* 1.23.458)." Zheng is not fooled by this ruse, declaring that his mother would never choose such a name. His awareness of the persistent undermining of his authority by his wife and mother is revealed in the scene where he beats Baoyu for supposed licentious crimes trumped up by Jia Huan. Lady Wang begs him to cease his beating, arguing that it would kill Grandmother Jia if Baoyu was killed. In his rage Zheng shouts, "'Don't try that sort of talk with me!' said Jia Zheng bitterly. 'Merely by fathering a monster like this I have proved myself an unfilial son; yet whenever in the past I have tried to discipline him, the rest of you have all conspired against me to protect him. Now that I have the opportunity at last, I may as well finish off what I have begun and put him down,

---

[7] In Gao E's final forty chapters Grandmother Jia and Jia Zheng undergo unconvincing and unexplained personality transformations. Grandmother Jia supports Jia Zheng's efforts to encourage Baoyu to attend school and she refuses to be persuaded otherwise despite Baoyu's pleas. Jia Zheng similarly softens his attitude to Baoyu and shows a personal interest in his progress, going as far as personally taking Baoyu to school on his first day. Both these transformations are unexplained and appear to reflect Gao E's more pedestrian talents and pedestrian morality. See for example chapters eighty to eighty-two.

like the vermin he is, before he can do any more damage' (*SS* 2.33.149)."
However, Jia Zheng's ability to withstand the pleas of his wife proves weak
and he is reduced to tears only to be confronted with the wrath of his mother
who proceeds to berate him for his lack of filiality. The kneeling Zheng en-
treated, "How can I bear it, Mother, if you speak to me like that? What I did
to the boy I did for the honour of the family." Grandmother Jia's reply
reveals Zheng's weakness in the face of his women, "A single harsh word
from me and you start whining that you can't bear it? How do you think
Baoyu could bear your cruel rod? And you say you've been punishing him
for the honour of the family, but you just tell me this: did your own father
ever punish *you* in such a way?—I think not." Zheng's failing resolve has
now evaporated completely as he replies, "From now on I'll never beat him
again, if that's what you wish." Lady Jia's scornful reply and her immediate
actions complete the destruction of Zheng's authority as father and a man.
She declares "He's your son. If you want to beat him, that's up to you. If
we women are in your way, we'll leave you alone to get on with it (*SS*
2.33.151)." However, the words are immediately exposed as being empty because she proceeds to make arrangements to have Baoyu transferred away to
Nanking with his mother and herself. Baoyu is duly carried off amongst a
bevvy of women leaving Zheng devoid of any male prerogative as a 'stern father.' The dominance of the women over Zheng is complete at this moment.[8]

Lady Wang's subsequent confession to Aroma leaves the reader in no
doubt as to the source of the conflict between the *yan fu* and the *ci mu*.

> I know perfectly well that Baoyu is in need of discipline; and anyone who
> saw how strict I used to be with Mr Zhu would realize that I am capable of
> exercising it. But I have my reasons. A woman of fifty cannot expect to
> bear any more children and Baoyu is now the only son I have. He is not a
> very strong boy; and his Grannie dotes on him. I daren't *risk* being strict.
> I daren't risk losing another son. I daren't risk angering Her Old Ladyship
> and upsetting the whole household (*SS* 2.34.163).

The selfishness and fear of the mother leads her to harm her child by not
providing adequate discipline. The PRC critic Bai Dun notes this in his
article on Jia Zheng and Lady Wang titled "'The stern father' and
'compassionate mother' and other things." Bai Dun suggests that Lady
Wang was far from a *ci mu* because she protected Baoyu out of sheer self-

---

[8] Confucian precepts for women practiced by Aunt Xue include the notion that "If you
have a husband you obey your husband, if you have no husband obey your son."
Grandmother Jia clearly rejects this notion in favour of the more commonly propounded notion of filial piety to parents in her dealings with Jia Zheng. In chapter eighty-five Aunt Xue
refuses to commit Baochai to marriage with Baoyu until she has received permission from her
son, Xue Pan, despite the latter's wanton and unreliable behaviour. For further discussion of
Aunt Xue see Yan Wang, "Lun Xue Yima xingxiang de dianxing yiyi" (Discussing the typicality of Aunt Xue's image), *Xinyang shifan xueyuan xuebao (she ke ban)*, No. 2 (1984), pp.
97-105, rpt. in *RD*, No. 4 (1984), pp. 83-92.

interest. If Baoyu dies she would be placed lower in the family than the
concubine Aunt Zhao whose son Jia Huan would take prime place. Her
continued enjoyment of security of position depended upon Baoyu.
According to Bai Dun, she has no real maternal love for Baoyu, just self
interest. All her dealings with Baoyu show that she is not really a *ci mu*
because she is self-centred, self interested in her dealings with him.[9] Her
own partiality for her first son, now dead, is also cited by Bai Dun as
evidence of her failure to achieve the model *ci mu* status. She cries for Zhu
during the beating. "Oh, Zhu! Zhu! If only you had lived, I shouldn't have
minded losing a *hundred* other sons! (*SS* 2.33.150)."

Her personal responsibility for the deaths of at least two people in the
novel develops from her opposition to Jia Zheng's harsh attitude to her only
remaining son. Rather than punish Baoyu for misbehaviour, Lady Wang
passes blame for his deeds onto those around him. As Jiang Hesen wrote,
"Unlike Jia Zheng, she often blames Baoyu's 'unworthy' behaviour on those
around him, and particularly the 'seductive' behaviour of his maids. To use
her own phrase, 'a perfectly good gentleman has been corrupted by them'."
And so, Jiang states, she eradicates the perceived sources of Baoyu's 'bad behaviour.' This leads to the death of Golden and Skybright.[10] Golden commits suicide after Lady Wang accuses her of attempting to seduce Baoyu
when it was indeed the reverse, with Baoyu persistently harassing Golden.
Skybright dies of illness after having been sent home under the suspicion
that she was a bad influence on Baoyu. Singled out as the most beautiful
and lively of Baoyu's maids, Skybright is accused of leading Baoyu astray.
It is indeed Lady Wang who orders the search of the garden when she sus-
pects illicit relations amongst its inhabitants. Tu Ying described Lady Wang
as one who "believes slander and tolerates licentiousness, and so she killed
Golden the first time she was angry, and kills Skybright the next time she
was angry."[11]

Each of Lady Wang's rash acts are described by Tai Yu in his critique of
1948 to be Lady Wang's emotional reactions to Baoyu's problems which are

---

[9] Bai Dun, "'Yan fu,' 'ci mu' ji qita—cong Jia Zheng, Wang Furen de xingxiang suzao
kan Cao Xueqin de chuangzao weiji" (The 'severe father,' 'indulgent mother' and other
things—A view of Cao Xueqin's creative crisis from the construction of Jia Zheng's and
Lady Wang's image), *Anhui shida xuebao*, No. 3 (1981), pp. 67-74, rpt. in *RD*, No. 11 (1981),
pp. 34-35. This point is also made by others, see for example Jiang Hesen's 1979 book-length
critique. Jiang declares that Lady Wang's "love for Baoyu is in fact love for herself." Jiang
Hesen, *Honglou meng gaishuo* (A commentary on *Honglou meng*) (Shanghai: Guji chubanshe, 1979), p. 90.

[10] Jiang Hesen, *Honglou meng gaishuo*, p. 91. Others who wrote along these lines include
Shi Yepin, "Lun Wang Furen" (Discussing Lady Wang), *Yangzhou shiyuan xuebao*, No. 4
(1983), pp. 58-63, rpt. in *RD*, No. 12 (1983), p. 64.

[11] Tu Ying, "*Honglou meng* lunzan," p. 133. Zhu Zuolin, another Qing critic described
Lady Wang as destroying the people nurtured by the matriarch, Grandmother Jia, because of
her inability to use talent and in her own lack of talent. Zhu Zuolin, "Honglou wenku: jie lu"
(Red chamber series [excerpts]), rpt. in *Honglou meng juan*, pp. 159-60.

partly the result of his mother's failure to supervise his activities. Left to his own devices in the Garden, Baoyu lacks the proper motherly guidance he should receive, according to Tai Yu.[12] Baoyu's childhood education is described by Tai Yu as being the result of Yuanchun's concerted efforts before she entered the Palace, not his mother's. Tai Yu cites the following passage as evidence, "When he [Baoyu] was still a very little boy of only three or four and had not yet begun his schooling, she [Yuanchun] had taught him to recite several texts and to recognize several thousand characters (*SS* 1.18.358)." Both Yuanchun and Baoyu lived with Grandmother Jia, further revealing the extent of Lady Wang's isolation from her children. Lady Wang concerns herself with her Buddhist pursuits rather than her children's education and intercedes in their lives only in fits of anger.

Zhang Bilai wrote in 1985 that this indulgent attitude towards her son, accompanied by Jia Zheng's rigidity, leads to the situation where Baoyu "regards his mother with closeness but without respect and regards his father with respect but not closeness." He cites the differing attitudes Baoyu takes towards them, such as Baoyu's cuddling of his mother in chapters twenty-five and twenty-eight and Baoyu disdain of her knowledge of medicine when she is inquiring after Daiyu's health. Lady Wang can't remember the name of a medicine she wanted to recommend for Daiyu and, suspecting that it included the word "Vajra," Baoyu laughs at her and says "I've never heard of 'Vajra Pills.' If there are 'Vajra Pills,' I suppose there must be 'Buddha Boluses'!" Lady Wang replies to his bantering in jest, "You're a naughty boy to make fun of your poor mother. A good whipping from your Pa is what you need (*SS* 2.28.45)." Zhang summarizes Baoyu's feelings for his mother as replicating the phrase from the *Jia shu meng qiu* which lays down Confucian precepts on family and educational affairs. "The mother is close but not respected, while the father has respect but not closeness." Zhang argues that Baoyu does not view his mother with 'respect,' but expects that she will be 'indulgent' (*ci*)."[13] Lady Wang on the other hand is perceived as finding Baoyu's cheeky behaviour as 'adorable.' Zhang proceeds to examine Baoyu's relationship with his father under the general understanding that "Jia Zheng is a father and the distinguishing characteristic of fathers is 'severity' (*yan*)... Indeed if the father is not severe then he will lose the honour (*zunyan*) due to a father." Zhang's discussion of the parental qualities of *yan* and *ci* makes clear the point made earlier about *ci* not being a quality that generates respect whereas *yan* implicitly connotes dignity and right to respect.[14] A *ci mu* is thereby, inherently tainted. Zhang goes on to say that "Those who are fathers must be severe. Severity is their founding point and

---

[12] Tai Yu, *Honglou meng renwu lun*, p. 113.

[13] Zhang Bilai, *Tan Honglou meng* (Talking on *Honglou meng*) (Shanghai: Zhishi chubanshe, 1985), p. 37.

[14] Zhang Bilai, *Tan Honglou meng*, p. 38.

respect follows." In chapter twenty-six Xue Pan tricks Baoyu into hurrying out of the garden to see him by saying that Jia Zheng wants to see Baoyu. Baoyu finds this intolerable and says, "I don't mind being made a fool of but I think it was going a bit far to bring my father into it (*SS* 1.26.518-19)." As Zhang reiterates "No matter whether he is being beaten or cursed, his thoughts and actions [towards his father] are always full of respect."[15]

Yuanchun, as surrogate mother, made the point about the delicacy of the balance between severity and pampering in several letters to her father regarding Baoyu's progress. "I beg you to be most careful in your handling of this child. If you are not strict with him, he will never grow up into a proper man. But if you are too strict, you may endanger his health and cause Grandmother to be distressed (*SS* 1.18.358)." The ideal recommended by the Imperial concubine is a moderate severity. Severity is then the male principle which serves to prevent the female's 'natural' tendency towards indulgence or over-kindness from ruining the children, realized in Grandmother Jia's 'opposition' to strictness.

It becomes evident that the women actively plot to keep Baoyu away from the men and find petty ruses to achieve this end. Lady Xing, Baoyu's aunt, for example, is described in chapter twenty-four as detaining Baoyu on false grounds simply to keep him in her company. Baoyu, Jia Huan and Jia Lan arrive to pay courtesy calls to their ailing Uncle, Jia She. Jia She later sends them into the women's quarters to see their Aunt, Lady Xing. After a brief time the boys prepare to leave but Lady Xing "stopped him [Baoyu] with a gracious smile" saying "I've got something else to say to you." She sends the other boys away pleading that she can't have them to dinner because her girls are causing a rumpus and giving her a headache. It emerges that the girls are nowhere to be seen (or heard) and when Baoyu asks "What was it you wanted to tell me?" Lady Xing replies gaily, "Oh nothing at all! I only said that because I wanted you to stay and have dinner here with me and the girls. And I've got something nice for you to take back with you afterwards (*SS* 1.24.472)." Baoyu has been carefully extracted from the male world of Jia She and also his male peers. This separation of Baoyu from the men's world becomes an important weapon in the women's sabotage of Jia Zheng's paternal authority. In some respects this reveals the extent to which the women have become immensely powerful through their active development of the uterine family with a key member of the Jia clan. However, the efficacy of this tactic is tempered by rivalries within the women's group and by sexual ideologies which undermine this power. Excessive time with women is seen as being over-feminizing for boys and carries with it the subsequent problems of declining family fortunes.

During the Imperial Visitation, Yuanchun singles out Baoyu for a personal greeting, emphasizing the female's role in separating him and distin-

---

[15] Zhang Bilai, *Tan Honglou meng*, p. 40.

guishing him from the menfolk. On not seeing Baoyu she asks his where-abouts and is told, "The menfolk of the family are not supposed to see you without special reason (*SS* 1.18.363)." To this she promptly orders that he be summonsed. This occurs immediately after Jia Zheng has greeted her from behind a screen. Yuanchun saw fit to make an exception for her brother but not her father.

After Baoyu's beating Grandmother Jia is more direct in her separation of Baoyu from Jia Zheng. She calls Jia Zheng's chief page and issues the fol-lowing instructions:

> In future, whenever the Master is entertaining guests or seeing anybody and asks for Baoyu, you are to say, straight away, without needing to see me about it, first of all that Master Bao was seriously injured by his beating and will need several months' complete rest before he can walk properly; and secondly that he has just made an offering to his star-guardian because of an unlucky conjunction in his horoscope and isn't allowed to see out-siders or go outside the inner gate until the beginning of the eighth month (*SS* 2.36.194).

Grandmother Jia then, not only controls Jia Zheng's access to his son (and incidentally Baoyu's movements too), but also openly reduces Jia Zheng's authority in the eyes of his pages.

The women of the household constantly battle against losing control of their children to the male exterior of the household. They contrive to limit the efficaciousness of male prerogative to educate/remove sons. This is achieved by physical isolation and direct opposition to male authority. Grandmother Jia's elder status as an elder, is used to undermine Jia Zheng's paternal responsibilities. The *ci mu* defeats the *yan fu* but simultaneously aids in the destruction of the clan.

Immoral sons: products of bad mothering

Baoyu is perceived as a problematic son by his parents who still remember fondly their model son, Jia Zhu. However, when compared to the other young men of the Jia family, Baoyu is still acceptable in polite company and generally a credit to his parents. Baoyu's half-brother, Jia Huan, on the other hand, is constantly proving himself to be a despicable and jealous char-acter. Similarly, Baoyu's cousin Xue Pan, performs deeds of considerable licentiousness, barbarity and stupidity throughout the novel. When we ex-amine the novel's explanation of the faults of these failed sons, Jia Huan and Xue Pan, we can see that indulgent or errant 'mothering' is often invoked as the causal factor.

In chapter four the reader is treated to a description of Xue Pan as follows,

> He [Xue Pan] was a native of Nanking and came of a refined and highly cul-tivated family, but having lost his father in infancy and been, as sole re-maining scion of the stock, excessively indulged by a doting widowed mother, he had grown up into a useless lout... He had been educated after a

fashion, but could barely read and write. He devoted the greater part of his
time to cock-fighting, horse-racing, and outings to places of scenic interest (*SS* 1.4.117-8).

An indulgent mother creates a monster who is incapable of supporting himself and in his impulsive licentious life-style generates numerous scandals,
including murder. This point is also made by Yan Wang in a 1984 critique.
Yan asks whether we can separate Xue Pan's wanton behaviour from his
mother's indulgence and pampering parenting?[16]

Xue Pan's pampered upbringing is echoed in that of his demonic wife,
Xia Jingui.

> It is true that she was not at all bad-looking, she could even read quite a
> number of words; and if subtle deviousness of character had been an exam-
> inable qualification, she might have come out a good second to Xifeng. Her
> chief drawback sprang from the fact that she had lost her father at a very
> early age; and as her widowed mother had no other child of her own and
> doted on her excessively, she had been thoroughly spoiled. By treating her
> every whim as law and gainsaying her nothing, her mother had turned her
> into a monster (*SS* 3.79.591).

So the spoiled son married the spoiled daughter in a marital combination that
causes chaos and drives Xue Pan to further immoral excesses.

Baochai is depicted as being cognizant of her mother's complicity in Xue
Pan's unbridled behaviour, just as Yan Wang was above. Indeed, Baochai
voices this suspicion several times in the novel. In chapter forty-seven for
example Xue Pan wrongly assumed that Liu Xianglian is homosexual and
after insulting him with repeated lewd assertions is beaten by Liu. Reaching
home Aunt Xue is both anxious at the extent of her sons wounds and angry
at both men for their folly. She wants to call Lady Wang in and ensure that
Liu is arrested but Baochai warns against this saying,

> Everyone knows what a lawless, ungovernable creature Pan is. It's only
> because you're his mother that you feel differently…If you insist on mak-
> ing an issue of it *now* and telling Aunt about it, you will make it appear that
> you are so blind to Pan's faults that you allow him to go around provoking
> other people, but that as soon as someone stands up to him, you fly up in
> arms and use our relations' influence to oppress them (*SS* 2.47.446-7).

Baochai's advice is basically aimed at limiting the extent to which the Xue
family's scandals reach the outside. There is no solution proffered by
Baochai, just a simple plan for damage control. This leaves the reader and
the critic in no doubt that the Xue family's problems will continue and that
they stem from a partial, unrestrained indulgent mother whose failure to recognize errant behaviour in her son has resulted in the development of an anti-

---

[16] Yan Wang, "Lun Xue Yima xingxiang de dianxing yiyi" (Discussing the typical significance of Aunt Xue's image), *Xinyang shifan xueyuan xuebao* (zhe she ban), No. 2 (1984),
pp. 97-105, rpt. in *RD*, No. 4 (1984), p. 90.

social buffoon. Baochai is warning her mother to keep her bad-mothering as quiet as possible. Yan Wang summarizes the connection between Aunt Xue's indulgence and Xue Pan's dissoluteness as "It is not hard to see that, under Aunt Xue's pampering and spoiling (*fangzong niai*), Xue Pan has really become a person who acts wildly in defiance of public opinion and the laws, and uses powerful connections to bully others right down to committing acts of murderous violence. In the end although he was exempt from capital punishment, his family fortunes declined. Can we still say that Aunt Xue is not the arch criminal and chief culprit for facilitating Xue Pan's crimes?"[17] In Baochai's comments and critics appraisals it is clear that some form of condemnation of Aunt Xue evolves from her son's wanton behaviour. The problem being overindulgence due to the absence of a restraining *yan fu*.

The case of Jia Huan is more complicated as a result of his ambiguous position in the family hierarchy. As the son of a concubine, Aunt Zhao, Huan is not quite a master and his natal mother is not quite his mother since his prime loyalty is supposed to rest with the main wife, Lady Wang. However, Lady Wang's partiality for Baoyu leaves Huan in an unenviable situation. Prompted by Aunt Zhao's own jealousy and resentment of her lowly place in the household, Huan's jealousy is unbounded. When Huan tips hot wax on Baoyu (Baoyu has been flirting with Huan's favourite maid Sunset), Xifeng says "Huan, you are *the* most cack-handed creature I have ever met! You are simply not fit for decent company. I don't know why Aunt Zhao hasn't taught you better." Lady Wang's reprimand to Aunt Zhao makes similar implication regarding the latter's poor mothering skills. "This is a fine son you bore us, I must say! He is a black-hearted little monster! You might at least *try* to teach him better. But no. Time and again I have overlooked this sort of thing, but instead of feeling sorry, you glory in it. You think that when I do nothing, you have got the better of me (*SS* 1.25.491)."

The confusion of parenting duties for concubines is clear in chapter twenty. Although the mother of Huan, Aunt Zhao has no rights to parent him, but still bears responsibility for his errant behaviour when it suits the family power holders. As Xifeng reveals when she overhears Aunt Zhao reprimanding Huan she replies tartly, "What do you want to go carrying on at him like that for? No matter *where* he's been, Sir Zheng and Lady Wang are quite capable of looking after him themselves. There's no cause for *you* to go biting his head off! After all, he *is* one of the masters. If he's misbehaved himself, you should leave the telling-off to those whose job it is. It's no business of yours (*SS* 1.20.409)." Xifeng regards Huan as lacking self-respect, because he repeatedly returns to his mother and remains influenced by her servile resentment and petty jealousies. As a concubine Aunt Zhao

---

[17] Yan Wang, "Lun Xue Yima xingxiang he dianxing yiyi," p. 90

lacks the authority and the knowledge to either educate or indulge her son and because he is ignored by Lady Wang, the young man develops a malicious and cowardly streak under the influence of his vicious and unhappy mother.

Of all the parents in the novel, Li Wan, the young widow emerges as having correctly balanced the degree of severity and closeness in her education of Jia Lan. Although fatherless since the death of his model father, Jia Zhu, Lan emerges as the complete Confucian son. Successful in the examinations and filial to his elders, untainted by the licentiousness of the other Jia family males, Jia Lan continues the tradition all had envisaged for his father. He, like Xue Pan, lost his father in infancy, but unlike Xue Pan, Lan was not indulged by an unrestrained *ci mu*. Indeed, Li Wan is the novel's epitome of self-restraint, self-sacrifice and dedication and stands as a condemnation of the other unrestrained mothers who abound in the mansions. Her restrained celibate life is described as being the result of her strict conservative upbringing. "This young widow living in the midst of luxury and self-indulgence was able to keep herself like the 'withered tree and dead ashes' of the philosopher, shutting out everything that did not concern her and attending only to the duties of serving her husband's parents and bringing up her child" who at the age of five had "already begun his schooling (*SS* 1.4.108)."

Li Wan's dedication to her son's education is repeatedly revealed. When the rest of the household is celebrating Baoyu's wedding, Li Wan is at home correcting Jia Lan's poems since, as a widow, she is excluded from attending the ceremony (*SS* 4.97.356). Li Wan's dedication and self-effacing devotion to Lan's education is thorough and she does not even welcome praise for coaching him. Lan's skills are made apparent, for example, in chapter eighty-eight when Baoyu describes Lan's progress at school and compares it favourably with Huan's. Huan was unable to complete a couplet without Baoyu's help but Lan 'managed perfectly well on his own. The Preceptor was very pleased and said he had a brilliant future ahead of him.' Grandmother Jia is rather sceptical of Baoyu's praise of Lan saying "If he really can do such things at his age, he may well distinguish himself when he grows up (*SS* 4.88.181)." Li Wan's reply to Baoyu's fulsome praise of her son is "please don't you go giving him exaggerated ideas of his achievements, Bao. He is only a child, remember. He may take you seriously and not realize that you are only trying to encourage him; and then he will become proud and conceited and *never* do well (*SS* 4.88.182)." Clearly, the boy has achieved Confucian success when he passes the imperial exams at the close of the novel. As a result of his remarkable abilities he wins a reprieve for those members of his family, the licentious Jia Zhen and Jia She, still in exile. The ultimate Confucian son, product of supreme conservative mothering makes amends for the misdeeds of his elders.

Thus we can see that the mothering of children is regarded as being of immense importance to their later development. The importance of the *yan fu*'s role in balancing the *ci mu*'s tendency towards pampering and spoiling is clear throughout. Womanly indulgence is at once indicative of their own lack of restraint as well as the men's failure to curb the women's lack of restraint. Ruined children are depicted as the inevitable result of such a combination and critical condemnation of the elder women has been the literary legacy.

CHAPTER EIGHT

MEN OF THE JIA CLAN: RESPONSIBLE OR DEGENERATE

While the Jia men, with the exception of Jia Baoyu, are not the novel's central characters their behaviour is pivotal in determining the ultimate fate of the Jia clan. Moreover, the various significances of the women in the novel discussed in previous chapters, assume their full importance only when their connection to the men is considered. In previous chapters we considered men within the context of parenting, female purity and bisexuality among other themes. Here I would like to focus specifically upon *Honglou meng*'s depiction of the men in relation to the underlying structures that inform the vision of degeneracy, licentiousness and incompetence that can broadly be said to encapsulate *Honglou meng*'s depiction of the Jia men. One paradigm of masculinity that explains the declining state of the Jia family is the conflict between responsibility and duty on the one hand, and indulgence and lack of self-restraint on the other. Men are appraised within criteria that assess their level of self-control and the extent to which they have mastered their desires. While there are external restraints imposed upon men by social and family regulations, the choice about whether or not to adhere to these remains largely one of individual male volition. The notion of the severe father (*yan fu*) who demands rigid adherence to certain codes from his sons, discussed in the previous chapter, is demonstrating his self-control as well as control over his sons within a Confucian notion of strictness and restraint.

In *Honglou meng* this tension between the self-controlled male and the man who gives free reign to his desires and whims with little regard for the social and political consequences of his actions is clear. Indeed, as will become evident through the remainder of the chapter, self-control and social responsibility are depicted as being inextricably linked throughout the novel. Those who have no control over their own desires are depicted as being unwilling to conform to duties and responsibilities expected of them by society. Those who are licentious are necessarily those who are unfilial. However, there is also a concurrent discourse whereby tensions between the roles expected of a man in his differing private and public functions are depicted as being irreconcilable for the individual involved. Duties to family order conflict with duties to the state, as do filial duties conflict with the individual's wish to adhere to broad moral or educational codes.

The Qing critic "Er zhi dao ren" believed that Cao Xueqin wrote *Honglou meng* as a way of "illuminating the depravity of the young gentlemen playboys."[1] Wang Xuexiang's critique from the same era similarly describes all of the elder men as being lacking in 'virtue' except for Jia Zheng. Similarly, the Jia men were regarded as lacking in 'talent' except for Jia Lian who was regarded as having 'a little.'[2] However, the intricate details of family life depicted in *Honglou meng* also enable us to see the conflicting needs and duties imposed upon men at various stages in their lives and careers. Within the broad theme of personal and social responsibility this chapter will unravel the complications for men as social beings in the mid-Qing world of fiction.

In the Rong mansions of the Jia clan the dichotomy between these social and moral positions is exemplified by the split between the brothers Jia Zheng and Jia She. One is lacking in virtue and devoid of a sense of responsibility, while the other aspires to virtue and regards family responsibility with the utmost gravity. Jia Zheng, although the younger of the two, has assumed responsibility in both the governmental and family spheres. However, Jia She pays little attention to anything except the potential expansion of the number of his concubines in his household and rare curios in his collections. Leng Zixing's introductory comments provide the readers' first summary of the difference between the two: "The elder son, Jia She, has inherited; but he's only a very middling sort of person and doesn't play much part in running the family. The second son though, Jia Zheng, has been mad keen on study ever since he was a lad. He is a very upright sort of person, straight as a die. He was his grandfather's favourite (*SS* 1.2.75)." Jia She inherited his father's rank at the orders of the emperor and Jia Zheng was granted an official post, that of Supernumerary Executive Officer, circumventing the arduous examination process.

The dichotomy between irresponsibility and responsibility is clearly divided between the two brothers. The generation below is similarly balanced with Jia Zheng's eldest son, Zhu described as a "Licensed Scholar at the age of fourteen (*SS* 1.2.75)" while Jia She's eldest, Lian, is described as follows: "Holds the Rank of a Sub-prefect by purchase. He's another member of the family who doesn't find responsibilities congenial. He knows his way round, though, and has a great gift of the gab, so at present he stays at home with his Uncle Zheng and helps him manage the family affairs (*SS* 1.2.83)." With the death of Jia Zhu before the commencement of the novel, the Jia clan is devoid of great prospects. There is nobody among the next generation who is suitable to as leader and Jia Zheng's efforts to curb the decline are erratic and prove futile.

In the senior Ning branch of the Jia clan there is no restraining influence at all, because the head of the household, Jia Jing, (from the same generation as Jia Zheng and Jia She), has decided to devote his life to Daoism in the

---

[1] "Er zhi dao ren", "*Honglou meng* shuo meng," p. 83.
[2] Wang Xuexiang, "*Honglou meng* zongping," rpt. in *Honglou meng juan*, p. 150.

pursuit of immortality. He leaves his family responsibilities to his son, Jia Zhen who, as Leng Zixing's comments reveal, is no self-restrained gentleman. "This Jia Zhen has got a son of his own, a lad called Jia Rong, just turned sixteen. With old Jia Jing out of the way and refusing to exercize any authority, Jia Zhen has thrown his responsibilities to the winds and given himself up to a life of pleasure. He has turned that Ningguo mansion upside down, but there is no one around who dares gainsay him (*SS* 1.2.74)."

The men of the Jia clan are then, in a manner similar to the novel's introduction to Jia Baoyu, described in terms of their position along the continuum between responsibility and unbridled indulgence in pleasure. Jia Zheng anticipated that Baoyu would develop into a wanton pleasure seeker, as I described in chapter three above, but ultimately Baoyu adopted another tangent, indeed one that was altogether removed from the mundane dichotomy between pleasure and responsibility prescribed by Leng Zixing. However, the other men of the Jia Clan are locked into this paradigm by their own ordinariness.

Education: An indicator of morality

Honglou meng invokes, within its depictions of the Jia men, the notions that the self-restraint and self-discipline expected of a responsible man is mirrored within their level of educational attainment. This level is then equated directly with personal morality. The ignorant men are necessarily the most immoral while the educated and refined are the least immoral. Once again the contrast between Jia Zheng and Jia She elucidates this point. Take for example the attitudes to learning and scholarship adopted by each man during the Mid-Autumn festival celebrations in chapter seventy-five. Jia Zheng regards scholarship seriously. Even a poem written at a family gathering should reflect the poet's breadth of learning and aspirations to excellence. Jia She, on the other hand, regards scholarship as a fashion accessory or a social lubricant to accompany drinking. When Jia Huan, Zheng's son by a concubine, writes a poem as part of the party games, Zheng remains unimpressed by his efforts and indeed proceeds to humiliate Huan for having failed to excel despite extensive schooling. Jia She takes sides with Huan on the matter saying,

> I like this poem, it's got guts in it. Boys from families like ours don't need to read themselves half blind in order to get started on a career. Provided they've read enough to show that they are better educated than the rabble and are capable of holding down a job, they can hardly fail to get on. Why waste a lot of time and energy on turning the boy into a book-worm? What I like about this poem is that it is just the sort of good amateur, not-too-brainy poem you'd *expect* a young chap of our class to write.

Jia She then bestows numerous gifts upon Huan and makes grand predictions about the boy's glorious future. Zheng replies "Whatever you think of the poem, it hardly justifies talking in this way about the boy's future (*SS* 3.75.506)."

Jia She's notion of 'good-enough' education is anathema to Jia Zheng who maintains extremely high standards for his sons and is sparing in his praise of their achievements. In chapter seventy-eight when the boys are asked to compose poems in honour of Fourth Sister Lin, analysed in chapter six above, we see Jia Zheng's attitude to his sons' efforts. The literary gentlemen praise Jia Huan and Jia Lan's efforts and Jia Zheng replies, "Come, come, they are not as good as that! They don't study hard enough, that's their trouble (*SS* 3.78.569)." Similarly, after each line composed by Baoyu, Jia Zheng makes a sarcastic or negative comment. This scene duplicates a scene earlier in the novel where Baoyu is asked to name the various scenic spots and pavilions of the newly constructed Prospect Garden by his father prior to the Imperial Visitation. While the names Baoyu recommends please Jia Zheng, he is careful not to 'ruin' the boy with praise. Instead he makes comments to the effect "You mustn't flatter the boy!...I only asked him as a joke, to see what he would say (*SS* 1.17.328)." His more effusive comments are those which put Baoyu back in his subordinate position such as "He always insists on criticizing everyone else's suggestions before he will deign to make one of his own. He is a worthless creature (*SS* 1.17.331)." Jia Zheng adopts the attitude that one can never stop aspiring to better one's scholarship and learning. Approximations and 'good efforts' are not sufficient for his sons. As was noted in the previous chapter, Li Wan was similarly reluctant to accept public praise for her son's efforts lest it spoil Jia Lan's attitude to his education. Indeed, Baoyu's casual attitude to learning was interpreted by Jia Zheng as indicating moral delinquency, since it lacked the seriousness of attitude Jia Zheng associated with proper education. Jia She on the other hand regarded elementary social poetic skills and a frivolous demeanour as being more than adequate for the needs of the aristocratic man.

Characters like Xue Pan, Jia She and Jia Rong are described in the novel as devoid of the self-control necessary to ensure a level of education beyond the elementary. Their morality is thereby implicitly questionable. Leng Zixing, as noted above, described Jia She as 'middling' and similarly Jia Rong is described in chapter seventy-five as having "no aptitude for book-learning." Neither man has any self-restraint. Rong is linked with several family scandals, the most notorious of which is his presumed affair with Xifeng. However, compared to Xue Pan, Jia She and Jia Rong are but mild examples of the discourse that directly links the educational level attained with moral restraint and moral rectitude. In chapter twenty-eight Xue Pan's gross ignorance is exposed. He is unable to compose the simple rhymes required in the drinking games which he and his class frequently indulged.

When it is time for Pan to pay his forfeit by completing a series of couplets his efforts reveal a boarish, oafish, Calibanish personality that is steeped in mindless sexual gratification. His friends are disgusted with his ignorance and uncouth versification. Xue Pan's couplets read as follows:

> The girl's upset:
> She's married to a marmoset.
> The girl looks glum:
> His dad's a baboon with a big red bum.
> The girl feels blest:
> In bridal bower she takes her rest.
> The girl's content:
> She's got a big prick up her vent (*SS* 2.28.58-59).

Xue Pan's exceptional barbarism and ignorance is reflected in the repeated severity of the scrapes in which he becomes embroiled. The beginning of the book features Xue Pan in jail for murder. He then uses his family's powerful connections to gain a reprieve. Mid-way through the novel he is beaten by Liu Xianglian for repeated insulting sexual advances and near the close of the book he is once again jailed for murder and once again wins reprieve through his family's wealth and influence. These public scandals complement the more discreet and subtle scandals of the Jia men as we will see below. Other than Jia Zheng and Baoyu, none of these characters has been sufficiently educated to restrain himself since they all lack the 'ideal' attitude to learning and self-improvement.

Adherence to legal and ritual customs

Honglou meng has set out in some considerable detail the many social and ritual conventions within aristocratic Qing society. The extent to which these elaborate social codes are adhered to by the various characters is indicative of their moral position, in the same way that educational attainment was indicative of self-restraint. However, as will become evident in the following section, an outward show of adherence to rituals does not ensure the family's continued strength and well-being.

Jia She, in particular, reveals himself to be completely devoid of basic moral codes. He is avaricious and selfish in his dealings with both his family and the outside world. Showing scant regard for the legal code, he also frequently reveals an irresponsible attitude to the various familial customs maintained in the Jia household. One of the more memorable scenes in the novel is his glee at the callous ruin of an innocent man in chapter forty-eight. Jia She is ecstatic because he has obtained the ruined man's precious and rare collection of fans, unconcerned that in the process he, albeit with the connivance of Jia Yucun, has dragged this innocent man into court, causing his financial and personal ruin (and later suicide). When Jia She boasted of his latest acquisition to his son, Jia Lian, even the rather careless Lian is disgusted. Previously Jia She had ordered Lian to buy the fans off their owner but the owner had refused to sell. Jia Yucun, a local magistrate related to the Jias, however heard of this tension and decided to fix the matter up himself by dragging the fan's owner, a certain 'Stoney,' into the courts on some trumped up charges. Yucun took the fans as court compensation and then made a present of them to Jia She. Patience tells the reader, "Mr Lian couldn't help remarking that he didn't see anything very 'competent' about ruining a man and stripping him of all he possessed for so trifling a reason. That made Sir She very angry, because of course he assumed that Mr Lian was really getting at *him* (*SS* 2.48.455-56)." For his disapproving comment Lian earned a beating from his father that was so severe he was bedridden. This beating comes only a few chapters after Zheng's beating of Baoyu and the contrast between the two brothers is striking. Zheng beats Baoyu when he is told that Baoyu molested a maid and caused her death. Jia She beats Lian when the latter dares to proffer a differing, indeed more morally upstanding, position to that taken by his father. Jia She regards this action as unfilial.

Indeed, Jia She's lack of self-restraint reaches the extent of completely disregarding, not only the lives of those outside the Jia family but also the well-being and feelings of his mother and daughter. His daughter, Yingchun, nicknamed Miss Doddy-block by the servants, is married to a callous and vicious man as settlement for Jia She's debts. Little concerned for the life she would lead married into such a family under such conditions, Jia She shows no remorse when Yingchun visits her natal family and relates the horrors of her married life. She dies within a year of marriage. Yingchun gives her Aunt and cousins a tearful description of her marital life:

> Sun Shaozu is an out-and-out libertine. Gambling, drinking and chasing after women are the only things he cares about. He has corrupted practically every maid and young woman in the house. I have protested to him about it more than once, but he only swears at me. He calls me a 'jealous little bitch.' He says that Father borrowed five thousand taels from him and spent it all, and that though he has been round time and again to ask for it, Father refuses to pay it back. Then he points his finger at me and shouts: "Don't put on the lady wife act with me, my girl! You're no better than a bought slave—payment in kind for the five thousand taels your old man owes me—and if you're not very careful I shall give you a good beating and send you to sleep with the maids (*SS* 3.80.611)."

Lady Wang explains that Jia Zheng had tried unsuccessfully to persuade She against the marriage. "I remember your Uncle Zheng speaking very strongly against the marriage to your father, but your father was so set on it, he wouldn't listen. It's a bad business (*SS* 3.80.611)." Yingchun's death is clearly a result of Jia She's selfishness just as is Faithful's suicide later on in the novel.

When Jia She seeks to expand the ranks of his concubines he decides that Faithful, his mother's principle and trusted maid, would be a desirable asset.

During the negotiation process, which is kept secret from Grandmother Jia until the very end, Jia She reveals that he has little concern for his mother's well-being and happiness. Everyone in the mansions is aware of the extent to which she relies upon Faithful, but Jia She is blinded by lust. Jia She contacts Faithful's family regarding the match but negotiations are halted by Faithful's expression of disgust at the idea of marriage to Jia She. Faithful staunchly rejects the idea of leaving Lady Jia. Jia She's servant relays his employer's position to Faithful's family as follows:

> No doubt she [Faithful] thinks him [Jia She] too old for her and has set her heart on one of the younger ones—Baoyu, probably, or my son Lian. Tell her, if she has, the sooner she abandons hope in *that* direction the better, because if *I* can't have her, she may be very sure that no one else in this family will dare to. That's one thing. And here's another. She may think that because she's Lady Jia's favourite, she can look forward to marrying outside one day and becoming someone's regular wife. Well if so, just let her get this firmly into her mind: whoever or wherever she marries, she needn't think she will ever escape me. If she dies or is prepared to live all her life an old maid, I might admit myself beaten; but otherwise, never (*SS* 2.46.422).

His threats are clearly taken seriously by Faithful for she commits suicide as soon as Grandmother Jia is dead, consciously realizing her vow to escape Jia She's clutches. The ruthless lust for control and possession revealed in the incident with the fans is echoed here in Jia She's bullying treatment of Faithful.

When Grandmother Jia heard of Jia She's plan to take Faithful as a concubine she is incensed. Xifeng, Lady Wang and Jia Lian had all seen the foolish nature of Jia She's choice but he refused to listen and enlisted his equally foolish wife, Lady Xing, to help. Jia Lian's reluctance to support his father in his silly venture caused him to face another rebuke. Lian is accused of being unfilial to his father. Lian says "This is all Father's doing. Now *we* have to face the consequences." "Unfilial wretch!' said Lady Xing. "Some people would *die* for their fathers, but *you*—a few harmless words and you are already whining and complaining. What's the matter with you? (*SS* 2.47.436)." Clearly, *Honglou meng* has established the dilemma men faced within the Qing social structure. If they had debauched fathers and chose not to support their parent's illegal and immoral acts then they themselves stand accused of unfilial acts. Men lower down the family hierarchy, like Jia Lian, suffer the whims of those above.

Jia Zhen and Jia Rong, from the Ning side, are involved in equally scandalous and illegal acts. We learnt from the Zhiyanzhai commentary that Jia Zhen has been involved in an incestuous relationship with his daughter-in-law, Qin Keqing. The shame and fear of discovery causes her to commit suicide. After her death Zhen goes to enormous lengths to organize a grand and expensive funeral. He uses an exquisite and expensive timber for the coffin which "Jia Zheng doubted the propriety of using such material for the burial of a person not of royal blood...but Cousin Zhen refused to listen (*SS* 1.13.261)." This example is at once indicative of Zhen's guilty conscience as it is of Jia Zheng's preoccupation with propriety and correct form.

Under Zhen's careful eye Keqing's funeral is one of exceptional splendour but after the death of his father, Jia Jing, Zhen is less enthusiastic about mourning rituals. Before the end of the official mourning period Zhen had arranged for illegal gambling parties to be held. In chapter seventy-five we read that Zhen was unable to adhere to the ban on recreation during the "seemingly interminable period of mourning." Under the guise of holding archery competitions, which were permitted, Zhen manages to ensure a return to his normal patterns of gambling and drinking.

> But it was not of course in the archery that Cousin Zhen was interested. On the grounds that resting the muscles was an important part of one's training, he was soon advocating a little cards or dice in the evenings as a means of relaxation. At first they played only for drinks, but soon they were playing more and more for money; the time spent on gaming gradually encroached on the time devoted to archery; betting became more open; and finally, with the formal opening of a 'bank' some three or four months previously, regular, organized gambling for heavy stakes had become a daily routine (*SS* 3.75.492).

The problem for Jia Zheng, upholder of proper rites and rituals, was that the servants, who profited from the tips and bribes that came their way, connived with the gentlemen participating in this deception to ensure that the true account of events did not ever become public knowledge. So Zheng and She spoke approvingly of the archery saying "Since Rong obviously has no aptitude for book-learning, Cousin Zhen does right to encourage him in the martial arts. The boy does, after all, hold a military commission (*SS* 3.75.492)." They then instructed that Baoyu, Jia Huan, Jia Lan and Jia Cong participate in these 'archery' lessons. So, Zheng implicates his own sons in the illegal act of gambling during an official mourning period.

Jia Zhen's relationship with Jia Rong is not entirely that of the father exploiting and leading his son astray. There are clear divisions in power between the two that are maintained at all times. For example, in chapter twenty-nine when the ladies journey to a Daoist temple for a day trip Jia Zhen catches Rong sitting in the cool while he is roasting in the heat.

> "Look at him!," said Cousin Zhen irately. "Enjoying himself in the cool while I am roasting down here! Spit at him, someone." Long familiarity with Cousin Zhen's temper had taught the boys that he would brook no opposition when roused. One of them obediently stepped forward and spat in Jia Rong's face; then, as Cousin Zhen continued to glare at him, he rebuked Jia Rong for presuming to be cool while his father was still sweating outside in the sun. Jia Rong was obliged to stand with his arms hanging submissively at his sides throughout this public humiliation, not daring to utter a word (*SS* 2.29.74).

Once again this strictness with a son is accepted as part of the paternal duty and right. However, the reasons causing fathers to exercize this power in the novel have vastly different inspirations as we saw in the example of Jia Lian's beating (for daring to disagree), and Jia Baoyu's beating (for the assumed violation of a maid). Jia Rong, in a fashion similar to Jia Lian, suffers his licentious father's venom. Ideals of paternal strictness and severity intended to further educate sons, are degraded and serve to reveal the father's inability to show restraint.

As was evident in Jia Lian's dealings with the You Sisters, he is similarly unconcerned about issues of legality and propriety. The two sisters were rumoured to be Jia Zhen's 'playthings' for a while and when Lian met the elder of the two, You Erjie, his lust was aroused. He then spent much of his time plotting ways to seduce her. Jia Jing's funeral provided the perfect excuse to escape Xifeng's jealous eyes. With a harebrained scheme dreamed up by Jia Rong, Jia Lian decides to marry You Erjie in secret. The narrator warns the reader of the folly of this path, emphasizing its illegal and immoral nature.

> There is an old saying 'Desire maketh the wise man a fool.' Jia Lian was so intoxicated by his desire for Erjie that Jia Rong's idiotic plan struck him as unassailable. The fact that he was in mourning, the fact that a secret marriage of the kind he was contemplating was bigamous and illegal, the fact that he had an extremely strict father and an exceptionally jealous wife—all those things which ought to have given him pause were lightly brushed aside (*SS* 3.64.266).

It also becomes obvious that Rong hit upon the plan of a secret marriage and a separate household so that he would have "unlimited opportunities for larks with her [You Erjie] whenever Jia Lian was away (*SS* 3.64.266)." Both father and son of the Ning mansions, Jia Zhen and Jia Rong, then are engaged in the seduction of the You sisters and Jia Lian rather foolishly joins the same illegal and immoral game led by his lack of restraint.

Empty attention to propriety

The irresponsible and illegal behaviour of the Jia men is the main cause of the family's decline and within this group the sole upholder of the moral and righteous path is Jia Zheng. However, Jia Zheng is also proven to be inadequate for the required task. Ultimately, Jia Zheng emerges as a character who is a stickler for form lacking in the substance which propriety requires for the successful protection of the clan's long-term interests.

The others see him as being a rather staid, strict and unimaginative person for when he is asked to tell a joke by Grandmother Jia at the Mid-Autumn festival the younger clan members, "to whom the notion of Jia Zheng telling a joke was in itself unbelievably funny (*SS* 3.75.502)" broke out in laughter before he had begun. Grandmother Jia threatens to punish him if he does not make her laugh. Next it is Baoyu's turn to tell a joke. He is extremely unhappy about his father's presence and fears that telling a joke would confirm his father's opinion that he is given to excessive frivolity. So he asks for an alternative penalty and his father then asks him to write a poem on the understanding that, if it is not up to standard, Jia Zheng would punish him. So the hierarchy is established; Grandmother Jia over Jia Zheng, and Jia Zheng over Baoyu.

Jia Zheng is consistently described as rigidly adhering to rules and rituals. In chapter thirty-seven we read of Jia Zheng's attention to conventions of departure when he is on the point of leaving to take up his new post as Commissioner for Education in one of the Provinces. His parting is described in intricate detail whereas none of the many other departures that occur in the novel are described in such detail. Jia Zheng first pays his respects to his ancestors in the family shrine, then farewells his mother and finally is accompanied as far as the first post-stage by Baoyu and the other men of the family. His tenure as Education Commissioner reveals Jia Zheng to be a man of mediocre talent with little vision or skill in leadership. It is only through good-fortune that he manages to avoid major disgrace while in his posting. His return in chapter seventy-one is similarly ceremonious and proceeds according to correct ritual. Although keen to see his family, Jia Zheng knows that he must first "report on his commission," but he nevertheless sends a message inquiring after his mother's health to the Jia mansions while continuing on his way to the Ministry. His feelings are described as follows:

> Jia Zheng was beginning to age now, and the worries and responsibilities of office had taken their toll of his health. It was good to be back after so long an absence from those nearest and dearest to him; he was determined to relax and enjoy himself to the utmost, refused even to think about money matters or domestic responsibilities, and spent all his time reading, or, when he felt in need of company, drinking and playing Go with his literary gentlemen (*SS* 3.71.394).

It becomes clear that Jia Zheng was not capable of balancing responsibilities in both the public and private spheres even though, as Grandmother Jia comments during the Mid-Autumn feast, the Jia clan was actually diminishing in size.

So we see Jia Zheng's dilemma when his clan is becoming increasingly depraved and unruly.

> It was not that Jia Zheng was a slack disciplinarian, incapable of keeping his house in order; but the clan was so numerous that he simply could not keep an eye on everyone at once.... Besides Jia Zheng was kept busy with public and private business of his own and, being by nature a quiet, retiring man who attached little importance to mundane affairs, tended to use whatever leisure time he had for reading and playing Go.

So in this situation, Xue Pan, who was already a known criminal escaping from a murder scandal, is described as becoming "ten times worse under their [the Jia men's] expert guidance (*SS* 1.4.123)." As the most morally upright male member of the clan, Jia Zheng feels it his duty to serve as a restraining influence. However, his abilities are limited and ultimately he is reduced to performing empty rituals and ineffectually invoking moral codes to an unresponsive clan.

Jia Zheng constantly struggles with his responsibilities as we see in his comments on hearing that Golden had thrown herself in the well. "I suppose it is because I have been too neglectful of household matters during these last few years. Those in charge have felt encouraged to abuse their authority, until finally an appalling thing like this can happen (*SS* 2.33.145)." So, while Jia Zheng is aware that he is failing in his duties as moral leader of the Rong mansions he appears ineffectual and takes no identifiable counter-measures. Jia Zheng's wishes are curtailed by his mother's dominance of the household and his junior position in the clan hierarchy relative to Jia Zhen. Jia Zheng's skills and talents are of an ordinary nature and clearly do not enable him to mediate these barriers of status and rank.

At the close of the novel, in chapter one hundred and seven, the rule of law finally catches up with the licentious Jia men. Jia She's part in ruining Stoney, the fan owner, leads to She's banishment to Mongolia. Jia Zhen's part in the seduction, betrothal and death of the You sisters and the disregard for normal process in reporting the death of You Sanjie leads to his banishment to the maritime frontier. These two delinquent fathers are then held responsible for the misdemeanours of their sons. Both Jia She and Jia Zhen are stripped of their hereditary titles and ordered to leave almost immediately that the order was issued. Jia Zheng's position remains comparatively secure and, although he apologizes for his neglect of the family affairs, the edict returns "Jia Zheng has for many years held provincial posts in which he has served conscientiously and prudently, and he is absolved from the consequences of his failure to govern his household correctly (*SS* 5.107.142)."

Thus Zheng's ritualistic and often incompetent performance of his official duties has saved him from banishment but it has, nevertheless, been entirely ineffectual in preventing his family from declining. Jia Zheng's talents are best typified by his statement after the Imperial raid, "I have had a word with various friends, and am confident they will do whatever they can." This comment is described by the narrator as being "characteristically ineffectual (*SS* 5.106.133)." For the Jia men, then, the combination of complete lack of self-restraint and mimicking of empty social rites combines to cause the family decline. As irresponsible degenerates they have presided over their own destruction. Moral leadership over the men was absent in the Jia clan. Those who held the positions of authority to exercize control over clan affairs, Jia Jing and Jia Zhen, were reluctant and licentious. Jia Zheng aspired to conservative clan management but was of mediocre talent and this combination ensured the destruction of the clan. *Honglou meng*, then, reveals a great deal about the constraints of masculinity and the restrictions on actions within male hierarchies of Chinese society in the Qing aristocracy. The novel is thus equally as insightful on men and masculinity as it is on the position of women in Qing China.

CHAPTER NINE

HONGXUE AFTER 1949 AND GENDER EQUALITY

As has become evident from the preceding discussion, the assertion that *Honglou meng*, China's great Qing 'novel of manners,' is concerned about the problems women faced in 'feudal' China is commonplace among the *Hongxue* scholars of the PRC more so than among critics from other periods in the last two hundred years.[1] The consistency with which this notion is propounded and the contradictory, cursory nature of the arguments used in this relatively new *Hongxue* casts doubt upon the authenticity of *Hongxue* scholars' claims to be concerned about gender or sexual equality.[2] Indeed, here in the conclusion of this book, I intend to reveal that canonization of the novel, and thereby the perpetuation of the interests of PRC *Hongxue* scholars, is the greater concern, and not women's rights.[3] Moreover, because the current academic scene in China encourages the publication of copious repetitive articles rather than originality, this rather narrow view of the significance of the novel is perpetuated rather than critically challenged. By canonization I mean the continued assurance that the novel will maintain its high profile through a constant process of correcting, reconstructing and revalorizing the text. The task of the PRC *Hongxue* critic, thereby, has been to ensure that *Honglou meng* does not suffer the same ignominious fate as had such Confucian texts as *The Mean* after the Communist Party's victory in 1949.

The purported concern for sexual equality, it will emerge, is little more than a superficial homily recited to grant the book or article a semblance of 'political correctness.' Moreover, implicit in the critics' discourse of sexual equality are values which perpetuate the oppression of women such as the eulogizing of purity, innocence, vulnerability and passivity. The discourse of sexual equality is however an exceptionally flexible signifier of political correctness and one that has become particularly useful in the post 1979 era of *Hongxue* when 'class analysis' has reduced credibility.

---

[1] I have used the term 'feudal' throughout this chapter in the sense that it is commonly used in the PRC today. This term has a loose relationship to modes of production and is generally used to refer to the values of the social system that existed in pre Socialist China in a pejorative manner.

[2] The Chinese term for sexual equality is literally 'male female equal status'—*nan nü pingdeng*.

[3] My concern in this chapter is not to critique *Honglou meng* but rather to critique the critiques of *Honglou meng*—that is to write a meta-critique.

Of paramount importance to my approach is the historicity of critical practice. The value of a piece of writing is regarded as being transient and moreover, linked specifically to critical practice. Thereby, while *Honglou meng* is part of the literary canon of today in the PRC, there is no guarantee that it will continue to be so highly prized in a hundred year's time. The criteria for selecting, processing and correcting texts, that has become known as literary criticism, are always historically variable and as such one cannot talk of the immutable value of *Honglou meng* to Chinese culture. The appearance of the retention of its literary worth over the last hundred years is related more to the flexibility and ambiguity of the novel, that allows the 'same' text to be re-evaluated (and thereby 'rewritten') in the light of contemporary concerns, than it is to the intrinsic and unchanging essential value of the novel. Terry Eagleton has summarized this understanding of literary criticism as "The history of a piece of writing is the history of its functions—of the varied, often conflicting ways in which it is constructed, granted a home, valorized, devalorized, put to use, within the different ideological systems its inhabits. And since the 'same' text may inhabit contradictory systems, either sequentially or simultaneously, it is clear that its career can be rather fraught."[4] Indeed the various interpretations of *Honglou meng* since its appearance attest to the importance of recognizing the historicity of critical practice. As we saw in chapter two above, *Honglou meng* has been valorized as a licentious, frivolous text, a Buddhist treatise on the folly of desire, a historical analogy and more recently canonized as a great realist text. The history of *Honglou meng* reveals the firm material grounding of a piece of writing, including literary criticism.

Origins 'Hongxue's' discourse of sexual equality

What then are the features that are deemed as valuable in the PRC that have been invoked by critics to ensure a place for *Honglou meng* in the great literary canon? Mao Zedong's "Talks at the Yan'an Conference on Literature and Art" clearly explain the criteria that came to influence *Hongxue* in the 1954 "Criticize Yu Pingbo campaign," and to a diminishing but not insignificant extent through to the current times.[5] Mao's conception of literary work, including literary criticism, was that it had a definite responsibility

---

[4] Terry Eagleton, "Literature and Politics now," p. 66.

[5] Essentially the "Yu Pingbo campaign" served to educate literary intellectuals in the new Maoist literary techniques and to establish a break with the pre-revolutionary styles of criticism. 1954 and 1920 are regarded as the two major junctures in the history of *Hongxue*—the former for establishing Maoist methodology and the later for establishing New *Hongxue* methodology. Guo Yushi, *Honglou yanjiu xiaoshi xugao*, p. 317. See the following works for a discussion of the 1954 campaign and its literary/political ramifications. Lucien Miller, *Masks of Fiction*; Joey Bonner, "Yü P'ing-po and the Literary Dimensions of the Controversy over *Hung lou meng*," *The China Quarterly*, No. 67, (1976), pp. 546-81; Jerome B. Grieder, "The Communist Critique of *Hung lou meng*," *Papers on China*, No. 10 (October, 1956), pp. 142-68.

to aid in the transformation of society. All literary work should serve the masses. For those critics dealing with a novel already written the task was reconstructing the old texts so that they became useful to the development of socialism. "We do not by any means refuse to use the old forms [of literature and art] of the feudal class and the bourgeoisie, but in our hands these old forms are reconstructed and filled with new content so that they also become revolutionary and serve the people."[6] Inheriting the intellectual tradition of which *Honglou meng* was a significant part thereby became a matter of providing a reading of the text that was ideologically correct and useful to the Chinese Communist Party and the masses. Thus for literary critics of the post 1949 era, *Hongxue* assumed the social function of re-appraising the past culture to help create a new socialist culture. This was a prerequisite for membership of the literary canon.

The ideologically correct reading of *Honglou meng* became the understanding that the novel was a realist work that revealed the evils of the feudal society and, by implication, the virtues of the present and the perceived future.[7] Typicality was the dominant feature of characterization in realist works. A typical character embodies historical forces and in some cases was reduced to be little more than a symbol of a particular class. In this respect a work could perform the function of being socially useful by providing, for example, positive role models or examples of negative behaviour, either simultaneously or consecutively.

As a realist text, the novel's perceived anti-feudal sentiment was constructed in a number of ways including the depiction of the treatment of servants, family relationships and the connections between the aristocracy and the Emperor. Another of these important signifiers, and the one of concern to this book, was the position of women in Imperial China. In the depiction of the tragic lives and fates of the women, and the young female protagonists called the Twelve Beauties in particular, *Honglou meng* was read as showing the author's and the novel's opposition to old customs regarding women. The 'women problem' thereby became an important signifier of the author's and the realist novel's political correctness and literary worth.

---

6   Mao Zedong, "Talks at the Yan'an Conference on Literature and Art," in *Mao Zedong's "Talks at the Yan'an Conference on Literature and Art:" A Translation of the 1943 Text With Commentary*, ed. and trans. Bonnie S. McDougall (Ann Arbor: Center for Chinese Studies, University of Michigan, 1980), p. 65.

7   Realist literary theory regards literature as being able to reveal the broad, underlying social movements within the depiction of tangible life events. In the *Hongxue* world, realism as a creative style and a critical tool, was constructed against naturalism which had been advocated by the New *Hongxue* scholars. The latter purported to objectively and scientifically depict actual events and, in contrast, realism purported to be able to discover or express the deeper social movements within narrative discourse, such as class struggle and the decline of feudalism into capitalism. Raymond Williams, *Keywords* (1976; rpt. London: Fontana, 1988), p. 217 and p. 261.

The broad social effects of *Honglou meng*'s high status as a socially useful, literary masterpiece has been the development of a veritable *Honglou
meng* industry. This includes the development of tele-movies, museums,
souvenirs and audio-cassettes of music from the movie. In the academic
world the post 1949 canonization of *Honglou meng* has been evidenced by
the production of three major journals devoted solely to *Hongxue*, two insti-
tutes in Beijing devoted to its study and regional official *Hongxue* groups
throughout China. Each year the *Wenxue nianjian* (Literature Year Book)
devotes a special section of several pages long in its classical literature seg-
ment to developments in *Hongxue*. This is an honour not afforded any other
classical novel.[8]

In the analyses of the novel, this style of socially responsible critical
practice necessarily came to focus upon the suffering of women under the
feudal system. Yu Pingbo's essay "On the depiction of the 'Twelve
Beauties' in *Honglou meng*" published in 1963 revealed this new emphasis
towards the issue of the treatment of women under feudalism. Yu wrote that
Baoyu's statements such as "Girls are made of water and boys are made of
mud (*SS* 1.2.76)" are evidence of his reversal of the discourse that favoured
men over women and that for a member of the feudal aristocratic class of the
eighteenth century to express such sentiments is indeed a rare occurrence.[9]
Previously his analysis had declared that the novel was a Buddhist text revealing the folly of human desire. Within the new matrix all the characters
in the novel were judged according to their position on the 'feudal' prescriptions of morality for women. Thus Baochai's place as a negative character is
confirmed by her propounding of the dictums on women's education to
Daiyu in chapter sixty-four. Similarly, You Sanjie's place as a rebellious
positive character is confirmed by her humiliation of the lecherous Jia Zhen
and Jia Lian in chapter sixty-five.

The origins of the discourse of sexual equality lie then in the Maoist prescriptions that literature and literary criticism be able to perform a positive
educational function and participate in the development of a new socialist
China rather than a specific concern with the position of women. Having
drawn *Honglou meng* into sexual politics of its own volition, *Hongxue* deserves to be examined within such a realm. My criticism is not that PRC

---

[8] In 1985 a lengthy television series of the novel was released for viewing and this generated a considerable amount of interest in the novel and its characters among the wider
population. The romance between Baoyu and Daiyu as portrayed on the series so captured
the imagination of viewers that speculation abounded about an off-screen romance between
the two. The garden reconstructed for the filming, in the form of Prospect Garden was
opened to the public and is now a popular tourist location. Within its walls is a museum of
Honglou meng paraphernalia and a small shop where momentos can be purchased. The three
journals mentioned above are the Academy of Social Sciences' *Honglou meng yanjiu jikan*,
the Beijing Arts Academy's *Honglou meng xuekan* and the Guiyang branch of the *Honglou
meng* association's *Honglou*.

9 Yu Pingbo, "*Honglou meng* zhong guanyu 'Shier chai' de miaoxie," p. 990.

critics have failed to supply a 'correct feminist' reading of *Honglou meng*, but rather that they have appropriated the issues of women's oppression without concern for women. Here I will reveal how critics have appropriated sexual politics and reveal the ends such appropriation serves. It is, moreover, important to unravel the manner in which the cause of sexual equality has been absorbed by the state socialism of China. *Hongxue*'s appropriation of sexual equality is in this respect a case study of the general strategic 'use' of women's issues in socialist China.

Interaction between sex and class

The eclectic nature of the discourse of sexual equality's theoretical foundation is evident from the early days of *Hongxue*'s interaction with Maoist literary precepts. Contradictions between class and gender as dual systems of oppression were rarely clearly explicated and when they were class was usually upheld as being the predominant category of oppression. Jiang Hesen's work *Honglou meng lungao* published in 1959 is an example of the problematic nature of the lack of rigorous theorizing of the connection between gender and class. *Honglou meng lungao* includes a section on characters' thinking and was written in a relatively accessible style that made it a 'popular' academic work. Jiang's discussion of Wang Xifeng draws out the increased importance of the issue of the position of women in feudal society and reveals how the new socialist order saw Xifeng as typical of the oppressive feudalists. The conceptual contradictions between women as the oppressed sex and aristocratic women as the oppressing class are vital in the analyses of Xifeng. For example, Jiang says of Xifeng, "The oppression and suffering of women in feudal society does not appear to have affected Xifeng." To Jiang, and the vast majority of critics, Xifeng was a feudal oppressor and not a suffering victim. Jiang then attempts to rationalize the contradiction in his analysis whereby Xifeng is placed on the side of the feudalists when much of her behaviour is immoral by feudal standards of femininity. Jiang states that the feudal classes embraced whatever was to their profit and morality was upheld only in so far as this profit was protected.[10] Xifeng was then able to be placed on the side of the feudalists despite her personal failing to adopt the feudal virtues for women. The embracing of these very virtues had been, ironically, one of the prime reasons given for Baochai's categorization as a 'feudal/negative character.'

After the "downfall of the Gang of Four" class analysis was tainted with extreme radicalism and anti-intellectualism. Indeed, most of the post 1979 *Hongxue*, the period which is the prime focus of this current chapter, is written consciously in reaction against the radical critiques of the 1973-74

---

10 Jiang Hesen, *Honglou meng lungao* (Outline of *Honglou meng*) (1959; rpt. Beijing: Renmin wenxue chubanshe, 1981), pp. 148-49.

Honglou meng campaign.[11] Nevertheless, prescriptions that literature be socially responsible remained in comments by Deng Xiaoping to the Fourth Congress of Writers and Artists in 1979. Here, Deng reasserted the importance of Maoist literary theory. "We must adhere to Comrade Mao Zedong's principle that art and literature should serve the people, particularly the worker-peasant-soldier masses and follow his policies of... 'weeding out the old to bring forth the new,' and 'making foreign and ancient things serve China'."[12] However, unlike Mao, Deng asserts that "the sole criterion for deciding the correctness of all work should be whether that work is helpful or harmful to the accomplishment of the Four Modernizations... We must criticize the ideas of the exploiting classes, the influence of conservatism, and the narrow-minded small producer mentality, as well as anarchism, extreme individualism, and bureaucracy."[13] While achieving all of these, writers and artists are assured that "Writers and artists must have the freedom to choose their subject matter and method of presentation based upon artistic practice and exploration."[14] At the same conference Zhou Yang declared that "A writer should be free to write what he wants in any way he wants."[15]

Here, in the 1980s and 1990s search for a balance between correctness and freedom, the discourse of sexual equality has proved itself to be an immensely useful literary tool.[16] Signifying a correct ideological position it is simultaneously free from the destabilizing, anti-intellectual effects of the ultimately correct, but anathematized class analysis. However, in the *Hongxue* world none of the tension between 'freedom' and 'correctness' generated an incisive explication of the mechanisms that perpetuate sexual inequality.

---

[11] This campaign was a smaller part of the anti-Confucius campaign and has been regarded by analysts as a failure. However, it generated a considerable body of radical *Hongxue* written by writing groups and worker study groups. See Tien-wei Wu's discussion in *Lin Biao and the Gang of Four: Contra-Confucianism in Historical and Intellectual Perspective* (Carbondale: Southern Illinois University Press, 1983), p. 152. For examples of the radical *Hongxue* produced during this time see Wang Xiaoqi and Wang Xiaopang, "Ba boxue zhidu yongyuan maizang—du *Honglou meng* di wushisan hui" (Bury the oppressive system forever—reading chapter fifty-three of *Honglou meng*) *Guangming ribao*, 8.7.1975; Hong Guangsi, "*Honglou meng* shi yi bu xie jieji douzhang de shu" (*Honglou meng* is a book about class struggle), *Beijing ribao* (Beijing daily), 2.11.1973; Zhonggong Jiaozuo shi wei xuanzhuan bu (ed.) (Chinese communist party's Jiaozuo city propaganda committee), *Ping "Honglou meng"* (A critique of *Honglou meng*) (Zhengzhou: Henan renmin chubanshe, 1976).

[12] Deng Xiaoping, "Congratulatory Message to the Fourth Congress of Chinese Writers and Artists," trans. George Cheng, in *Chinese Literature for the 1980s: The Fourth Congress of Writers and Artists*, ed. Howard Goldblatt (Armonk: M.E. Sharpe, 1982), p. 10.

[13] Deng Xiaoping, "Congratulatory Message to the Fourth Congress," p. 9

[14] Deng Xiaoping, "Congratulatory Message to the Fourth Congress," pp. 13-14.

[15] Zhou Yang, "Inherit the Past and Usher In the Future," trans. Betty Ting in *Chinese Literature for the 1980s: The Fourth Congress of Writers and Artists*, p. 30.

[16] Merle Goldman has noted the continuation of this tension between professed support for artistic freedom and the simultaneous demands for political and social responsibility up to the Congress of the Chinese Writers Association of December 1984 and January 1985. Merle Goldman, "The Zigs and Zags in the Treatment of Intellectuals," *The China Quarterly*, No. 102 (1985), pp. 709-15.

Rather, sexual equality simply became a tool for dismantling the strictures intellectuals felt class analysis had placed upon *Hongxue*.

Maoist demands that a character be either negative or positive left little room for character analysis which sought to unravel contradictions in characters' personalities. Just as demands that critics adhere to the view that *Honglou meng* was documenting the inevitable decline of the decadent and rotten feudal culture to pave the way for a new socialist China left no space for the eulogies to the splendour and grander of late Imperial Chinese elite culture so intricately documented in the novel. The process of dismantling these and other such strictures was carried out surreptitiously and often under the 'politically correct' banner of 'sexual equality' so as not to jeopardize the ultimate security of *Honglou meng*'s place in the Communist canon. Women, it seems were simply to become tools of the elite *Hongxue* scholars in their bid to expand the content of 'correct' *Hongxue* in the Dengist years of comparative liberalism.

Comparing social systems

Invoking the horrors of the treatment of women in feudal China necessarily implied a positive comparison of the socialist present with the feudal past. For example Guan Hua's 1986 *Renmin ribao* article titled "Cao Xueqin and Women" cited in the introduction "makes the past serve the present" on this issue and is representative of the general position of *Hongxue* scholars that the present socialist system is unproblematically providing women with equality of opportunity and freedom from oppression.[17] In *Hongxue*'s critique of feudal China's treatment of women, socialist China is the realization of the ideal state for women. Within this reading *Honglou meng* thereby serves to reveal the wonders of the current situation with regards to the position of women.

The lyricism of *Hongxue*'s laments to life for women in feudal China are expansive. In a 1985 critique of Li Wan, the young widow, Li Dejun wrote that Cao Xueqin wrote of the tragedies of the girls of the 'Department of Ill-fated Fair'[18] with tears in his eyes because "whether they were young girls and mothers of the aristocratic classes or maids and hand maidens from the slave class, each had a tragic end,... they were all innocent objects of sacrifice under the butcher's knife of feudal ethics." Among these innocent victims of feudal thought is the character of Li Wan who is described as an "outstanding model of tragedy."[19] Clearly, the likening of the experiences of

---

[17] Guan Hua, "Cao Xueqin he nüxing."

[18] The women in the 'Department of Ill-fate Fair' (*baoming ce*) are those whose fate Baoyu previewed in his visit to the Land of Illusion in chapter five. The Twelve Beauties form a subset of this larger group.

[19] Li Dejun, "Li Wan xingxiang jianlun" (A brief discussion of Li Wan's image), *Jining shizhuan xuebao* (Jining teachers' training college journal), No. 2 (1984), pp. 60-65, rpt. in *RD*, No. 4 (1984), p. 95. This article was republished in 1985 under a different name and ar-

aristocratic women with women of the slave class would have been impossible a decade earlier when class analysis divided both male and female characters' experiences strictly along class lines. In the Deng years such strictures are relinquished and critics are able to justify *Honglou meng*'s worth to socialist China by simply proving the evils of the feudal past through the suffering of women regardless of class.[20]

Li Dejun regards Cao's vision of chaste widowhood, in particular, and feudal ethics in general, to be one of loathing and distaste. Through the character of Li Wan, who is the literary image of someone destroyed by Cheng-Zhu ethics, Cao Xueqin was making an indignant denunciation and a strong protest against such practices, according to Li. The foundation of these customs is that after her husband's death she must close off her spirit and maintain a composure of complete apathy, represented by the four character expression "withered tree and dead ashes" (*gaomu sihui*).[21] "'The three obediences and the four virtues,' 'chastity' and 'martyrdom' and this sort of feudal dogma, were just like venomous snakes that fiercely and maliciously engulfed the spirit of many women and ruthlessly deprived millions and millions of women of their lives!"[22]

---

ticle title see Li Yin, "Mei de huimie—Li Wan xingxiang jianlun" (The destruction of beauty—a brief discussion of the image of Li Wan), *Honglou meng xuekan*, No. 1 (1985), pp. 139-50.

[20] Contrast Li's disregard for class with Guo Yushi's critique written in 1964 and published in 1979. "On the one hand *Honglou meng* ... has etched portrait after portrait of the tragedy of young girls oppressed and engulfed, stating clearly that feudal rites, the feudal marriage system, and feudal society treats these women, regardless of class status or difference in thinking, in a heartless manner; on the other hand Cao Xueqin has not been able to show, as we would today in a society that recognizes [the importance of] class, that the problem of women is at its foundation a problem of class oppression." Moreover Guo warns his audience against reading the message that "life is but a dream" into the tragedy of love and the tragedy of women depicted by Cao Xueqin as had the earlier *Hongxue* scholars, Yu Pingbo and Wang Guowei. Guo Yushi, *"Honglou meng" wenti pinglun ji* (A collection of critiques on questions arising from *Honglou meng*) (Shanghai: Guji chubanshe, 1981), pp. 223-26.

[21] This phrase is used in the novel to describe Li Wan as well (*SS* 1.4.108) and has its origins in the *Zhuangzi* in the essay "The Equality of Things." Wing-tsit Chan translates the sentence from which the expression has come as "The body may be allowed to be like dry wood but should the mind be allowed to be like dead ashes?" and goes on to explain that from the *Zhuangzi* "dry wood and dead ashes have become common idioms in Chinese literature and philosophy. They represent the persistent questions whether man is a spirit and whether the mind is alert." Wing-tsit Chan, ed., trans., *A Source Book in Chinese Philosophy* (1963; rpt. Princeton: Princeton University Press, 1973), pp. 179-80. An interpretation of the phrase along less philosophical lines is that it is an allusion to someone without the slightest vitality, suffering extreme depression or someone who is indifferent and emotionless. Wang Li, ed., *Zhongguo chengyu da cidian* (Shanghai: Shanghai cishu chubanshe, 1987), p. 428.

[22] The three obediences are to father before marriage, to husband after marriage, and to son after the death of the husband. The four virtues are morality, proper speech, modest manner and diligent work. Beijing waiguoyu xueyuan Yingwen xi (Beijing foreign languages institute English department), *Han Ying cidian* (A Chinese-English Dictionary) (Beijing: Shangwuyin shuguan, 1985), p. 585. Li Dejun, "Li Wan xingxiang jianlun," p. 95.

Just as *Honglou meng*'s portrayal of chaste widowhood was regarded as being evidence of the author's abhorrence of feudal ethics so were the incorporation of descriptions of parentally arranged marriage and polygamy. In an article first written in 1964 and then amended for publication in 1979, Guo Yushi, asserted the notion that "The depiction of love in *Honglou meng* can not be separated from the author's attitudes to women." The attitude is one of deep sympathy for women's suffering under an oppressive system.[23] Jiang Hesen's 1979 *Honglou meng gaishuo* similarly wrote of the importance of love to *Honglou meng*'s social value. "If freedom in love and self determination in marriage are permitted then the string of feudal practices such as [the morality of] 'honouring men and denigrating women,' the polygamous marriage system, and the clan structures etc. would all be destroyed."[24]

Discussion surrounding the death of Yingchun through maltreatment after only a year of marriage to Sun Shaozu is typical. In a 1989 chapter on Cao's advocacy of freedom in love and marriage, Huang Lixin reiterates the interpretation that Yingchun's life reveals the evils of the feudal marriage system. Huang states that Yingchun's marriage to the so called "Zhongshan wolf" is the event in the novel which reveals Cao's opposition to the practice of following the dictates of one's parents (*fu mu zhi ming*) in all matters of marriage. Being the daughter of a long deceased concubine Yingchun's position is more vulnerable than most because she lacks the concern of a birth mother and receives no attention from Lady Xing either. This leaves her entirely in the hands of Jia She who dictates a marriage that serves himself and his lecherous, wanton lifestyle. Yingchun is powerless to object to Jia She's choice because of the dictum that one should follow the orders of one's parents that underpins the entire feudal marriage system.[25]

The critiques which cite the tragedy for women of parentally arranged marriages most consistently are those that deal with the triangular romance between Lin Daiyu, Jia Baoyu and Xue Baochai that provides the novel with its main thread of plot. In the critiques that appeared in the mid 1980s it is possible to see that 'love' has been transformed into a socially useful concept. Previous decades had regarded love as a bourgeois indulgence at worst and, at best, based entirely upon mutual revolutionary feelings to a symbol of progressive social values simply for its challenge to the feudal marriage system. Thus by 1988 critics such as Xu Shanhe were attempting to prove that Baochai loved Baoyu just as much as Daiyu, but in a different way.

---

[23] Guo Yushi, *"Honglou meng" wenti pinglun ji*, p. 216.

[24] Jiang Hesen, *Honglou meng gaishuo* (A commentary on *Honglou meng*) (Shanghai: Shanghai guji chubanshe, 1979), pp. 59-60.

[25] Huang Lixin, "Ming Qing hunyin ziyou de shehui sichao yu *Honglou meng*" (*Honglou meng* and the trend in social thought towards freedom in marriage during the Ming and Qing). *Shanghai daxue xuebao: she ke ban* (Shanghai university journal: Social sciences edition), No. 4 (1989), pp. 29-35. Rpt. in *RD*, No. 4 (1989), p. 26.

Baochai's love was a pragmatic one whereas Daiyu's was romantic but it was no less in contradiction to feudal marriage practices. The subtext being that Baochai is thereby an equally admirable character who is capable of revealing the horrors of the feudal past to the contemporary readership. Indeed Xu proceeds to argue that both women are tragic figures destroyed by feudalism because although Baochai marries Baoyu, he is thoroughly deranged and after just over a year of marriage disappears leaving Baochai alone to spend the rest of her days as a widow.[26]

An important part of the search for a victim is the evocative repetition of the notion of tragedy. Zhang Qingshan wrote in a reappraisal of Shi Xiangyun that her role in the novel was not only to symbolize the decline of the Shi clan (on the way to reaching capitalism and socialism) but also that feudal society destroyed things of beauty and goodness such as the young Xiangyun. According to Zhang, Cao Xueqin loved Xiangyun but because he was a realist author he did not fall into the trap of granting characters he loved happy endings. Instead he sadly wrote of Xiangyun's tragic end to show the evils of feudalism and how badly it treated young women like Xiangyun. Zhang's assertion that Cao wrote a tragedy for the Twelve Beauties because feudalism destroyed all good and beautiful people and things is an important feature of the *Hongxue* of the post 1979 years because it assumes a classless notion of 'goodness' and 'beauty' that would have been anathema a decade earlier. The relative liberalism of these years has permitted Cao and his novel to be inherited positively upon this type of new criteria partly because these universal concepts of 'goodness' and 'beauty' are couched in a discourse of sexual equality. It proclaims Cao to be a realist author and thereby faithful to his material as well as being politically correct because he has 'realistically' shown the negative side of feudal society's treatment of women and, by implication, the positive side of the current system. [27]

Similarly the critics who addressed the vexed problem of Qin Keqing's suicide in chapter thirteen invoke the vulnerability of young daughters-in-law in the traditional Chinese family structure. Li Zili wrote in 1984 that her suicide came after the shame of her incestuous relationship with her father-in-law became too much to bear. Li points out that unlike the other young

---

[26] Examples of other critics who invoked the existence of Baochai's love for Baoyu in the attempt to positively appraise her include Han Wenzhi, "Dai-Chai xingxiang de yishu gousi jiantan" (A brief discussion of the artistic conception of the images of Daiyu and Baochai), *Shenyang jiaoyu xueyuan xuekan* (Shenyang education institute journal), No. 1 (1984), pp. 13-21, rpt. in *RD*, No. 3 (1984), pp. 85-94; Liu Kanlong, "Ye shi fengjian lijiao de shouhaizhe—jiantan Xue Baochai" (She is also a victim of feudal ethics—a brief discussion of Xue Baochai), *Xinjiang shifan daxue xuebao* (Xinjiang normal university journal), No. 2 (1981), pp. 85-89, rpt. in *RD*, No. 11 (1981), pp. 51-56.

[27] Zhang Qingshan, "Shi Xiangyun shi 'ludu' ma?—yu Ling Jiefang tongzhi shangque" (Is Shi Xiangyun a "Career Worm"?—a discussion with Comrade Ling Jiefang), *Honglou meng xuekan*, No. 2 (1983), p. 257.

daughter-in-law, Xifeng, Qin Keqing had no powerful family backing. She relied entirely upon her "Moon-like" looks to obtain the position of Mrs Rong, wife of the heir to the Jia clan's main line. This fundamental vulnerability, accompanied by the "Four Great Authorities" that bound women in feudal society meant that she was not in a position to reject her father-in-law's advances.[28] Had she done so, the head of the Jia clan could simply have discarded her. Li concludes that Keqing was not the image of a loose woman, as had been the dominant critical opinion, but rather was the image of the young woman trampled on by the feudal system. She was no less than a sacrificial offering to the patriarchal clan system.[29]

Thus, the tragedy of the Twelve Beauties in *Honglou meng* has been reconstructed by contemporary critics as evidence that Cao Xueqin and his *Honglou meng* were in opposition to feudal customs regarding the place of women in society. Contemporary China compares very favourably with the uniformly negative vision of women's lot in Imperial China described by *Hongxue* scholars. Most importantly of all *Honglou meng*'s social function has been reaffirmed in this process.

A discourse perpetuating inequality

That the reaffirmation of *Honglou meng*'s place in the literary canon is of paramount importance to *Hongxue* scholars is evident by their failure to adequately address, or address at all, the effects of their discourse of sexual equality on women. The search for oppression and suffering in the feudal system implicit in the 'correct' *Hongxue* of the 'free' Deng years produces the search for female characters that are convincingly oppressed and suffering. Passivity, vulnerability, misery, weakness and long-sufferance have become the characteristics of the oppressed women of feudal China. The result of the recreation of *Honglou meng*'s female characters in the search for vulnerability implicit in the discourse of sexual equality is the eulogizing of qualities which serve to further subjugate women. *Hongxue* scholars' oft-stated concern for the position of women in Chinese society is belied by the recreations of female characters in their own texts.

The most common method with which the *Hongxue* scholars recreate female characters as oppressed by feudal society is by emphasizing their status as victims. This weakness is mostly found when previously negatively ap-

---

[28] The Four Great Authorities—political, clan, religious, patriarchal—were noted in 1927 by Mao Zedong in his "Report on an Investigation of the Peasant Movement in Hunan," *Selected Works of Mao Tse-tung: Volume 1*, by Mao Zedong (1965; rpt. Beijing: Foreign Languages Press, 1967), pp. 44-47. They became a common analytical tool in the 1970s. See for example Zhang Bilai, *Manshuo Honglou* (Talking about the red chamber) (Beijing: renmin wenxue chubanshe, 1978) which devoted over 100 pages of length to the Four Authorities and how they emerge within *Honglou meng*.

[29] Li Zili, "Qin Keqing guankui" (A narrow view of Qin Keqing), *Henan shida xuebao: she ke ban* (Henan teachers' university journal: Social sciences edition), No. 2 (1984), pp. 74-77, rpt. in *RD*, No. 2 (1984), pp. 100-102.

praised characters are re-appraised. To ensure that a women is politically correct she must first be proved to be oppressed. Denying the female characters' agency, proclaiming their victim status and eulogizing their helplessness in the face of tragedy and feudal oppression is a major feature of the discourse of sexual equality.

For example in the case of Xue Baochai, who had been negatively appraised for the decades prior to 1979, re-appraisal is made possible by stressing her status as a victim. Zhang Jinchi wrote of Xue Baochai that she was a victim of feudal poisoning. Her advocacy of feudal prescriptions on appropriate female behaviour reveal that she had been tricked and duped by social morality. "Being a young girl, Baochai also suffered oppression from feudal ethics. Unable to determine her own fate she too was a victim."[30]

The problems with this type of reappraisal are abundantly clear. Baochai is regarded by Zhang, and the many others who wrote along these lines, as being a victim of poisoning, She is poisoned by feudal teachings and thereby should be redeemed as a complex character who can show contemporary readers the insidious nature of feudal ethics. This line of argument implicitly eulogizes the virtues of naivety and innocence in young girls. Zhang laments the loss of these female virtues that occurs through worldly pollution and claims for Baochai the status of victim.

The extent to which Zhang's critique is only a partial redemption is great when one considers that he laments the loss of naivety and innocence by criticizing Baochai's most active participation in her life. Zhang writes that "The most important quality of Xue Baochai, depicted by Cao Xueqin, is that she is worldly-wise and consequently we should not use criteria that are normally applied to naive and romantic girls to judge her inner thoughts and actions."[31]

From within this eulogy to female innocence and condemnation of female activeness, the problems of the discourse of sexual equality, whereby women should be sympathized with because they are victims of feudal oppression, clearly emerge. Zhang's critique of Baochai's worldly-wise behaviour is

---

[30] Zhang Jinchi, *Honglou shier lun* (Twelve essays on the red mansions). (Tianjin: Baihua wenyi chubanshe, 1982), p. 245. An identical logic was used in the critiques of Tanchun which are attempting to salvage her from the 'feudalist' label she had been granted in the early 1970s. See the invocation of trickery and poisoning by feudalism in Mo Zhu's article, "Tanchun lun" (On Tanchun), *Shandong shida xuebao* (Shandong teachers' university journal), No. 6 (1981), pp. 76-82, rpt. in *RD*, No. 12 (1981), p. 49.

[31] Zhang Jinchi, *Honglou shier lun*, p. 258. Other critics who followed this line include Fan Guoliang, "Cong *Honglou meng* hui mu kan Cao Xueqin dui Xue Baochai de yiyang taidu" (Looking at Cao Xueqin's modulating attitudes to Xue Baochai from the chapter headings of *Honglou meng*), *Honglou meng xuekan*, No. 1 (1987), p. 217. Another example of a critique which asserts that Baochai is neither bad nor good is Gu Yujie's article "Jin yu qi wai—bai xu qi zhong—shi tan Xue Baochai de xingge tedian" (Gold and jade on the outside—decaying cotton on the inside—an attempt to talk about the personality characteristics of Xue Baochai), *Liaoning jiaoyu xueyuan xuebao: she ke ban* (Liaoning education institute journal: Social science edition), No. 3 (1987), pp. 69-74, rpt. in *RD*, No. 4 (1987), pp. 56-61.

thorough. It proceeds from the rejection of the previous decade's appraisal of Baochai as an upholder of feudalism. By first narrating at length the events that had previously been use to describe her as a feudal maiden, Zhang then announces that Baochai is not a model feudal maiden at all, and should not be criticized on these grounds. Instead she should be criticized for her cunning manipulation of the feudal system and her hypocritical promotion of its morality to others around her. As a young girl, she is briefly redeemed as a victim of feudal poisoning, but is then invoked as a negative example for precisely those qualities that make her less of a passive victim. This type of argument is typical and clearly reveals the limited concern the discourse of sexual equality has with explicating the manner in which women functioned within the patriarchal society of Qing China because of its overriding concerns with notions of passivity.[32]

As well as emphasizing the vulnerability and passivity of female suffering critics stress the importance of youthful beauty, purity, naivety and sexual innocence among those recreated as symbols revealing the horrors of feudal China. For example Zhao Rong's 1982 critique describes *Honglou meng* as a "eulogy to equality between the sexes" and then proceeds to list the admirable qualities of the women described by Cao Xueqin. These include a pure mind and spirit, high character and the praiseworthy quality of looking upon death as "returning home" by preferring death to loss of chastity.[33]

Loss of virginal purity is promoted as an integral part of the tragedy for feudal women by *Hongxue* critics of the post 1979 years. This is most succinctly revealed in Cai Yijiang's discussion of the end of Wang Xifeng's daughter, Jia Qiaojie. The history of debate about Qiaojie's fate is lengthy. In the Gao E version Qiaojie is rescued by Granny Liu just before she is to be sold into a harem of a Mongol Prince by Xifeng's enemies. However, Yu Pingbo suggested in the 1920s that Cao intended to write that she was first sold into a brothel before being rescued by Granny Liu.[34] Cai adopts the position that Yu Pingbo was correct in his proposed 'real ending' because the Gao E ending is insufficiently tragic for a women in feudal China. Gao E, according to Cai, tried to make a happy ending in a society that could never have provided it. Cai argues that Cao Xueqin, as a great realist author,

---

[32] Lin Jinhong's 1984 critique is another example of *Hongxue*'s eulogizing of female passivity and rejection female activity. Lin divides his analysis into two sections: Xue Baochai's beauty and Xue Baochai's ugliness. Lin then searches for Cao Xueqin's attitude to Baochai to serve as the correct measure. As a realist author, and not a naturalist author, Cao Xueqin certainly takes a political stand in this respect according to Lin. Cao Xueqin is thus regarded as loving her literary knowledge and her physical beauty but loathing her reactionary politics and her hypocritical scheming. The rejection of her active manipulation of the social system and Lin's praise of her physical beauty ensure that little understanding of the mechanisms of sexual oppression has been reached. Lin Jinhong, "Renwu xingxiang de keguanxing yu zuozhe de qing xiangxing" (Objectivity of characters' images and the writer's tendencies), *Honglou meng xuekan*, No. 4 (1984), pp. 29-38.
[33] Zhao Rong, "Hunyin ziyou de nahan—nannü pingdeng de ouge," pp. 55-65.
[34] Yu Pingbo, *Honglou meng bian*, pp. 234-43.

did not create happy endings simply to satisfy his readers. Instead Cao has shown how in feudal society all beautiful things are trampled upon, causing their tragic ends.[35] Using the logic of Cai Yijiang and others who wrote along these lines, as a 'beautiful thing,' Jia Qiaojie, like the other Twelve Beauties, should have a more tragic ending than that narrated by Gao E.

This search for a heightened level of tragedy is then realized in the scenario where the young virgin's chastity is polluted in a brothel. It is from here, Cai proposes, that she is rescued by Grannie Liu and taken back to the village where she marries Liu's grandson, the young impoverished peasant, Baner. From here Qiaojie lives the life of a self-sufficient working peasant woman.[36] As Granny Liu had predicted when giving her the lucky name, Qiaojie, some good fortune will arise out of a seemingly bad situation.[37] According to Cai, the bad situation is her life in a brothel and the good fortune is that she is rescued by Liu.

Cai then addresses one potential problem in his preferred scheme. If Qiaojie had been working in a brothel would Grannie Liu want a sexually compromised girl to marry her grandson? Cai counters this query by saying that during Cao's time peasants were not as concerned with chastity as were the upper classes. For Grannie Liu to take an ex-prostitute as a grand-daughter-in-law would thereby be possible. There may have been some local gossip and laughter but nothing too extreme.[38] The loss of virginal purity in the young Qiaojie is then the tragedy enforced upon the beautiful and good things in feudal China, according to Cai.

The critiques surrounding the character of Adamantina, the young nun, also provide evidence of *Hongxue*'s eulogy to female purity and chastity. Adamantina observes a life of religious chastity and seclusion but near the end of the novel finds herself abducted and raped by a gang of ruffians. Previous analyses have argued that this fate is the necessary result of her failure to truly extinguish her desires and is duly punished by the gods for her false sincerity. Moreover, critics like Lin Yutang have described her as an "abnormal sex maniac."[39] However, Yi Qian and Shi Yuan reject this reading and argue that her personal decline comes about as the result of the

---

[35] Cai Yijiang, "Liu Laolao yu Jia Qiaojie" (Grannie Liu and Jia Qiaojie), *Honglou meng yanjiu jikan*, No. 3 (June, 1980), p. 270.

[36] Cai Yijiang, "Liu Laolao yu Jia Qiaojie," p. 266.

[37] On one of Grannie Liu's visits to the Jia mansions she is asked by Xifeng to name her baby saying that being named by an old and poor person is sure to bring her long-life and good luck. As Qiaojie was born at the unlucky time of the seventh day of the seventh month, Granny Liu decides to "fight poison with poison and fire with fire" by calling her "lucky sister" or Qiaojie. Liu then prophesies "she may for a time find that things are not going her way; but thanks to this name, all her misfortunes will turn into blessings, and what at first looked like bad luck will turn out to be good luck in the end (*SS* 2.42.325)."

[38] Cai Yijiang, "Liu Laolao yu Jia Qiaojie," pp. 270-71.

[39] Lin Yutang in Yi Qian and Shi Yuan, "Lun Miaoyu," (On Adamantina). *Shanghai shifan xueyuan xuebao* (Shanghai teachers' college journal), No. 1 (1979), pp. 82-86. Rpt. in *RD*, No. 11 (1979), p. 110.

necessary decline of the feudal system as it progresses towards socialism. "Contrary to her own aspirations she sinks into hardship, but this is not the result of her failure to truly 'break off with emotions and lust' (*qing yu wei duan*). Rather it is connected with the decline of the four great clans because they make it difficult for a young nun to protect her purity! That is to say Adamantina's tragedy is not self-generated but rather it is caused by a society that devours human-kind."[40] The critics summarize by saying that "her tragedy certainly is not God's punishment of a hypocrite, but rather it reveals the fact that a high and pure minded rebel is finally overcome by the dark society."[41]

The critics' approval of values such as chastity and purity in women is often in contradiction with their purported opposition to practices such as religious chastity, as was common for Buddhist and Daoist nuns, and, as we saw in a previous example, also to chastity imposed on widows. Discussion surrounding the young widow Li Wan draws out many of the features of *Hongxue*'s discourse of sexual equality that buttress the further oppression of women. These include praise of self-sacrifice, long-sufferance, purity and innocence and laments to the loss of beauty, youth and access to sex.

Li Dejun, for example, bemoans the misery the young chaste widow must suffer in feudal society. Indeed, this leads Li Wan to a situation where, "she does not notice the passing seasons, in limitless loneliness she accompanies the rotating stars. So it goes—with the beauty of youth and precious life allowed to fade away on life's river! These are the traces of the life of the young widow's steadfast preservation of her chastity... Beauty is turned to ash—feudal teachings and beautiful objects are as different as fire and water."[42] Indeed, Li exclaims "A young widow even has the right to wear cosmetics...stripped away allowing us to see that the Cheng-Zhu school's advocacy of 'extinguishing human desire' extinguishes with an extreme thoroughness!"[43] In this statement we can see how close is the relationship between suffering and loss of youth and beauty in Li's discourse of sexual equality. Moreover, the preoccupation of critics such as Li, with the loss of a woman's physical beauty suggests a limited comprehension with the manner in which identifying women as the aesthetic sex participates in their continued subordination. In the case of the discourse of sexual equality within

---

[40] Yi Qian and Shi Yuan, "Lun Miaoyu," p. 112.
[41] Yi Qian and Shi Yuan, "Lun Miaoyu," p. 113.
[42] Li Dejun, "Li Wan xingxiang jianlun," p. 96.
[43] Li Dejun, "Li Wan xingxiang jianlun," p. 100. Gu Piaoguang's critic makes the same point in his comment that Li Wan forgoes "a woman's fundamental right" to wear cosmetics. The loss of the right to facial decoration is symbolic of her wasted youth through steadfast adherence to preservation of her chastity. Gu Piaoguang, "Daoxiang cunli weiwang ren—Li Wan sanlun" (The not yet deceased person of Sweet-rice village—a discussion of Li Wan), *Honglou meng renwu lun* (Discussion of *Honglou meng*'s characters), ed. Guizhou sheng Hongxue hui (Guizhou city *Hongxue* academy) (Guiyang: Guizhou renmin chubanshe, 1988), p. 385.

Hongxue, the destruction of 'beautiful women' has also come to symbolize the destruction of all that is inherently beautiful and virtuous in Chinese culture. The feudal social system is held culpable for this destruction and no attempt is made within these analyses, to elucidate the links between beauty and power differentials between the sexes or even power differentials between classes.

The intimacy of the discourse of sexual equality's link with vulnerability and sexual innocence is revealed when critics discuss two young female characters who have traditionally been described as licentious, cunning manipulators—Qin Keqing and Wang Xifeng. The discourse of sexual equality is never applied to older married women, such as Grandmother Jia or Lady Wang because they have lost their innocence and naivety. It is thereby important that critiques of those transitional characters, the young daughters-in-law Xifeng and Keqing, be examined to reveal the lacunae in the discourse of sexual equality.

Those critics who seek to re-appraise in a positive light these two characters who have previously been described as negative characters, do so within the discourse of sexual equality by stressing their vulnerability as young daughters-in-law in a rotting and decadent feudal aristocratic family. However, those who still wish to maintain a negative appraisal argue that the notion that these women were oppressed because of their sex is inapplicable. Here class remains the dominant classifier.

Chen Shujing's 1987 chapter on Keqing is indicative of this viewpoint, and his basic argument became increasingly common in *Hongxue* publications as the 1980s progressed. Chen describes her as "a one hundred percent bad woman," arguing that Keqing is the point of symbolic convergence of chaos and disorder that led to the Jia family's decline. Chen discredits the view of many critics who "a little like Jia Baoyu, regard the women of the novel (and particularly the women in the three volumes of registers) with favouritism, while regarding the men of the novel with hate and loathing. The critiques of the men (with the exception of Baoyu) deliver harsh censure and demand perfection [in their behaviour]; but on the other side, the treatment of women is totally forgiving with explanations full of sighs of dejection."[44]

This view is taking Cao Xueqin's notion of "Girls are made of water and boys are made of mud (*SS* 1.2.77)" too literally, according to Chen, who regards Cao's play on reality and illusion and truth and falsehood in the line "Truth becomes fiction when the fiction's true; Real becomes not-real where the unreal's real (*SS* 1.1.55)" as evidence of the importance of ambiguity and reversal in the novel. Chen goes on to discredit the view that the novel contains "praise for some sort of rebellious spirit in feudal women and has taken the 'Twelve Beauties of Jinling' as representatives of persecuted women."

---

[44] Chen Shujing, "Jinxiu ronghua qing ke jin," p. 224.

Chen regards this viewpoint as being weak in analysis because both Xifeng and Qin Keqing are "out and out bad women." In Qin Keqing's case, Chen regards the two verses that foretell her fate in chapter five as exposing her as a morally corrupt, sexually licentious, thoroughly evil person.[45] However, while Chen perceives the dominant analysis, that the novel is showing the opposition to the oppression of women to be inaccurate in the case of these two women, he supports its general application to other women of the registers. The discourse of sexual equality is thereby most readily applied to those characters who are easily placed in the innocent, passive victim role. The fact that it is not applied generally to characters like Keqing must be argued by critics like Chen in terms of traditional sexual morality and traditional notions of harmony and stability. Incest is read by Chen as symbolic of social chaos pointing to the decline of the feudal family and was granted no significance as a manifestation of a particular form of sexual power. Invoked in this manner, as a symbol of decline, even within a materialist discourse, it has strong resonances with Confucian conceptions of propriety and social harmony. Chen's critique reveals the limitations of the discourse of sexual equality precisely because it makes clear the distinction between which girls (sexually pure, passive and powerless) can be included for analysis within its realm and which women (sexually tainted, active and powerful) are to be excluded. These limitations are the result of *Hongxue*'s lack of genuine concern, despite protestations to the contrary, with elucidating the problems of women in China, and their considerable concern with eulogizing the novel.

Ge Chuying's 1983 critique of Wang Xifeng is similarly disdainful of the view that would forgive Xifeng her faults on the grounds that she was a women in a misogynistic society. Ge's argument is that Xifeng is not a typical oppressed woman and thereby should not be judged on the grounds of her sex. The general notion that women were oppressed in feudal society is correct, according to Ge, but knowledge of this has led to the incorrect assumption that all men are bad and all women have been maltreated."[46] Ge proceeds to cite from Lu Xun's story of Ah Qin, suggesting that Lu Xun's view is one that should not look at the sex of the culprit, but rather at that person's position and whether or not they have power, because the trouble caused by a powerful women is not less than that caused by men. Xifeng's position was one of considerable power according to Ge.[47] Having established Xifeng as a member of the feudal aristocracy who should not be ab-

---

[45] Chen Shujing, "Jinxiu ronghua qing ke jin," pp. 224-25.

[46] Ge Chuying, "Wang Xifeng de beiju," pp. 78-79.

[47] Lu Xun, "Ah Qin" (Ah Qin), *Lun Xun quanji: di liu juan* (Complete works of Lu Xun: Volume six), by Lu Xun (1934; rpt. Beijing: Renmin wenxue chubanshe, 1973), pp. 199-204. In this story Lu Xun grapples with his desire to 'sympathize' with the plight of women and his feelings of anger at a female neighbour whose life-style causes chaos and disruption to his scholarly quietude.

solved of her crimes as a member of an oppressing class, simply on the grounds of her sex, Ge addresses the problem of her tragedy. In chapter seventy-three Lady Xing tells Xifeng, through a servant, to "go back home and take care of her illness" (*SS* 3.73.445). Ge suggests that this phrase foretells Xifeng's fate as a divorced woman being sent back to her natal home.[48] Once Xifeng's patron, Grandmother Jia, is dead, Lady Xing is free to seek her revenge on this disrespectful daughter-in-law and so sends her back to her parents. Her divorce is however, not the essence of her tragedy, in Ge's reading. Ge argued that Xifeng's tragedy was unlike that of the average woman in feudal society because "it is not based on a love or marriage tragedy nor is it the tragedy of one who has suffered oppression or humiliation." Xifeng's tragedy, to Ge is one that is outside of the issues subsumed under the title of 'sexual equality' and has a broader "social and political nature."[49] As an aristocrat, Xifeng's tragedy can only be that of a manipulator of power and it "serves as a warning to those in power 'Be careful not to dig your own grave'."[50] To Ge, Xifeng's tragedy is not that of a victim of feudal oppression but rather that of one who gains power and then misuses it to the extent that it threatens her own position. As a holder of power and an active manipulator of social situations, Xifeng is no longer regarded as an average woman to critics like Ge. Women who do not assume the roles of passive, weak, miserable victims, and who are not young, beautiful and chaste are beyond the scope of the discourse of sexual equality's abilities to theorize social/sexual power. In these respects the discourse of sexual equality consistently perpetuates values that are supportive of continued patriarchal power.

The fundamental subordination of women's concerns to Maoist conceptions of literary worth and Maoist preoccupations with Marxist categories of class and historical materialism emerge then as one of the major keys to comprehending the many lacunae in the discourse of sexual equality's logic of knowledge. Indeed, the parameters of the discourse of sexual equality alter in direct response to the changing strength of class as an analytical tool. Sexual equality is in a subordinate and dependent relationship to the overriding category of class. The discourse of sexual equality, did not develop a coherent methodology that would aid in the elucidation of the mechanisms of women's oppression. In its eclectic nature and with its reactive role, the discourse of sexual equality often perpetuated values and notions that buttressed the system that subordinates women.

---

[48] The view that Cao Xueqin's intended ending for Xifeng was divorce from Jia Lian and expulsion from the family is derived from Yu Pingbo. See Yu Pingbo, *Honglou meng bian*, pp. 235-36.

[49] Ge Chuying, "Wang Xifeng de beiju," p. 71.

[50] Ge Chuying, "Wang Xifeng de beiju," p. 79. Ge makes a direct connection to the 'ten years of chaos' of the Cultural Revolution and Jiang Qing's dream of becoming a female Empress immediately after this warning.

Establishing the considerable extent of a woman's suffering under feudal prescriptions of love, marriage or celibacy, could ensure her the credibility needed to serve as an example of the sort of evil perpetuated by the feudal system. It did, however, also reveal the limited degree of critics' comprehension of the manner in which women continue to be oppressed. By eulogizing the extent to which a woman is a victim of suffering and hardship without analyzing the functions such behaviour performs in a patriarchal society, female passivity is further encouraged. If the discourse of sexual equality had been generated with a concern for comprehending the mechanisms of the oppression of women then it would have been able to incorporate the experiences of a broader spectrum of women than those few young, naive innocents.

This is most clearly revealed by the critics' reconstruction of the notion of tragedy in the novel. As the novel depicts the tragic fates of the Twelve Beauties, *Hongxue* scholars invoked the discourse of sexual equality to reveal how the past feudal system necessarily created tragic ends for women. That is to say, the feudal past was regarded as inevitably creating suffering and often ensured an early death for women who were unlucky enough to be born in this dark period of Chinese history. However, while critics were concerned to reconstruct women as victims of an oppressive feudal system, they made no attempt to enunciate the discursive function of female suffering in *Honglou meng*. As dead virgins, dead concubines, beaten wives, lonely nuns, long-suffering widows and maltreated prostitutes, images of these women can serve simply to canonize the novel by revealing the evils of the past. In this respect *Honglou meng* is read as a romanticized lament to the destruction of women. In PRC *Hongxue*'s failure to elucidate the aesthetic function that female tragedy performs in Chinese culture, the notion of tragedy in the discourse of sexual equality serves to perpetuate female oppression. *Honglou meng* stands at the apex of a lengthy tradition of literary romanticization of female suffering and death, but the discourse of sexual equality has been content to simply use the notion of tragedy to canonize the novel and has not concerned itself with drawing out the broader implications for women's status.

While ensuring that the present is compared favourably with the past, through the elaboration of female suffering and hardship, critics do not only romanticize female passivity, they also eulogize personal qualities for women that suggest a limited appreciation of how women are oppressed. For example, the discourse of sexual equality requires for its successful reconstruction of a character, the praise of qualities such as purity, innocence, naivety, long-sufferance and physical beauty. Qualities of cunning, manipulativeness and active participation in family politics were de-emphasized when the discourse of sexual equality was invoked. The former group of qualities (purity, innocence and passivity) ensures that women do not disrupt the social order but instead serve to represent social ideals of beauty and virtue within a patriarchal social order. The later group of qualities (cunning and manipulativeness) includes those traits that would possibly undermine the status quo because women with these qualities would be more able to act in their own self-interest. These may or may not be the interests of a patriarchal society.

In their efforts to ensure the continuity of *Honglou meng*'s status as a socially useful text, while simultaneously freeing it of the radical anti-intellectualism of the pre 1979 decades, *Hongxue* critics have participated in the perpetuation of values and morality that do not further the cause of sexual equality. Perpetuating the cultural construct that has become a veritable *Hongxue* industry, is clearly providing the dominant impetus with the discourse of sexual equality a mere convenient tool.

Clearly then, from the perspective of a feminist critic each form of *Hongxue* has its implicit discourse of gender which informs its production. The issue then becomes not only one of examining texts but also examining the manner in which these texts are put to use throughout time. In this respect we can learn a great deal about prescription of gender, amongst a host of other social concerns, across lengthy periods of time.

BIBLIOGRAPHY OF ENGLISH MATERIALS

Ahern, Emily. "The Power and Pollution of Chinese Women." *Women in Chinese Society.* Ed. Margery Wolf and Roxanne Witke. Taipei: Caves Books, 1979, pp. 169-90.

Ban Zhao. "Lessons for Women." In *Pan Chao: Foremost Woman Scholar of China.* Ed. and trans. Nancy Lee Swann. New York: Russell and Russell, 1968, pp. 82-99.

Barthes, Roland. "The death of the Author." In *Image Music Text.* Ed. and trans. Stephen Heath. London: Fontana, 1977.

———, *The Grain of the Voice.* Trans. Linda Coverdale. New York: Hill and Wang, 1985.

Bauer, W. and Franke, H. eds. *The Golden Casket: Chinese Novellas of Two Millenia.* London: George Allen and Unwin, 1965.

Belsey, Catherine. *Critical Practice.* 1980; rpt. London: Methuen, 1985.

Bonner, Joey. "Yü P'ing-po and the Literary Dimensions of the Controversy over *Hung lou meng.*" *The China Quarterly,* No. 67, (1976), pp. 546-81.

Brandauer, Frederick P. "Women in the *Ching-hua yüan*: Emancipation toward a Confucian Ideal." *Journal of Asian Studies,* 36, No. 4 (August, 1977), pp. 647-60.

Cao Xueqin. *The Story of the Stone, Vol. 1: The Golden Days.* Trans. David Hawkes. 2nd ed., 1973; rpt. Harmondsworth: Penguin, 1978.

———, *The Story of the Stone, Vol. 2: The Crab-Flower Club.* Trans. David Hawkes. 2nd ed., 1977; rpt. Harmondsworth: Penguin, 1979.

———, *The Story of the Stone, Vol. 3: The Warning Voice.* Trans. David Hawkes. Harmondsworth: Penguin, 1980.

———, *The Story of the Stone, Vol. 4: The Debt of Tears.* Ed. Gao E, trans. John Minford. Harmondsworth: Penguin, 1982.

———, *The Story of the Stone, Vol. 5: The Dreamer Wakes.* Ed. Gao E, trans. John Minford. Harmondsworth: Penguin, 1986.

Chan, Ping-leung. "Myth and Psyche in *Hung-lou meng.*" In *Critical Essays on Chinese Fiction.* Ed. Winston L.Y. Yang and Curtis P. Adkins. Hong Kong: Chinese University Press, 1980, pp. 165-79.

Chan, Wing-tsit ed., trans. *A Source Book in Chinese Philosophy.* 1963; rpt. Princeton: Princeton University Press, 1973.

Chao, Chien. "Female Chastity in Chinese Culture." *Bulletin of the Institute of Ethnology: Academia Sinica,* No. 31 (Spring, 1971), pp. 205-11.

Cheng Weiyuan. "Preface by Cheng Weiyuan." In *The Story of the Stone, Vol. 4: The Debt of Tears.* By Cao Xueqin, ed. Gao E, trans. John Minford. Harmondsworth: Penguin, 1982, pp. 385-86.

Cixous, Hélène. "The Laugh of the Medusa." Trans. by Keith Cohen and Paula Cohen. In *New French Feminisms.* Ed. Elaine Marks and Isabelle de Courtivron. New York: Schocken, 1980.

———, "Castration or decapitation?" Trans. Annette Kuhn. *Signs: Journal of Women in Culture and Society,* 7, No. 1 (1981), pp. 41-55.

Connell, R.W. *Gender and Power: Society, the Person, and Sexual Politics.* Sydney: Allen and Unwin, 1987.

Coward, Rosalind. *Female Desire.* London: Paladin, 1984.

Culler, Jonathan. *On Deconstruction: Theory and Criticism after Structuralism.* 1983; rpt. London: Routledge and Kegan Paul, 1985.

Deng Xiaoping. "Congratulatory Message to the Fourth Congress of Chinese Writers and Artists." *Chinese Literature for the 1980s: The Fourth Congress of Writers and Artists.* Ed. Howard Goldblatt, trans. George Cheng. Armonk: M.E. Sharpe, 1982, pp. 7-14.

——, "Our Work in All Fields Should Contribute to the Building of Socialism with Chinese Characteristics." *Build Socialism with Chinese Characteristics.* No trans. given. Beijing: Foreign Languages Press, 1985, pp. 10-13.

Douglas, Mary. *Purity and Danger: An analysis of concepts of pollution and taboo.* London: Routledge and Kegan Paul, 1966.

Dugaw, Dianne. *Warrior Women and Popular Balladry, 1650-1850.* Cambridge: Cambridge University Press, 1989.

Eagleton, Terry. *Marxism and Literary Criticism.* London: Methuen, 1976.

——, "Literature and politics now." *Critical Quarterly,* 20, No. 3, (1978), pp. 65-69.

——, *Literary Theory: An Introduction.* 1983; rpt. Oxford: Basil Blackwell, 1985.

Eberhard, Wolfram. "Ideas about Social Reforms in the Novel *Ching-hua yuan.*" In *Festschrift für Ad.E. Jensen.* Ed. Eike Haberland, Meinhard Schuster and Helmut Straube. Munisch: Runner, 1964, pp. 113-21.

——, *Dictionary of Chinese Symbols.* Singapore: Federal Publications, 1990.

Edwards, Louise. "Historiography of Lin Siniang: Desirability and Virtue in Eighteenth Century China." *New Zealand Journal of East Asian Studies,* 1, No. 2 (December, 1993), pp. 63-75.

Elman, Mary. *Thinking About Women.* London: McMillan and Co., 1968.

Elvin, Mark. "Female Virtue and the State in China." *Past and Present,* No. 104 (August, 1984), pp. 110-52.

Evans, Nancy. "Social Criticism in the Ch'ing: The Novel *Ching-hua yuan.*" *Papers on China, Volume 23.* Cambridge, Mass.: East Asia Research Center, 1970, pp. 52-66.

Féral, Josette. "The Powers of Difference." In *The Future of Difference.* Ed. Hester Eisenstein and Alice Jardine. Boston: G.K. Hall, 1980, pp. 89-94.

Fitzgerald, John. "Continuity Within Discontinuity: The Case of Water Margin Mythology." *Modern China,* 12, No. 3 (July, 1986), pp. 361-400.

Foreman, Ann. *Femininity as Alienation: Women and the Family in Marxism and Psychoanalysis.* London: Pluto Press, 1978.

Foucault, Michel. *The History of Sexuality: An Introduction.* Trans. Robert Hurley. 1976; rpt. Harmondsworth: Penguin, 1987.

——, "What Is an Author?." In *The Foucault Reader.* Ed. Paul Rabinow. 1984; rpt. Harmondsworth: Penguin, 1987, pp. 101-20.

Foulkes, A.P. *Literature and Propaganda.* London: Methuen, 1983.

Furman, Nelly. "The politics of language: beyond the gender principle?" *Making a Difference: Feminist Literary Criticism.* Ed. Gayle Greene and Coppélia Kahn. 1985; rpt. New York, Methuen, 1986, pp. 59-79.

Furth, Charlotte. "Blood, Body and Gender—Medical Images of the Female Condition in China 1600-1850." *Chinese Science,* No. 7 (1986), pp. 43-66.

——, "Concepts of Pregnancy, Childbirth and Infancy in Ch'ing Dynasty China." *Journal of Asian Studies,* 46, No. 1 (February, 1987), pp. 7-33.

——, "Androgynous Males and Deficient Females: Biology and Gender Boundaries in Sixteenth and Seventeenth-Century China." *Late Imperial China,* 9, No. 2 (December, 1988), pp. 1-31.

Gao E. "Preface by Gao E." In *The Story of the Stone, Vol. 4: The Debt of Tears.* By Cao Xueqin, ed. Gao E, trans. John Minford. Harmondsworth: Penguin, 1982, p. 386.

Gelfand, Elissa D. and Hules, Virginia Thorndike, ed. *French Feminist Criticism: Women, Language, and Literature: An Annotated Bibliography.* New York: Garland Pub. Inc.,1985

Goldman, Merle. *Literary Dissent in Communist China.* Cambridge, Mass.: Harvard University Press, 1967.

——, *China's Intellectuals: Advise and Dissent.* Cambridge, Mass.: Harvard University Press, 1981.

——, "The Zigs and Zags in the Treatment of Intellectuals." *The China Quarterly,* No. 102 (1985), pp. 709-715.

——, with Cheek, Timothy and Hamrin, Carol Lee. *China's Intellectuals and the State: In Search of a New Relationship.* Cambridge, Mass.: Harvard University Press, 1987.

Grant, Joan. "Power and Pitfalls: The Possibilities of Real Political Power for Women in 20th Century China." In *Class, Ideology and Women in Asian Societies*. Ed. Gail Pearson and Lenore Manderson. Hong Kong: Asian Research Services, 1987, pp. 17-45.

Greene, Gayle and Kahn, Coppélia. "Feminist scholarship and the social construction of woman." *Making a Difference: Feminist Literary Criticism*. Ed. Gayle Greene and Coppélia Kahn. 1985; rpt. New York, Methuen, 1986, pp. 1-36.

Grieder, Jerome B. "The Communist Critique of *Hung lou meng*." *Papers on China*, No. 10 (October, 1956), pp. 142-68.

Hawkes, David. "Introduction." *The Story of the Stone, Vol. 1: The Golden Days*. By Cao Xueqin, trans. David Hawkes. 2nd ed., 1973; rpt. Harmondsworth: Penguin, 1978, pp. 15-46.

——, "The 'Twelve Beauties of Jinling' and the 'Dream of Golden Days' Song-cycle." *The Story of the Stone, Vol. 1: The Golden Days*. By Cao Xueqin, trans. David Hawkes. 2nd ed., 1973; rpt. Harmondsworth: Penguin, 1978, pp. 527-34.

Hegel, G.W. F. *Lectures on the History of Philosophy: Volume 1*. Trans. E.S. Haldane. London: Routledge and Kegan Paul, 1955.

Holmgren, J. "Myth, Fantasy or Scholarship: Images of the Status of Women in Traditional China." *The Australian Journal of Chinese Affairs*, No. 6 (1981), pp. 147-59.

Hooper, Beverly. "China's Modernization: Are Young Women Going to Lose Out?" *Modern China*, 10, No. 3 (July, 1984), pp. 317-43.

——, "'Serve the Consumer': the Creation of the Chinese Pinup Girl." Paper presented to the Eighth Biennial Asian Studies Association of Australia Conference held in Brisbane at Griffith University in July 1990.

Hsia, C.T. *The Classic Chinese Novel: A Critical Introduction*. New York: Columbia University Press, 1968.

——, "The Scholar-Novelist and Chinese Culture: A Study of *Ching Hua Yuan*." *Tamkang Review*, 5, No. 2 (October, 1974), pp. 1-32.

Huang, Wang Pi-twan. "Utopian Imagination in Traditional Chinese Fiction." Unpublished Ph.D. Dissertation. University of Wisconsin-Madison, 1980.

Hung, Chang-tai. "Female Symbols of Resistance in Chinese Wartime Spoken Drama." *Modern China*, 15, No. 2 (April, 1989), pp. 149-77.

Jameson, Fredric. *Marxism and Form: Twentieth-Century Dialectical Theories of Literature*. Princeton: Princeton University Press , 1971.

——, *The Political Unconscious: Narrative as a Socially Symbolic Act*. London: Methuen, 1981.

Jones, Ann Rosalind. "Inscribing Femininity: French Theories of the Feminine." In *Making a Difference: Feminist Literary Criticism*. Ed. Gayle Greene and Coppélia Kahn. London: Methuen, 1986, pp. 80-112.

Kao, Hsin-sheng C. *Li Ju-chen*. Boston: Twayne, 1981.

Kao, Karl S.Y. *Classical Chinese Tales of the Supernatural and the Fantastic: Selections from the Third to the Tenth Century*. Bloomington: Indiana University Press, 1985.

Kasuko, Ono. *Chinese Women in a Century of Revolution, 1850-1950*. Ed. Joshua A. Fogel. Stanford: Stanford University Press, 1989.

Knoerle, Jeanne. *The Dream of the Red Chamber: A Critical Study*. Bloomington: Indiana University Press, 1972.

Ko, Dorothy. "Pursuing Talent and Virtue: Education and Women's Culture in Seventeenth and Eighteenth-Century China," *Late Imperial China*, 13, No. 1 (1992), pp. 9-39.

Kristeva, Julia. *About Chinese Women*. Trans. Anita Barrows. New York: Urizen Press, 1977.

——, "Oscillation Between Power and Denial." Trans. Marilyn A. August. In *New French Feminisms*. Ed. by Elaine Marks and Isabelle de Courtivron. New York: Schocken, 1980.

Lacan, Jacques. *Ecrits: A Selection*. Trans. Alan Sheridan. London: Tavistock, 1980.

Lee, Lily Hsiao Hung. "The Emergence of Buddhist Nuns in China and Its Social Ramifications." *Journal of the Oriental Society of Australia*, No. 18,19 (1986-1987), pp. 82-100.

Li Ju-chen. *Flowers in the Mirror*. Trans. Lin Taiyi. Berkeley: University of California Press, 1965.

Liao, Hsien-hao. "Tai-yü or Pao-ch'ai: The Paradox of Existence as Manifested in Pao-yü's Existential Struggle." *Tamkang Review*, 15, No. 1,2,3,4 (Autumn, 1984-Summer, 1985), pp. 485-93.

Lin Yutang. "Feminist Thought in Ancient China." *T'ien Hsia Monthly*, 1, No. 2 (September, 1935), pp. 127-50.

Liu Wu-chi. *An Introduction to Chinese Literature*. Bloomington: Indiana University Press, 1966.

Lo, Dai-yee. *Enchantment and Disenchantment: Love and Illusion in Chinese Literature*. Princeton: Princeton University Press, 1993.

Louie, Kam. *Inheriting Tradition: Interpretations of the Classical Philosophers in Communist China 1949-1966*. Hong Kong: Oxford University Press, 1986.

Lu Xun. *A Brief History of Chinese Fiction*. Trans. Yang Hsien-yi and Gladys Yang. 1925; rpt. Beijing: Foreign Languages Press, 1959.

Macherey, Pierre. *A Theory of Literary Production*. Trans. Geoffrey Wall. London: Routledge and Kegan Paul, 1978.

Makward, Christiane Perrin. "La Critique Féministe, Éléments d'une Problematique." *Revue des Sciences Humaines*, No. 168 (1977). Cited in "Aspects of Current French Literary Criticism." By Meaghan Morris, *Hecate*, 5, No. 2 (1979).

Mann, Susan. "Widows in the Kinship, Class, and Community Structures of Qing Dynasty China." *Journal of Asian Studies*, 46, No. 1 (February, 1987), pp. 37-55.

———, "*Fuxue* (Women's Learning) by Zhang Xuechang (1738-1801): China's First History of Women's Culture." *Late Imperial China*, 13, No. 1 (1992), pp. 40-62.

Mao Zedong. "Report on an Investigation of the Peasant Movement in Hunan." Rpt. in *Selected Works of Mao Tse-tung: Volume 1*. By Mao Zedong. 1965; rpt. Beijing: Foreign Languages Press, 1967, pp. 23-62.

———, "The Role of the Chinese Communist Party in the National War." Rpt. in *Selected Works of Mao Tse-tung: Volume 2*. By Mao Zedong. 1965; rpt. Beijing: Foreign Languages Press, 1967, pp. 195-211.

———, "Talks at the Yan'an Conference on Literature and Art." In *Mao Zedong's "Talks at the Yan'an Conference on Literature and Art:" A Translation of the 1943 Text With Commentary*. Ed. and trans. Bonnie S. McDougall. Ann Arbor: Center for Chinese Studies, University of Michigan, 1980, pp. 55-86.

McDougall, Bonnie S. *The Introduction of Western Literary Theories into Modern China: 1919-1925*. Tokyo: The Centre for East Asian Cultural Studies, 1971.

———, *Mao Zedong's "Talks at the Yan'an Conference on Literature and Art": A Translation of the 1943 Text With Commentary*. Ann Arbor: Center for Chinese Studies, University of Michigan, 1980.

McMahon, R.K. "Eroticism in Late Ming, Early Qing Fiction: The Beauteous Realm and the Sexual Battlefield." *T'oung Pao*, No. 73 (1987), pp. 217-64.

———, "A Case for Confucian Sexuality: The Eighteenth-Century Novel 'Yesou puyan'." *Late Imperial China*, 9, No. 2 (December, 1988), pp. 32-55.

Miller, Lucien. *Masks of Fiction in the "Dream of the Red Chamber": Myth, Mimesis, and Persona*. Tucson: University of Arizona Press, 1975.

———, "Naming the Whirlwind: Cao Xueqin and Heidegger." *Tamkang Review*, 12, No. 2 (Winter, 1981), pp. 143-63.

———, "Children of the Dream: The Adolescent World in Cao Xueqin's *Honglou meng*." Paper presented to the Symposium on Children in Pre-Modern China. May 25-27, 1990 at the Center for Advanced Studies, University of Virginia, Charlottesville.

Minford, John. "Preface." In *The Story of the Stone, Vol. 4: The Debt of Tears*. By Cao Xueqin, ed. Gao E, trans. John Minford. Harmondsworth: Penguin, 1982, pp. 15-30.

Moi, Toril. *Sexual/Textual Politics: Feminist Literary Theory*. 1985; rpt. London: Methuen, 1988.

Ng, Vivien, W. "Ideology and Sexuality: Rape Laws in Qing China." *Journal of Asian Studies*, 46, No. 1 (February, 1987), pp. 57-70.

O'Brien, Mary. *The Politics of Reproduction*. London: Routledge and Kegan Paul, 1983.

Palandri, Angela Jung. "Women in the *Dream of the Red Chamber*." *Literature East and West*, 12, No. 2,3,4 (1968), pp. 226-38.

Plaks, Andrew. *Archetype and Allegory in the "Dream of the Red Chamber".* Princeton: Princeton University Press, 1976.

"Record of Forum Held for the Study of the Dream of the Red Chamber." *Current Background*, No. 315, 4.3.1955.

Red Detachment of Women: A Modern Revolutionary Ballet. Beijing: Foreign Languages Press, 1972.

Roberts, Moss. "Neo-Confucianism in the *Dream of the Red Chamber*: A Critical Note." *Bulletin of Concerned Asian Scholars*, 10, No. 1 (January-March, 1978), pp. 63-66.

Roddy, S. J. "'Rulin waishi' and the Representation of Literati in Qing Fiction." Unpublished PhD. dissertation. Princeton University, 1990.

Rolston, David, ed. *How to Read the Chinese Novel.* Princeton: Princeton University Press, 1990.

——, "Chang Hsin-chih on How to Read the *Hung-lou meng* (Dream of the Red Chamber)." In *How to Read the Chinese Novel.* Ed. David Rolston. Princeton: Princeton University Press, 1990, pp. 316-322.

Ropp, P.S. "The Seeds of Change: Reflections on the Condition of Women in the Early and Mid Ch'ing." *Signs: Journal of Women in Culture and Society*, (Autumn, 1976), pp. 5-23.

Ruthven, K.K. *Feminist Literary Studies.* Cambridge: Cambridge University Press, 1984.

Shan Hai Ching: Legendary Geography and Wonders of Ancient China. Commentary by Kuo P'o—Chin dynasty, explanatory notes by Hao Yi-hsing—Ch'ing dynasty. Trans. Hsiao-Chieh Cheng, Hui-Chen Pai Cheng and Kenneth Lawrence Thern. Taipei: National Institute for Compilation and Translation, 1985.

Spence, Johnathan. *Ts'ao Yin and the Kang-hsi Emperor: Bondservant and Master.* New Haven: Yale University Press, 1966.

Stanton, Domna C. "Language and revolution: the Franco-American dis-connection." *The Future of Difference.* Ed. Hester Eisenstein and Alice Jardine. Boston, Mass.: G.K. Hall, 1980, pp. 73-87.

Sychov, L. and V. "The Role of Costume in Ts'ao Hsueh-chin's novel *The Dream of the Red Chamber*." Trans. Cecelia Shickman. *Tamkang Review*, 11, No. 3 (Spring, 1981), pp. 287-305.

T'ien Ju-k'ang. *Male Anxiety and Female Chastity: A Comparative Study of Chinese Ethical Values in Ming-Ch'ing Times.* Leiden: E.J. Brill, 1988.

Tsai, Kathryn A. "The Chinese Buddhist Monastic Order for Women: The First Two Centuries." *Historical Reflections*, 8, No. 3 (Fall, 1981), pp. 1-20.

Tsao Hsueh-chin and Kao Ngo. *A Dream of Red Mansions: Vol. 1.* Trans. Yang Hsien-yi and Gladys Yang. Beijing: Foreign Languages Press, 1978.

Van Gulik, R.H. *Sexual Life in Ancient China.* Leiden: E.J. Brill, 1974.

Wagner, Marsha L. "Maids and Servants in Dream of the Red Chamber: Individuality and the Social Order." In *Expressions of Self in Chinese Literature.* Ed. Robert E. Hegel and Richard C. Hessney. New York: Columbia University Press, 1985, pp. 251-81.

Waltner, Ann. "Widows and Remarriage in Ming and Early Qing China." *Historical Reflections*, 8, No. 3 (Fall, 1981), pp. 129-46.

——, "On Not Becoming a Heroine: Lin Dai-yu and Cui Ying-ying." *Signs: Journal of Women in Culture and Society*, 15, No. 1 (Autumn, 1989), pp. 61-78.

——, "The Grand Secretary's Family: Three Generations of Women in the Family of Wang Hsi-chüeh." *Family Process and Politicial Process in Modern Chinese History: Part I.* Taipei: Zhongyang yanjiu yuan jindai shi yanjiu suo, 1992, pp. 543-77.

Wang, Jing. *The Story of Stone.* Durham: Duke University Press, 1992.

Wheelwright, Julie. *Amazons and Military Maids: Women Who Dressed as Men in the Pursuit of Life, Liberty and Happiness.* London: Pandora, 1989.

Williams, Raymond. *Keywords.* 1976; rpt. London: Fontana, 1988.

Wolf, Margery. *Women and the Family in Rural Taiwan.* Stanford: Stanford University Press, 1972.

Wu, Fatima. "Foxes in Chinese Supernatural Tales (Part I)." *Tamkang Review*, 17, No. 2 (Winter, 1986).

Wu Qingyun. "Transformations of female rule: Feminist utopians in Chinese and English literature." Unpublished Ph.D. dissertation. Pennsylvania State University, 1991.

Wu Shichang. *On the Red Chamber Dream.* Oxford: Clarendon, 1961.

Wu Tien-wei. *Lin Biao and the Gang of Four: Contra-Confucianism in Historical and Intellectual Perspective.* Carbondale: Southern Illinois University Press, 1983.

Yee, Angelina C. "Counterpoise in *Honglou meng.*" *Harvard Journal of Asiatic Studies*, 50, No. 2 (1990), pp. 613-50.

——, "Sympathy, counterpoise and symbolism: Aspects of Structure in 'Dream of Red Chamber'." Unpublished Ph.D. dissertation. Harvard University, 1986.

Yu, Anthony C. "Self and the Family in the *Hung-lou Mêng*: A New Look at Lin Tai-yü as Tragic Heroine." *Chinese Literature: Essays, Articles and Reviews*, 2, No. 2 (July, 1980), pp. 199-223.

Yu Yingshi. "The Two Worlds of *Hung-lou meng.*" Trans. Diana Yu. *Renditions*, No. 2 (Spring, 1974), pp. 5-22.

Zeitlin, Judith T. "Pu Songling's (1640-1715) *Liaozhai zhiyi* and the Chinese Discourse on the Strange." Unpublished Ph.D. dissertation. Harvard University, 1988.

Zhang Xinzhi. "*Honglou meng* dufa" (How to read the *Honglou meng*). Trans. Andrew Plaks. In *How to Read the Chinese Novel*. Ed. David Rolston. Princeton: Princeton University Press, 1990, pp. 316-40.

Zhou Yang. "Inherit the Past and Usher In the Future." *Chinese Literature for the 1980s: The Fourth Congress of Writers and Artists*. Ed. Howard Goldblatt, trans. Betty Ting. Armonk: M.E. Sharpe, 1982, pp. 15-38.

BIBLIOGRAPHY OF CHINESE MATERIALS

Abbreviation: I have use the abbreviation *RD* to represent the works compiled in the People's University's collection of photocopied material—Zhongguo renmin daxue shubao ziliao she (Compilers of books and materials, China's People's University), *Fuyin baokan ziliao "Honglou meng" yanjiu* (Copied materials of journals and newspapers on *Honglou meng* research).

Bai Dun. "'Yan fu,' 'ci mu' ji qita—Cong Jia Zheng, Wang Furen de xingxiang suzao kan Cao Xueqin de chuangzao weiji" (The 'severe father', indulgent mother' and other things—A view of Cao Xueqin's creative crisis from the construction of Jia Zheng's and Lady Wang's image). *Anhui shida xuebao* (Anhui teachers' university journal), No. 3 (1981), pp. 67-74. Rpt. in *RD*, No. 11 (1981), pp. 34-35.

——, "Lun Wang Xifeng xingge de beiju yiyi" (On the tragic significance of Wang Xifeng's personality). *Honglou meng xuekan* (*Honglou meng* journal), No. 1 (1982), pp. 121-36.

——, *Honglou meng xinping* (A new critique of *Honglou meng*). Shanghai: Shanghai wenyi chubanshe, 1986.

Bai Yun. "Gudai funü de yingxiong xingxiang" (Images of ancient heroines). *Jiefang junbao* (Liberation army daily), 7.3.1951.

Beijing waiguoyu xueyuan Yingwen xi (Beijing foreign language institute English department). *Han Ying cidian* (A Chinese-English Dictionary). Beijing: Shangwuyin shuguan, 1985.

Cai Yijiang. "Liu Laolao yu Jia Qiaojie" (Grannie Liu and Jia Qiaojie). *Honglou meng yanjiu jikan* (Journal of research on *Honglou meng*), No. 3 (June, 1980), pp. 261-73.

Cai Yuanpei. "Shitou ji suoyin" (An index to *The Story of the Stone*). *Xiaoshuo yuebao* (Fiction monthly), 7, No. 1-6 (1916). Excerpts rpt. in *Honglou meng juan* (Collection of material on *Honglou meng*). Ed. Yi Su. 1963; rpt. Beijing: Zhonghua shuju, 1985, pp. 319-22.

Cao Xueqin. *Honglou meng: yi-si* (*Honglou meng*: Vols 1-4). Beijing: Beijing shifan daxue chubanshe, 1987.

Chen Dongyuan. *Zhongguo funü shenghuo shi* (A history of the lives of Chinese women). No original publishing date given; Taipei, Shangwuyin shuguan, 1986.

Chen Shujing. "Jinxiu ronghua qing ke jin—lun Qin Keqing de xiangzheng yiyi" (Good things come to an end—on the symbolic significance of Qin Keqing). *Honglou meng xuekan* (*Honglou meng* journal), No. 2 (1987), pp. 223-34.

Chen Weisong. *Furen ji* (Collections on women). Rpt. in *Congshu jicheng xinbian*, No. 101. Taipei: Xinwen feng chubangongsi, 1986, p. 712.

Cheng Weiyuan. "*Honglou meng* xu" (Preface to *Honglou meng*). Rpt. in *Honglou meng juan* (Collection of material on *Honglou meng*). Ed. Yi Su. 1963; rpt. Beijing: Zhonghua shuju, 1985, p. 31.

Cheng Weiyuan and Gao E. "*Honglou meng* yinyan" (Prefatory remarks on *Honglou meng*). Rpt. in *Honglou meng juan* (Collection of material on *Honglou meng*). Ed. Yi Su. 1963; rpt. Beijing: Zhonghua shuju, 1985, p. 32.

Dai Bufan. "Qin Keqing wan si kao" (Investigating Qin Keqing's late death). *Wenyi yanjiu* (Literature and art research), No. 1 (1979), pp. 87-92. Rpt. in *RD*, No. 7 (1979), pp. 41-46.

Deng Qing. "Deng qing 'Siren bang' zai *Honglou meng* yanjiu zhong zhizao de hunluan" (Clarifying the chaos created in the "Gang of Four's" research on *Honglou meng*). *Hongqi* (Red flag), No. 10 (1977), pp. 57-64.

"Er zhi dao ren." *"Honglou meng* shuo meng" (Dream Talk on the *Honglou meng*). Rpt. in *Honglou meng juan* (Collection of material on *Honglou meng*). Ed. Yi Su. 1963; rpt. Beijing: Zhonghua shuju, 1985, pp. 83-102.

Fan Yang. *Yanggang de huichen* (The demise of yang). Beijing: Guoji wenhua chuban gongsi, 1988.

Fu Ying. "Guangcai minmie de 'yü mu' shijie ji qi beiju—*Honglou meng* gui furen qunxiang fenxi" (The tragedy of the vanishing splendour of the 'fish eyes' world—an analysis of the images of the aristocratic women in *Honglou meng*). *Guangdong shehui kexue* (Guangdong's social sciences), No. 3 (1990), pp. 91-96. Rpt. in *RD*, No. 4 (1990), pp. 49-55.

Gao E. *"Honglou meng* xu" (Preface to *Honglou meng*). Rpt. in *Honglou meng juan* (Collection of material on *Honglou meng*). Ed. Yi Su. 1963; rpt. Beijing: Zhonghua shuju, 1985, p. 31.

Ge Chuying. "Wang Xifeng de beiju" (Wang Xifeng's tragedy). *Wu shi Xiaogan fen yuan xuebao* (Journal of Wuhan teachers' college Xiaogan branch), No. 2 (1982), pp. 23-30. Rpt. in *RD*, No. 1 (1983), pp. 71-79.

Gu Jiegang. "Gu xu" (Gu's preface). *Honglou meng bian* (Distinguishing *Honglou meng*). By Yu Pingbo, rpt. in *Yu Pingbo lun Honglou meng* (Yu Pingbo on *Honglou meng*), by Yu Pingbo. Shanghai: Shanghai guji chubanshe, 1988, pp. 73-81.

Gu Quanfang. *"Yang jia jiang* zayi" (Miscellany on the *Yang family Generals*). *Wenhui bao*, (Wenhui daily), 1.9.1980.

Gu Rong. "'Ban ge Hongxuejia' he yige yexinjia" ("Half a *Hongxue* scholar" and a Careerist). *Renmin ribao* (People's daily), 9.2.1977.

Guan Hua. "Cao Xueqin he nüxing" (Cao Xueqin and women). *Renmin ribao* (People's daily), 6.3.1986.

Guo Yushi. *Honglou yanjiu xiaoshi gao* (A short history of research into the red chamber). Shanghai: Shanghai wenyi chubanshe, 1980.

——, *Honglou yanjiu xiao shi xugao* (A further short history of research into the red chamber). Shanghai: Shanghai wenyi chubanshe, 1981.

——, *Honglou meng wenti pinglun ji* (A collection of critiques on questions arising from *Honglou meng*). Shanghai: Guji chubanshe, 1981.

Han Huiqiang. *"Honglou meng* zhong de xing guannian ji wenhua yiyi" (Sexual concepts and the cultural significance of *Honglou meng*). *Beijing daxue yanjiusheng xuekan* (Beijing university research students journal), No. 1 (1988), pp. 77-82. Rpt. in *RD*, No. 2 (1988), pp. 17-22.

Han Jinlian. "Qian hong yi ku; wan yan tong bei (shi lun shier chai de dianxing yiyi)" (Maiden's Tears and Lachrymae Rerum [A tentative discussion on the typical significance of the Twelve Beauties]). *Hebei shifan daxue xuebao: zhe she ban* (Hebei normal university journal: Social sciences and philosophy edition), No. 2 (1984), pp. 29-36. Rpt. in *RD*, No. 3 (1984), pp. 77-84.

Han Wenzhi. "Dai-Chai xingxiang de yishu gousi jiantan" (A brief discussion of the artistic conception of the images of Daiyu and Baochai). *Shenyang jiaoyu xueyuan xuekan* (Shenyang education institute journal), No. 1 (1984), pp. 13-21. Rpt. in *RD*, No. 3 (1984), pp. 85-94.

Hong Guangsi. *"Honglou meng* shi yi bu xie jieji douzheng de shu" (*Honglou meng* is a book about class struggle). *Beijing ribao* (Beijing daily), 2.11.1973.

Hu Shi. *Honglou meng kaozheng* (Textual research on *Honglou meng*). Rpt. in *Hu Shi Honglou meng yanjiu lunshu quan bian* (The complete work of Hu Shi's research and discussion on *Honglou meng*). By Hu Shi. Shanghai: Shanghai guji chubanshe, 1988, pp. 75-120.

——, "*Jinghua yuan* de yin lun" (Introductory discussion of *Jinghua yuan*). In *Hu Shi wencun di er ji* (Second volume of Hu Shi's literary writings). By Hu Shi. Taipei: Yuandong tushu gongsi, 1953, pp. 412-33.

——, "Hu Shi zhi kaozheng" (Hu Shi's textual criticism). In *Ernü yingxiong zhuan* (Heroic sons and daughters). By Wen Keng. Taipei: Xinwenfeng chuban gongsi, 1979, pp. 1-26.

——, "Jieshao wo ziji de sixiang" (A briefing on my own personal thinking). Excerpts rpt. in *Hu Shi Honglou meng yanjiu lunshu quan bian* (The complete work of Hu Shi's research and discussion on *Honglou meng*). By Hu Shi. Shanghai: Shanghai guji chubanshe, 1988, pp. 192-94.

——, "Kaozheng *Honglou meng* de xin cailiao" (New material on textual research into *Honglou meng*). Rpt. in *Hu Shi Honglou meng yanjiu lunshu quanbian* (Complete discussion and research of Hu Shi on *Honglou meng*), by Hu Shi. Shanghai: Guji chubanshe, 1988, pp. 158-91.

——, "Ba Qianlong jiaxu *Zhiyanzhai chongping "Shitou ji"* yingyin ben" (Postscript to the Qianlong copy of the "Repeated commentary on the *Story of the Stone* by Zhiyanzhai"). Rpt. in *Hu Shi Honglou meng yanjiu lunshu quan bian* (The complete work of Hu Shi's research and discussion on *Honglou meng*). By Hu Shi. Shanghai: Shanghai guji chubanshe, 1988, pp. 317-44.

Hu Shiming. "Ruhe renshi Qin Keqing xingxiang de sixiang yiyi" (How to understand the thought significance of Qin Keqing's image). *Honglou meng yanjiu jikan* (Journal of Research on *Honglou meng*), No. 13 (March, 1986), pp. 63-73.

Huang Changlin. "*Honglou meng* er bai yong (jie lu)" (200 odes on *Honglou meng* [excerpts]). Rpt. in *Honglou meng juan* (Collection of material on *Honglou meng*). Ed. Yi Su. 1963; rpt. Beijing: Zhonghua shuju, 1985, pp. 499-500.

Huang Lixin. "Ming Qing nan nü pingdeng de shehui sichao yu *Honglou meng*" (*Honglou meng* and trends in social thought towards sexual equality in the Ming and Qing). *Honglou meng xuekan* (*Honglou meng* journal), No. 2 (1986), pp. 303-25.

——, "Ming Qing hunyin ziyou de shehui sichao yu *Honglou meng*" (*Honglou meng* and the trend in social thought towards freedom in marriage during the Ming and Qing). *Shanghai daxue xuebao: she ke ban* (Shanghai university journal: Social sciences edition), No. 4 (1989), pp. 29-35. Rpt. in *RD*, No. 4 (1989), pp. 23-29. This article also appeared in an abbreviated form in *Honglou meng xuekan* (*Honglou meng* journal), No. 4 (1988), pp. 234-38.

Huang Tian. "Bodiao Jiang Qing 'ban ge Hongxuejia' de jia mian ju: xuexi 'Guanyu Honglou meng yanjiu wenti de xin'" (Strip off the mask of the "Half *Hongxue* scholar" Jiang Qing: Studying the "Letter regarding problems in the research on *Honglou meng*"). *Guangzhou ribao* (Guangzhou daily), 17.5.1977.

Jiang Chao. "Shier chai zhong san ge jinyu zhuyizhe ji qita" (The three ascetics within the Twelve Beauties and other matters). *Honglou meng xuekan* (*Honglou meng* journal), No. 3 (1985), pp. 181-97.

Jiang Hesen. *Honglou meng gaishuo* (A commentary on *Honglou meng*). Shanghai: Shanghai guji chubanshe, 1979.

——, *Honglou meng lungao* (Outline of *Honglou meng*). 1959; rpt. Beijing: Renmin wenxue chubanshe, 1981.

Jiang Wenqin. "'Nüer shijie' de liang ge ceng ci: Lun Daguan yuan yu Taixuhuan jing" ("Girls' World" at two levels: A discussion of Prospect Garden and the Land of Illusion). *Wenzhou shizhuan xuebao* (Wenzhou teachers' training college journal), No. 1 (1985), pp. 15-24. Rpt. in *RD*, No. 5 (1985), pp. 36-45.

Jiaozuo dian gongren *Honglou meng* pinglun zu (Jiaozuo electrical workers' group to criticize *Honglou meng*). "Shi ping Lin Daiyu" (An attempt to criticize Lin Daiyu). In *Ping "Honglou meng"* (A critique of *Honglou meng*). Ed. Zhonggong Jiaozuo shi wei xuanzhuan bu (Chinese communist party's Jiaozuo city propaganda committee). Zhengzhou: Henan renmin chubanshe, 1976, pp. 78-84.

Jiaozuo shi gongren, Kaifeng shiyuan Zhongwen xi gong nong bing xueyuan *Honglou meng* pinglun zu (Jiaozuo workers' and Kaifeng teachers' college worker, peasant, soldier students' collective study group for *Honglou meng*). "Tatian, butian, biantian" (Collapsing heaven, repairing heaven, changing heaven). *Henan ribao* (Henan daily), 21.8.1974.

Jing Meijiu. *Shitouji zhendi* (The true significance of *The Story of the Stone*). No place: Xijing chubanshe, 1934.

Lan Ling and Li Xifan. "Guanyu "Honglou meng jianlun" ji qita" (Regarding "A brief discussion on *Honglou meng*" and other matters). *Wen shi zhe* (Literature, history and philosophy), No. 9 (1954), rpt. in *Honglou meng pinglun ji* (Collection of critiques on *Honglou meng*). By Lan Ling and Li Xifan. Beijing: Renmin wenxue chubanshe 1973, pp. 1-20.

——, "Zou shenme yang de lu?" (Which road should we take?). *Renmin ribao* (People's daily), 24.10.1954.

——, "Ping *Honglou meng yanjiu*" (Criticizing *Research on "Honglou meng"*). *Guangming ribao* (Guangming daily), 10.10.1954.

——, "Honglou meng zhong liang ge duili de dianxing: Lin Daiyu and Xue Baochai" (Two opposing types in *Honglou meng*: Lin Daiyu and Xue Baochai). *Xin guancha* (New observations), No. 23 (December,1954), pp. 28-30.

——, "Ping Wang Guowei de *"Honglou meng* pinglun"' (Appraising Wang Guowei's "Critique of *Honglou meng*"). In Honglou meng pinglun ji (Collection of critiques on *Honglou meng*). By Lan Ling and Li Xifan. Beijing: Renmin wenxue chubanshe, 1973, pp. 83-103.

Li Chendong. *Honglou meng yanjiu* (Research on *Honglou meng*). 1942; rpt. Taipei: Xinxing shuju, 1962.

Li Dejun. "Li Wan xingxiang jianlun" (A brief discussion of Li Wan's image). *Jining shizhuan xuebao* (Jining teachers' training college journal), No. 2 (1984), pp. 60-65. Rpt. in *RD*, No. 4 (1984), pp. 95-100. This article was republished in 1985 under a different name and article title. Li Yin. "Mei de huimie: Li Wan xingxiang jianlun" (The destruction of beauty: A brief discussion of the image of Li Wan). *Honglou meng xuekan* (*Honglou meng* journal), No. 1 (1985), pp. 139-50.

Li Junxia. *Honglou meng renwu jieshao* (An introduction to the characters in *Honglou meng*). Taipei: Shangwuyin, 1988.

Li Ruzhen. *Jinghua yuan* (Flowers in the mirror). 1828; Taipei: Xuehai chubanshe, 1985.

Li Xifan and Feng Qiyong. *Honglou meng da cidian* (A comprehensive *Honglou meng* dictionary). Beijing: Wenhua yishu chubanshe, 1990.

Li Xifan (see also under Lan Ling).

Li Zili. "Qin Keqing guankui" (A narrow view of Qin Keqing). *Henan shida xuebao: she ke ban* (Henan teachers' university journal: Social sciences edition), No. 2 (1984), pp. 74-77. Rpt. in *RD*, No. 2 (1984), pp. 99-102.

Liang Xiao. "Pipan zichan jieji bu ting—xuexi 'Guanyu Honglou meng yanjiu wenti de xin'" (Do not stop criticizing the capitalist classes—studying the "Letter regarding problems in the research on *Honglou meng*"). *Renmin ribao* (People's daily),16.10.1974.

Liao Zhongan. "*Honglou meng* sixiang suyuan yi li—'Tian di jian lingshu zhi qi zhong yu nüzi' yi yu de chuchu he yuanliu" (An example of the source of *Honglou meng*'s thinking: "The purest essences of the universe are concentrated in the female of the species" the origin of one sentence) *Guangming ribao* (Guangming daily), 3 December, 1977.

Lin Jinhong. "Renwu xingxiang de keguanxing yu zuozhe de qing xiangxing" (Objectivity of characters' images and the writer's tendencies). *Honglou meng xuekan* (*Honglou meng* journal), No. 4 (1984), pp. 29-38.

Ling Jiefang. "Fenghuang chao he feng huan chao: ling yi ge Wang Xifeng" (The phoenix nest and the phoenix returns to the nest: Another Wang Xifeng). *Honglou meng xuekan* (*Honglou meng* journal), No. 4 (1983), pp. 151-72.

——, "Shi Xiangyun shi 'ludu' ma?" (Is Shi Xiangyun a "Career worm"?). *Honglou meng xuekan* (*Honglou meng* journal), No. 4 (1981), pp. 41-55.

Liu Caonan. "Qin Keqing zhi si xinlun" (A new appraisal of Qin Keqing's death). *Longfang luncong: Haerbin shida xuebao* (Collected essays from the dragon's place: Harbin teachers' university journal), No. 1 (1988), pp. 72-75. Rpt. in *RD*, No. 1 (1988), pp. 65-68.

Liu Guangsheng. "*Yang jia jiang* de gushi shifou fuhe lishi zhenshi?" (Does the tale of the *Yang Family Generals* represent the actual history or not?). *Lishi jiaoxue* (History education), No. 4 (1978).

Liu Kanlong. "Ye shi fengjian lijiao de shouhaizhe—jiantan Xue Baochai" (She is also a victim of feudal ethics—a brief discussion of Xue Baochai). *Xinjiang shifan daxue xuebao* (Xinjiang normal university journal), No. 2 (1981), pp. 85-89. Rpt. in *RD*, No. 11 (1981), pp. 51-56.

Liu Lanying et al., eds. *Honglou meng renwu cidian* (A dictionary of *Honglou meng* characters). Nanning: Guangxi renmin chubanshe, 1989.

Liu Mengxi. *Hongxue* (*Hongxue*). Beijing: Wenhua yishu chubanshe, 1990.

——, *Honglou meng xinlun* (A new discussion of *Honglou meng*). Beijing: Shehui kexue chubanshe, 1982.

——, ed. *Hongxue sanshi nian lunwen xuanbian: shang, zhong, xia* (Collected articles from thirty years of *Hongxue*: Three volumes). Tianjin: Baihua wenyi chubanshe, 1984.

Liu Shurong. "Sichuan nüxuetang kaixue zhi yanshuo" (Lecture at the opening of the women's school in Sichuan). Rpt. in *Jindai Zhongguo nüquan yundong shiliao 1842-1911* (Documents on the modern Chinese women's movement). Ed. Li Youning and Zhang Yufa. Taipei: Zhuanji wenxueshe, 1975, pp. 618-19.

Liu Wangli. "Xinhai geming qian de funü yundong" (The women's movement before the 1911 revolution). Rpt. in *Jindai Zhongguo nüquan yundong shiliao 1842-1911*. Ed. Li Youning and Zhang Yufa. Taipei: Zhuanji wenxueshe, 1975, pp. 759-63.

Lu Xun. "'Jiang dong hua zhu' xiaoyin" (Foreword to "Lord of the Flowers"). Rpt. in *Lu Xun quanji: ji wai ji she yi* (Complete Works of Lu Xun: Collected material omitted from the collections). By Lu Xun. 1927; rpt. Shanghai: Lu Xun quanji chubanshe, 1938, pp. 419-20.

——, "Ah Qin" (Ah Qin). Rpt. in *Lun Xun quanji: di liu juan* (Complete works of Lu Xun: volume six). By Lu Xun. 1934; rpt. Beijing: Renmin wenxue chubanshe, 1973, pp. 199-204.

Luo Di. "Guanyu Qin Keqing zhi si" (On Qin Keqing's death). *Honglou meng xuekan* (*Honglou meng* journal), No. 3 (1980), pp. 251-66.

Ma Qin. "Tongxing lian: Jia Baoyu tuifei xingge de mingzheng" (Homosexuality: Clear proof of Baoyu's decadent personality). *Xinjiang shifan daxue xuebao (she ke ban)* (Xingjiang teachers' university journal [humanities and social sciences]), No. 2 (1984), pp. 56-57.

Mao Yizhao. "*Guihua ci* shi shuo?" (What does the *Winsome Colonel* say?) *Honglou meng xuekan* (*Honglou meng* journal), No. 2 (1980), pp. 232-33.

Pu Songling. "Lin Siniang" (Fourth Sister Lin). In *Liaozhai zhiyi: di yi ce* (Tales of Liaozhai: vol. one). Jinan: Jilu shu she chuban faxing, 1981, pp. 437-42.

Qu Mu. "Lin Daiyu de xuefeng" (Lin Daiyu's scholarly style). *Guangzhou ribao* (Guangzhou daily), 26 October, 1983. Rpt in *RD*, No. 10 (1983), p. 53.

Shi Yepin. "Lun Wang Furen" (Discussing Lady Wang). *Yangzhou shiyuan xuebao*, (Yangzhou teachers' institute journal), No. 4 (1983), pp. 58-63. Rpt. in *RD*, No. 12 (1983), pp. 61-66.

Shou Pengfei. *Honglou meng benshi bianzheng* (Evidence for determining the original story of *Honglou meng*). 1927; rpt. Shanghai: Shangwu shuguan,1928.

Tai Yu (Wang Kunlun). *Honglou meng renwu lun* (Discussion of characters in *Honglou meng*). 1948; rpt. Taipei: Chang'an chubanshe, 1988. Revised version rpt. Hong Kong: Zhonghua shuju, 1987.

Tu Ying. "*Honglou meng* lunzan (An appraisal of *Honglou meng*). Rpt. in *Honglou meng juan* (Collection of material on *Honglou meng*). Ed. Yi Su. 1963; rpt. Beijing: Zhonghua shuju, 1985, pp. 125-45.

Wan Zhaofeng. "'Yi cong er ling san ren mu' xin jie" (A new explanation of "'Two' makes my riddle with a man and a tree"). *Honglou meng xuekan* (*Honglou meng* journal), No. 2 (1980), pp. 191-92, 234.

Wang Chaowen. *Lun Fengjie* (On Sister Feng). Tianjin: Baihua wenyi chubanshe, 1980.

Wang Guowei. "Honglou meng pinglun" (Critique of *Honglou meng*). Rpt. in *Honglou meng juan* (Collection of material on *Honglou meng*). Ed. Yi Su. 1963; rpt. Beijing: Zhonghua shuju, 1985, pp. 244-65.

Wang Li et al eds. *Zhongguo gudai wenxue cidian: di yi juan* (Dictionary of classical Chinese literature: volume one). Nanning: Guangxi renmin chubanshe, 1986.

Wang Li, ed. *Zhongguo chengyu da cidian* (Dictionary of Chinese proverbs). Shanghai: Shanghai cishu chubanshe, 1987.

Wang Mengyuan. "*Honglou meng* suoyin tiyao (jie lu)" (Synopsis of the hidden meaning of *Honglou meng* [excerpts]). Rpt. in *Honglou meng juan* (Collection of material on *Honglou meng*). Ed. Yi Su. 1963; rpt. Beijing: Zhonghua shuju, 1985, pp. 293-301.

Wang Shizhen. *Chi bei ou tan: xia ce* (Casual chats north of the pond: volume two). Taipei: Shangwuyin shuguan, 1976, *juan* 21.

Wang Xuexiang (Wang Xilian). *"Honglou meng* zongping" (General comments on *Honglou meng).* Rpt. in *Honglou meng juan* (Collection of material on *Honglou meng).* Ed. Yi Su. 1963; rpt. Beijing: Zhonghua shuju, 1985, pp. 146-53.

Wang Yigang. "Fengjie xingxiang de suzao yu e de lishi zuoyong" (The portrayal of Xifeng and the historical uses of evil). *Honglou meng xuekan (Honglou meng* journal), No. 4 (1982), pp. 233-49.

Wang Yongzhao, et al. *"Honglou meng"* shi yi bu zhengzhi lishi xiaoshuo *(Honglou meng* is a political and historical novel). Harbin: Renmin wenxue, 1975.

Wang Yukun, Wang Xiaoqi and Wang Xiaopang. "Ba boxue zhidu yongyuan maizang: Du *Honglou meng* di wushisan hui" (Bury the oppressive system forever: Reading chapter fifty-three of *Honglou meng). Guangming ribao* (Guangming daily), 8.7.1975.

Wang Zhichun. "Shusheng suibi" (Casual notes of Shusheng). Rpt. in *Honglou meng juan* (Collection of material on *Honglou meng).* Ed. Yi Su. 1963; rpt. Beijing: Zhonghua shuju, 1985, p. 386.

Wang Zhiwu. *"Honglou meng"* renwu chongtu lun (Discussion on the conflicts between the characters of *Honglou meng).* Xi'an: Renmin chubanshe, 1985.

Wang Zhiyao and Tong Haitian. "Lun Qin Keqing zhi si" (On Qin Keqing's death). *Henan daxue xuebao: zhe she ban* (Henan university journal: Social sciences and philosophy edition), No. 5 (1984), pp. 103-107. Rpt. in *RD,* No. 5 (1984), pp. 83-87.

Wei Jianlin et al. "'Ban ge Hongxuejia' de langzi yexin" (Wolfish careerism of the Half *Hongxue* scholar). *Guangming ribao* (Guangming daily), 29.1.1977.

Wu Shaonan. *"Chai Dai heyi"* xin lun (A new discussion of Chai-Dai combined). Hong Kong: Sanlian shudian, 1985.

Wu Shaoping. "'Yi cong er ling san ren mu' xi" (Analysis of "'Two' makes my riddle with a man and a tree"). *Honglou meng xuekan (Honglou meng* journal), No. 1 (1990), pp. 279-89.

Wu Shichang. "Zhiyanzhai shi shei" (Who is Zhiyanzhai). *Guangming ribao* (Guangming daily), 14.4.1962. Rpt. in *Hongxue sanshi nian lunwen xuanbian: xia* (Collected articles from thirty years of *Hongxue:* volume three). Ed. Liu Mengxi. Tianjin: Baihua wenyi chubanshe, 1984, pp. 231-37.

Wu Wenke. "Ye lun Fengjie" (Also on Sister Feng). *Honglou meng xuekan (Honglou meng* journal), No. 1 (1985), pp. 19-36.

Wu Ying. "Lun Lin Daiyu xingxiang de lishi yiyi" (On the historical significance of the image of Lin Daiyu). *Honglou meng yanjiu jikan* (Journal of research on *Honglou meng),* No. 12 (March, 1985), pp. 123-37.

Wuhan daxue Zhongwenxi qier ji ping *Hong* zu (Wuhan University Chinese department class of '72 group to criticize *Hong [lou meng]). Women shi zenme du "Honglou meng" de* (Our reading of *Honglou meng).* Beijing: Renmin wenxue, 1975.

Xiang Guanzhong et al ed. *Zhonghua chengyu da cidian* (A comprehensive dictionary of China's proverbs). Changchun: Jinlin chubanshe, 1986.

Xie Yafei et al ed. *Honglou meng zhuping* (Critical comments on *Honglou meng).* Nanning: Guangxi renmin chubanshe, 1982.

Xu Decheng and Tian Yuheng. "Qin Keqing yu Qin Zhong" (Qin Keqing and Qin Zhong). *Honglou meng xuekan (Honglou meng* journal), No. 1 (1985), pp. 151-59.

Xu Shinian ed. *Tangdai xiaoshuo xuan.* (Selected fiction from the Tang dynasty). Changchou: Changchou shuhua, 1982.

Yan Wang. "Lun Xue Yima xingxiang de dianxing yiyi" (Discussing the typicality of Aunt Xue's image). *Xinyang shifan xueyuan xuebao (she ke ban)* (Journal of Xinyang teachers' institute [social sciences edition]). Rpt. in *RD,* No. 4 (1984), pp. 83-92.

Yao Xie. "Du *Honglou meng* gangling" (An outline for reading the *Honglou meng).* Rpt. in *Honglou meng juan* (Collection of material on *Honglou meng).* Ed. Yi Su. 1963; rpt. Beijing: Zhonghua shuju, 1985, pp. 164-75.

Yi Qian and Shi Yuan. "Lun Miaoyu" (On Adamantina). *Shanghai shifan xueyuan xuebao* (Shanghai teachers' college journal), No. 1 (1979), pp. 82-86. Rpt. in *RD,* No. 11 (1979), pp. 110-14.

Yu Pingbo. *Honglou meng bian* (Distinguishing *Honglou meng).* Rpt. in *Yu Pingbo lun Honglou meng* (Yu Pingbo on *Honglou meng).* By Yu Pingbo. Shanghai: Shanghai guji chubanshe, 1988, pp. 96-323.

——, "Honglou meng jianlun" (A brief discussion of *Honglou meng*). *Xin jianshe* (New construction), No. 3 (1954). Rpt. in *Yu Pingbo lun Honglou meng* (Yu Pingbo on *Honglou meng*). By Yu Pingbo. Shanghai: Shanghai guji chubanshe, 1988, pp. 843-62.

——, *Honglou meng yanjiu* (Research on *Honglou meng*). Rpt. in *Yu Pingbo lun Honglou meng* (Yu Pingbo on *Honglou meng*). By Yu Pingbo. Shanghai: Shanghai guji chubanshe, 1988, pp. 369-599.

——, "*Honglou meng* zhong guanyu 'Shier chai' de miaoxie" (On the depiction of the "Twelve Beauties" in *Honglou meng*). *Wenxue pinglun* (Literary criticism), No. 4 (August, 1963). Rpt. in *Yu Pingbo lun Honglou meng* (Yu Pingbo on *Honglou meng*). By Yu Pingbo. Shanghai: Shanghai guji chubanshe, 1988, pp. 985-1049.

——, "Zhiyanzhai '*Honglou meng*' jiping yin yan" (Prefatory remarks to the *Collected Criticisms of Zhiyanzhai on "Honglou meng"*). Rpt. in *Yu Pingbo lun Honglou meng* (Yu Pingbo on *Honglou meng*). By Yu Pingbo. Shanghai: Shanghai guji chubanshe, 1988, pp. 919-32.

Yu Rui. "Zao chuang xian bi" (Casual jottings by the date tree window). Rpt. in *Honglou meng juan* (Collection of material on *Honglou meng*). Ed. Yi Su. 1963; rpt. Beijing: Zhonghua shuju, 1985, p. 14.

Yuan Mei. "Suiyuan shi hua" (Notes on Suiyuan poems). Rpt. in *Honglou meng juan* (Collection of material on *Honglou meng*). Ed. Yi Su. 1963; rpt. Beijing: Zhonghua shuju, 1985, pp. 12-13.

Yuan Shaoying and Yang Guizhen (eds), *Zhongguo funü mingren cidian* (A dictionary of famous women of China). Changchun: Beifang funü ertong chubanshe, 1989.

Yunnan dianzi guanchang gongren yeyu wenyi pinglun zu (Yunnan valve factory workers' after-hours literary criticism group). "Ba pipan zichan jieji weixin lun de douzheng jinxing daodi: Xuexi Mao Zedong 'Guanyu Honglou meng yanjiu wenti de xin'" (Taking the struggle to criticize the capitalist class' idealism to the end: Studying Mao Zedong's "Letter regarding problems in the research on *Honglou meng*"). *Yunnan wenyi* (Yunnan literature and art), No. 5 (1974).

Zhang Bilai. *Manshuo Honglou* (Talking about the red chamber). Beijing: Renmin wenxue chubanshe, 1978.

——, *Tan "Honglou meng"* (On *Honglou meng*). Shanghai: Zhishi chubanshe, 1985.

Zhang Jinchi. *Honglou shier lun* (Twelve essays on the red mansions). Tianjin: Baihua wenyi chubanshe, 1982.

Zhang Rufa. "*Mulan shi* de zhuti shi shenme?" (What is the main theme of *The Poem of Mulan*?). *Yuwen xuexi* (Language and literature studies), No. 11 (1981), pp. 14-15.

Zhang Tianlin. "Guanyu Yang jia jiang de chuanshuo he lishi" (On the history and legends of the Yang family Generals). *Tianjin ribao*, 24.10.1962.

Zhang Weiping. "Guochao shiren zhenglue" (Brief textual notes on poets under the nation's dynasties). Rpt. in *Honglou meng juan* (Collection of material on *Honglou meng*). Ed. Yi Su. 1963; rpt. Beijing: Zhonghua shuju, 1985, pp. 363-64.

Zhang Xinzhi. "Miaofu jianping *Shi touji ziji*" (A brief commentary on the *Story of the Stone* from the Miaofu studio). Rpt. in *Honglou meng juan* (Collection of material on *Honglou meng*). Ed. Yi Su. 1963; rpt. Beijing: Zhonghua shuju, 1985, pp. 34-35.

——, "*Honglou meng* dufa" (How to read the *Honglou meng*). Rpt. in *Honglou meng juan* (Collection of material on *Honglou meng*). Ed. Yi Su. 1963; rpt. Beijing: Zhonghua shuju, 1985, pp. 153-59.

Zhang Xun. "*Jinghua yuan* he *Honglou meng*." *Huaiyin shizhuan xuebao: zhe she ban*, No. 4 (1988), pp. 62-66. Rpt. in *RD*, No. 2 (1989), pp. 47-51.

Zhao Jiaqi. "Funü beiju mingyun de xiangxiang lishi—tan *Honglou meng* de zhongyao sixiang yinxiang" (Historical images of the tragic fates of women—talking about the major trends of thought in *Honglou meng*). *Xinjiang shifan daxue xuebao: she ke ban* (Xinjiang teachers' university journal). Rpt. in *RD*, No. 3 (1985), pp. 67-72.

Zhao Rong. "Hunyin ziyou de nahan, nan nü pingdeng de ouge" (A cry for freedom in marriage and a eulogy to equality of the sexes). *Guiyang shiyuan xuebao* (Guiyang teachers' college journal), No. 1 (1982), pp. 58-69. Rpt. in *RD*, No. 4 (1982), pp. 55-65.

Zhiyanzhai. *Zhiyanzhai "Honglou meng" jiping* (Collected criticisms of Zhiyanzhai on *Honglou meng*). Shanghai: Zhonghua shuju, 1960.

Zhongguo shehui kexueyuan wenxue yanjiusuo, ed. *Zhongguo wenxueshi.* (A history of Chinese literature). Beijing: Renmin wenxue chubanshe, 1985, pp. 324-27.

Zhongyang dianshitai (Central television studios). "Cao Xueqin meng duan xishan" (Cao Xueqin dreams in the Western mountains). Four parts (1988).

Zhou Chun. "Yue *Honglou meng* suibi" (Casual notes on reading Honglou meng). Rpt. in *Honglou meng juan* (Collection of material on *Honglou meng*). Ed. Yi Su. 1963; rpt. Beijing: Zhonghua shuju, 1985, pp. 66-77.

Zhou Jianyin. "Guanyu *Gui hua ci*" (On *The winsome colonel*). *Honglou meng xuekan* (*Honglou meng* journal), No. 1 (1983), pp. 187-90.

Zhou Lengqie. *Pei Xing chuanqi.* Shanghai: Guji chubanshe, 1980.

Zhou Ruchang. *Honglou meng xinzheng* (New evidence on *Honglou meng*). Shanghai: Tangdi chubanshe, 1953.

Zhou Yang et al. "Zhongguo zuoxie gudian wenxuebu zhaokai de *Honglou meng* yanjiu zuo tan hui jilu" (Chinese writers' association classical literature section's symposium on research in *Honglou meng*). *Guangming ribao* (Guangming daily), 14.11.1954.

Zhou Yibin. "Lun Daiyu Baochai de shixue guandian yu Ming Qing shige liu pai de guanxi" (Discussing Daiyu and Baochai's poetics in regard to Ming and Qing poetry schools). *Honglou meng xuekan* (*Honglou meng* journal), No. 1 (1986), pp. 57-74.

Zhou Zhongming. "Fengjie de xingxiang wei shenme zheyang shengdong huopo" (Why is Sister Feng's character so lively). *Honglou meng yanjiu jikan* (Journal of research on *Honglou meng*), No. 13 (March, 1986), pp. 75-95.

——, "Lun *Honglou meng* yu *Jin Ping Mei*" (Discussing *Honglou meng* and *Jin Ping Mei*). *Honglou meng xuekan* (*Honglou meng* journal), No. 3 (1989), pp. 195-233.

Zhu Danwei. *Honglou meng yanjiu* (Research into *Honglou meng*). Rpt. Taipei: Guiya wenhua, 1990).

Zhu Lian. "Honglou ping meng: xuanlu" (The red mansions criticize the dream: excerpts). Rpt. in *Zhongguo lidai xiaoshuo lun zhu xuan: shangce* (Selections of critiques of novels from China's past dynasties: volume one). Ed. Han Tongwen and Huang Lin. Nanchang: Jiangxi renmin chubanshe, 1982, pp. 542-45.

Zhu Meishu. "*Gui hua ci* xin jie" (A new understanding of *The winsome colonel*). *Liaoning daxue xuebao* (Liaoning university journal), No. 3 (1980), pp. 71-75.

Zhu Yaokuan. "Qin Keqing de shiming" (Qin Keqing's mission). *Honglou meng xuekan* (*Honglou meng* journal), No. 4 (1984), pp. 153-61.

Zhu Zuolin. "Honglou wenku (jie lu)" (Red chamber series [excerpts]). Rpt. in *Honglou meng juan* (Collection of material on *Honglou meng*). Ed. Yi Su. 1963; rpt. Beijing: Zhonghua shuju, 1985, pp. 159-63.

INDEX